HIDDEN MAGDALEN

FRONTISPIECE *Madonna and Child, with two Angels.* Attributed to Ambrogio Lorenzetti

HIDDEN MAGDALEN

Compiled by David Roberts

Edited by David Roberts and Richard Sheppard

Associate Editors
Robin Darwall-Smith
Christine Ferdinand
John Nightingale

Magdalen College Oxford

2008

Published in Great Britain by

Magdalen College

Oxford

OX1 4AU

© The President and Fellows of Magdalen College Oxford 2008

First published 2008 by Magdalen College Oxford

ISBN 978 0 9536435 3 0

Designed by Derek Brown at
Oblong Creative Ltd, Wetherby, West Yorkshire
using Monotype Bembo

British Library Cataloguing in Publication Data
Data available

Printed by Henry Ling Ltd, The Dorset Press, Dorchester

Contents

List of Contributors   vii

Foreword by David Clary, President of Magdalen College   ix

Acknowledgements   xi

Bibliographical Abbreviations   xi

Introduction: A Case for Curiosity by Robert Douglas-Fairhurst   I

THE DOCUMENTS   5

THE BUILDINGS   25

THE PEOPLE   45

THE ARTEFACTS   79

THE BEQUESTS   91

THE GIFTS   127

THE PURCHASES   157

THE LIBRARY   171

THE SCIENCE MEMORABILIA   193

THE SPORTING MEMORABILIA   211

Appendix: The Deed of Foundation   218

Index   221

Contributors

ADS — Anthony Smith CBE: Honorary Fellow; President of Magdalen 1988–2005

ARW — Alan Williams: Archaeometallurgist, The Wallace Collection, London

BJB — Brian Bellhouse: Emeritus Fellow; Fellow and Tutor in Engineering Science 1968–2003

BJS — Bernard Stone: Steward to the Oxford Society of Change Ringers

CFHT — Colin Tapper: Emeritus Fellow; Emeritus Professor of Law; Fellow and Tutor in Law 1965–2002

CGY — Charles Young: Fellow and Senior Bursar 1999–

CJGI — Bill Ives: Fellow and Informator Choristarum 1991–

CYF — Christine Ferdinand: Fellow Librarian 1992–

DBR — David Roberts: Emeritus Fellow; Fellow and Tutor in Biology 1970–2004

DCC — David Clary FRS: President of Magdalen 2005–

DJI — David Ibbetson FBA: Regius Professor of Civil Law, Cambridge; Fellow and Tutor in Law 1980–2000

GLH — Gerald Harriss FBA: Emeritus Fellow; Fellow and Tutor in History 1967–92

JACS — Andrew Smith: Fellow and Tutor in Biology 1990–

JBWN — John Nightingale: Fellow and Tutor in History 1993–

JCAF — Juliane Fürst: Junior Research Fellow in Modern History, St John's College, Oxford

JSTG — Toby Garfitt: Fellow and Tutor in French 1980–

LWBB — Laurence Brockliss: Fellow and Tutor in History 1984–

MAJW-B — Michael Wheeler-Booth KCB: Honorary Fellow; Special Lecturer in Politics 1998–

MJP — Michael Piret: Fellow and Dean of Divinity 1994–

MRB-B — Mark Blandford-Baker: Fellow and Home Bursar 2001–

NL — Nick Lambourn: Director, Christie's, Head of Topographical Pictures, Exploration, and Travel

RCSW — Ralph Walker: Fellow and Tutor in Philosophy 1972–

RGD — Bob Denning: Emeritus Fellow; Fellow and Tutor in Inorganic Chemistry 1968–2005

RH — Roger Hutchins: Secretary of the Magdalen Society 1999–2006

RHD-S — Robin Darwall-Smith: Archivist, University College 1993– , Magdalen 1996–

RJD-F — Robert Douglas-Fairhurst: Fellow and Tutor in English 2002–

RWS — Richard Sheppard: Emeritus Fellow; Fellow and Tutor in German 1987–2005

TJH — Tim Hunter: Magdalen (Modern History) 1985–92; Director, Christie's, Old Master and British Pictures

Foreword

David Clary, President, Magdalen College

Magdalen was founded by William of Waynflete 550 years ago in 1458. Since that time the College has been fortunate to receive or acquire a remarkable variety of items which have their own special beauty, curiosity, or history. Many of these precious objects are not often seen, being hidden in archives, safes, cases, and obscure rooms. This book provides a glimpse of some of them, and tells the stories of how they came to the College and why they are of interest.

There are many items in this book to highlight. Waynflete's Deed of Foundation of 12 June 1458 shows the arms of the College and a pot of lilies — Magdalen's flower, which features on items throughout the College. The College Muniment Room contains over 12,000 title deeds of lands which Waynflete gave to the College. This remarkable room preserves its original fittings intact and has been unchanged for over 500 years.

Thomas Wolsey is one of the most famous members of the College and a copy of his handwriting in the 'attendance register' of 1497 is included here, as is his lectionary, which contains magnificently detailed paintings of saints, plants, and flowers. The College has an exceptional collection of other books and manuscripts and *Hidden Magdalen* provides just a flavour of these. Examples include the papyrus fragment which is thought to be the earliest known part of the Gospel according to St Matthew; a handwritten manuscript by William of Malmesbury (*c.* 1125); a first edition of Ptolemy's *Geographia* (1482); and Oscar Wilde's hand-corrected draft of *Lady Windermere's Fan*.

Most of the College silver was lost to the Royalist cause in the Civil War, but this book describes some interesting pieces that remain or were subsequently donated. These include the Founder's Cup, which was saved at the last minute by President Frewen; the mysterious Magdalen Pot which also predates the Civil War; the Cup of the Restored Fellows; tankards and

tuns which are still regularly used on High Table; and a sake frame donated by the brother of the Emperor Hirohito of Japan, Prince Chichibu, who came up to Magdalen in 1926.

The College has been fortunate to acquire many exceptional works of art. Highlighted in this book are a fourteenth-century Madonna and Child attributed to the younger Lorenzetti; fine sixteenth-century portraits of Margaret of Lorraine, Jeanne d'Halluin, and Elizabeth I; a charming 400-year-old painting of the south front of Magdalen; a forest scene by Savery; Tonneau's interpretation of the 1687 extrusion of the Fellows; etchings by Turner; sunsets by Gilpin; paintings by Richard Wilson, John Ruskin, and Augustus John; and an exquisite drawing by Burne-Jones of Mary Magdalene at the feet of Jesus Christ. The Magdalen tradition of taking dessert after High Table is brilliantly portrayed in paintings of groups of Fellows in the Winter and Summer Common Rooms. The Port Railway also illustrates a quaint after-dinner custom. The College has a magnificent collection of Turkish Iznik pottery and this book shows some of the finest examples of these distinctively coloured tiles and plates. Another remarkable treasure is an Assyrian relief from the palace of Nimrud dating from around 880 BC.

Since its foundation Magdalen has been proud of its achievements in science. The 1947 Nobel Prize Medal of Robert Robinson is featured here, as are early globes and telescopes, a sketch of the great theoretical physicist and Fellow Erwin Schrödinger, and a picture of Daubeny's 1848 lecture room, where science teaching was pioneered in Oxford.

The Chapel and choir have always played a central role in College. The book features a cross and medal that are presented to choristers, and the pulpit cloth of 1617 which is still used when the College hosts University Sermons. Sport has been popular in the College for some time and a rare pre-1840 engraving captures the calm atmosphere of the cricket ground. Also included is a winning blade from Henley Regatta and a 1908 Olympic Games diploma. Other unusual items include a fine set of eighteenth-century guns that were thought to be kept by the Bursar as protection against highwaymen; the matriculation forms of three famous old members (Lord Alfred Douglas, Edward VIII, and John Betjeman); and the fossilized wig of the College's oldest President, Martin Routh.

Hidden Magdalen also reproduces a letter from the mother of Edward IV and Richard III requesting Waynflete to admit one of her protégés to the College. Some things have not changed in the five-and-a-half centuries of the College's existence!

Acknowledgements

We warmly acknowledge the help received by many of the authors who have contributed to this book. Most authors acknowledge their particular gratitude to the College Archivist, Robin Darwall-Smith, who has so willingly provided information on a great variety of topics. We would also like to thank: Jim Bennett (Museum of the History of Science), Sarah Boada-Momtahan (Sanders of Oxford), Ted Donohoe (undergraduate 1949–50), David Edge (The Wallace Collection), Walter Hooper, Tom Kemp (Natural History Museum), Mami Mizutori (Japanese Embassy), Susan North (Textiles and Fashion, Victoria and Albert Museum), Clare Pollard (Department of Eastern Art, Ashmolean Museum), Philip Powell (Natural History Museum), Clive Rassam (undergraduate 1966–69), and Tony Simcock (Museum of the History of Science).

We are grateful to the Stewards of Henley Royal Regatta for their kind permission to reproduce the race report in the piece on the Henley Blade. The photograph of *Mars as a Warrior* (p. 107) is reproduced by kind permission of V&A Images, Victoria and Albert Museum, London. We sought suggestions for what should be included from Fellows of the College and are most grateful to those who responded.

Nearly all the photographs in the book were taken by John Gibbons Studios, The Shambles, Lower Common, Uffington, Oxon SN7 7SQ, and we are most grateful to John for the care he has taken in coping with such a variety of subject matter. Additional photographs were taken: the James Short telescope (by Keiko Ikeuchi of the Museum of the History of Science); the two photographs of fritillaries (by Andrew Smith); the photograph of the Great War Memorial Cross at Wheatley and the two photographs of Magdalen's bells (all by David Roberts). Mary Franklin, who copy-edited the book, deserves our special thanks. The book was designed by Derek Brown of Oblong Creative.

Two items are so hidden that they are not even in Magdalen. The James Short telescope is on display in Oxford's Museum of the History of Science, and the Japanese armour has been lent to the Ashmolean Museum and will be on display in the new Japanese Gallery that is opening in 2009.

Bibliographical Abbreviations

The following abbreviations have been used for some of the books that are more commonly referred to:

Bloxam, *Register*: John Rouse Bloxam, *A register of the presidents, fellows, demies, instructors in grammar and in music, chaplains, clerks, choristers, and other members of Saint Mary Magdalen College in the University of Oxford: from the foundation of the College to the present time*, 8 vols, Oxford, 1853–85.

Macray, *Register of Members*: W. Macray, *A Register of the Members of St. Mary Magdalen College, Oxford: From the Foundation of the College*, new series, 8 vols, London, 1894–1915.

ODNB: *Oxford Dictionary of National Biography*, revised edition, Oxford, 2004.

Poole, *Catalogue of Portraits*: Mrs R. L. Poole, *Catalogue of Portraits in the Possession of the University, Colleges, City, and County of Oxford*, 3 vols, Oxford, 1912–26.

White and Darwall-Smith, *Architectural Drawings*: R. White and R. H. Darwall-Smith, *The Architectural Drawings of Magdalen College Oxford: A Catalogue*, Oxford, 2001.

Introduction: A Case for Curiosity

Robert Douglas-Fairhurst

Tucked away in a dusty corner of Oxford's Ashmolean Museum, far enough from the main corridors for the sounds of other visitors to be no more than a distant hum, is the Tradescant Room. It is a modest room, no larger than the average modern kitchen, but one crammed with treasures. Here, piled into display cases behind glass that has been smeared by generations of young fingers, and accompanied by carefully handwritten descriptions, all kinds of odd and unexpected objects jostle for the viewer's attention. Some are from overseas: two small lumps of mortar from the pyramids at Giza; 'the slough of a locust'; dainty wire and gauze Chinese lanterns that are crusted over with age. Others are from sources closer to home, but still seem like fragments from another world: an armour-plated hat worn by President Bradshaw 'as a protection against assassination attempts when he passed sentence on Charles I'; Guy Fawkes's lantern; the earliest surviving model ship in England, still displaying its delicate web of rigging. Many of these objects have quirky stories attached to them, like the huge patchwork shoes of the aptly named hermit John Bigg, who 'grew melancholy' in about 1660, 'and lived in a cave at Dryton, Bucks, between thirty and forty years'.

Other objects carry their stories around with them only in the form of dents and frayed edges: a little girl's embroidered corset, no larger than a doll's dress; some tiny twig sandals, the soles rubbed smooth with use; 'Figure and stories neatly carved upon Plum-stones, Apricock-stones, Cherry-stones, Peach-stones, &c'. And, peering down from the corner of one display case, overseeing all these wonders of the natural and human worlds, there is a diminutive portrait of John Tradescant (1608–62), the seventeenth-century collector who first put together this 'closet of rarities' or 'Ark' and who now forms one of its prize exhibits, 'curiously painted as though he were standing out from the clouds'.

Some of the strangest objects in 'Tradescant's Ark', straddling the worlds of fact and fiction, are no longer on public display: 'flea chains of silver and gold with 300 links a piece and yet but an inch long', 'two feathers of the Phoenix tayle', 'Blood that rained in the Isle of Wight', 'a bracelet made of the thighs of Indian flyes'.

Tradescant's collection is one of the finest surviving 'cabinets of curiosities', a relic of the seventeenth- and eighteenth-century fad for assembling objects that would show off the owner's travels, form a jigsaw puzzle of his or her experience, and 'excite wonder ... celebrate the marvellous strangeness of man and his world'. The 'cabinet of curiosities' offered a world seen in miniature and in glimpses.

As a product of the age of Enlightenment, it suggested both man's ability to master different kinds of knowledge and the world's undiminished capacity for mystery and surprise: the cabinet was at once a scientific laboratory and a bubble of fantasy. But even when the Enlightenment faded from view and many private collections were absorbed by the new public museums (as Tradescant's 'Ark' landed up in Oxford), the desire to marvel at edited highlights of the world did not stop altogether: it merely changed direction.

The 1851 Great Exhibition brought thousands of articles together from across the globe to the Crystal Palace, like a gigantic glass display case, and later on in the century Baudelaire described shop windows that appeared to contain 'the whole world in miniature'. Much the same might be said today about the Internet, which allows viewers to peer at anything and everything through the lens of a computer screen: another attempt to trap the whole world behind glass.

Such continuities suggest that it is not only professionally organized collections — museums, exhibitions, department stores — that reveal the human need to gather, assemble, and hoard. From neat rows of china dolls to teetering piles of old

I

theatre programmes, the urge to collect appears as natural and irresistible as breathing. Whether it manifests itself in the shape of a photograph album, with its carefully selected anthology of memories, or a car covered in bumper stickers (the keen motorist's equivalent of notches on the bedpost), a collection promises a tantalizing glimpse of patterns in an otherwise chaotic world. It offers a redemption of contingency, a local triumph of order over confusion.

But not always, for not all collections are planned. Some emerge over the years through habit or inertia, like the old newspapers and half-used pots of paint that people cannot bear to throw away. Such collections can seem puzzling to an outsider, even if they are perfectly logical to the person with whom they have grown up. In *Un cœur simple*, Flaubert describes the collection of relics and knick-knacks in the room of his heroine, the uneducated but faithful servant Félicité: 'It had the simultaneous air of a chapel and a bazaar'; and as the narrator of Julian Barnes's novel *Flaubert's Parrot* observes, in a world where other kinds of love can be unpredictable or unreliable, Félicité finds special consolation in 'an assembly of stray objects . . . united only by their owner's affection'.

Still, love being in the eye of the beholder, it can be as difficult to fathom what friends see in their cherished collection of beer mats or *Star Wars* memorabilia as it is to understand why they dote on their boring lover or mangy cat. I once visited the Barbie Museum in California as a bit of fun, and swiftly realized that for the soft-voiced woman conducting guided tours this was no joke: all her best friends were six inches tall. To a less loving eye, the chief object of curiosity in a collection is usually the taste of the person who put it together.

This is unlikely to be a problem for readers of *Hidden Magdalen*, because the items depicted here represent a rather different kind of collection. Some have been purchased or commissioned over the 550 years of the College's history, while others, such as the matriculation forms shown on pp. 22–23, have been deliberately stored in its archives; most have been gifts. So what unites them is not the shared taste of

successive Presidents or Fellows, but the donors' affection for a College that was either temporarily or permanently their home.

Perhaps this is why, for all their eclecticism, these items sit so happily together in one place. Like the people who assemble in Magdalen at the start of every academic year, they come from a diversity of backgrounds, but for all their local differences they have one thing in common: Magdalen is their home. From large bequests such as the Brocklebank Collection (see p. 92), to individual curiosities such as Routh's fossilized wig (p. 61), these are Magdalen's treasures — not in the sense that they are worth a great deal of money, but in the sense that they continue to be preserved and valued as key fragments of the College's human history. Like the worn flagstones of the Cloisters or the scribbles of ancient graffiti on the staircase of the Great Tower, they represent lasting traces of the lives that the College has gathered to itself over the years.

If the items in this book are fragments of the past, then, like all fragments, they are inevitably haunted by what is missing: the silver plate that was melted down during the Civil War; Oscar Wilde's stolen ring; the buildings that never materialized; parts of the historical record that nobody thought worth preserving. But they also bear witness to remarkable survivals against the odds, such as the gates from Addison's home which were discovered in a junkyard in the 1950s and now lead into the water meadow from Addison's Walk (see p. 188), or the cartoon of 'Little Mr Bouncer' etched by Oscar Wilde on the window of his undergraduate room (p. 68).

For several reasons — fragility, security, insurance — many of these items are not usually visible to the College's visitors. Every year thousands of people come to Magdalen to see the Cloisters, the New Building, and other guidebook highlights. Some crane their necks around the stern warning sign 'PRIVATE: NO ADMITTANCE' at the entrance to St Swithun's to get a glimpse of students playing frisbee. Others peer through the window of the Senior Common Room during lunch, in the hope of discovering a ghastly Inspector Morse-style crime scene. One or two even tap on the glass, like visitors to the zoo hoping to stir a case of spiders into life.

But by and large Magdalen manages to keep its public face and its private life separate. Tourists tend not to see the ordinary activities that make a college a living organism rather than a heritage centre. They also tend not to see some of the most remarkable pieces of architectural history, such as the Muniment Room (pp. 28–29), that distinguish Magdalen from other Oxford colleges. This is one kind of hidden Magdalen that this book celebrates, for it is hidden not in the sense that it is deliberately concealed, like buried treasure, but in the sense that it is not normally available to the public gaze.

You don't have to look too hard in Oxford to find other examples of collections that have been created more by accident than design. Like many other university towns, Oxford has always generated clutter, from piles of paperwork to rusting heaps of abandoned bicycles. Indeed, looked at from the air, Oxford colleges appear less like a carefully organized campus than a tattered spider's web, ready to catch any stray objects that come into its path. Perhaps this is inevitable, given the University's chief function as a place of learning. Philip Larkin once remarked that 'the impulse to preserve lies at the bottom of all art', and a similar impulse underlies all learning.

But if this impulse is visible in Magdalen's collection of treasures and curiosities, others are also at work, including a reluctance to take the past for granted. Perhaps this is equally inevitable, given the University's other main function as a place of research. For to research is to look again at what everyone thinks is already known; it involves revising old ideas in order to come up with new ones. This is one reason why academics' rooms tend to be cluttered places: not, by and large, out of eccentricity or slovenliness, but because they never know which scrap of paper or bit of apparatus will prove to be the missing piece of the jigsaw.

Several of the items featured here reflect the continuing conversation in university life between the backward-looking and the forward-thinking. The Port Railway in the Senior Common Room, for instance

(pp. 86–87), is an invention which, unlike most railways in Britain, has been tweaked and modified until it runs with beautiful smoothness and efficiency. But it will no doubt be tweaked and modified again, for there are some Magdalen Fellows who seem unable to use it without a glint in their eye and a twitch in their fingers. And this is another kind of hidden Magdalen — the future that research more serious than that involved in the construction of the Port Railway, such as Sir Robert Robinson's Nobel Prize-winning work in Chemistry (see pp. 70–71), sets out to bring to light.

But there is a third hidden aspect to Magdalen: when extraordinary things start to fade into the background and come to seem quite ordinary. The hardest things to see properly can be those we see all the time, just as new students at Magdalen quickly become habituated to having deer grazing a few feet away from their rooms. In their first week they eagerly watch the deer; in their second week they occasionally notice the deer; after their third week the deer attract about as much attention as anything else in the College with four legs, like tables or chairs or canoodling couples. Similarly, the regular trundle of the Port Railway rarely attracts the attention of those who use it every day: it is literally part of the furniture.

Hidden Magdalen is something other than a museum catalogue. Unlike the objects in a museum, many of Magdalen's treasures are still part of everyday College life: scholars from all over the world consult Cardinal Wolsey's lectionary (see p. 180–81) or the papyrus fragment of St Matthew (pp. 130–31), while every night on High Table the silver tuns (pp. 140–41) are used as water tumblers. Such objects are hidden not because they are safely tucked away from the public gaze, but because the eyes of people who know and love the College tend to glide over them without stopping.

And this is another reason for the publication of *Hidden Magdalen* 550 years after the founding of the College. It is an attempt to show something of the richness and variety of the life that is led here and the lives that have been led here which might otherwise

3

be taken for granted. Towards the end of Arthur Conan Doyle's mystery *A Case of Identity*, Watson blusters that 'You appeared to read a great deal in the suspect which was quite invisible to me', and receives the cool reply from Sherlock Holmes: 'Not invisible but unnoticed.' If the photographs and descriptions in this book offer a set of keyholes onto normally inaccessible parts of the College, we hope they will also give readers familiar with Magdalen the pleasure of seeing other parts of it with fresh eyes.

The Documents

The Scale of Perches.

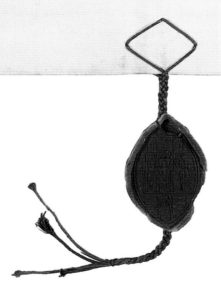

▲ The Deed of Foundation of 12 June 1458   35.5 x 58.5 cm

Hidden
Magdalen

Deed of Foundation of Magdalen College

Before becoming Bishop of Winchester in 1447, William of Waynflete had been Headmaster of Winchester College and Provost of Eton College, and was identified with the educational programme of King Henry VI. In 1448 he founded 'Maudeleyn Hall' on the site of the present Examination Schools. Its membership consisted of a President and graduate scholars studying Philosophy and Theology, and its purpose was 'to eradicate heresy and increase the number of clergy'. Ten years later, after becoming Lord Chancellor, Waynflete re-founded 'Maudeleyn Hall' as a College on the site of the Hospital of St John the Baptist outside the east gate of the city of Oxford, a process which involved protracted legal proceedings.

In October 1456 Henry VI granted the patronage of the Hospital to Waynflete and licensed its transfer into the ownership of 'Maudeleyn Hall'. In July 1457 the brethren surrendered the Hospital and were given pensions. Waynflete, with royal approval, then issued a deed founding a College on the site of the Hospital. Once the College was formally in being, he petitioned Pope Calixtus III in October 1457 to suppress the Hospital; and in March 1458 the Pope commissioned the Bishop of Hereford for this purpose. On 12 June Waynflete issued his foundation deed dedicating the College to the Virgin Mary, St Mary Magdalene, St John the Baptist, and the Apostles Peter and Paul. He named William Tybard (d. 1480) as President, and six Fellows, five of them from 'Maudeleyn Hall'. Some statutes were provided for the College's governance, though Waynflete reserved the right to change these and to remove the President and scholars at his discretion. The Hall and the Hospital were then conveyed to and amalgamated with the College, and on 19 June 1458 the Bishop of Hereford, as papal delegate, formally suppressed the Hospital and confirmed the College's foundation. For over ten years the new College occupied the former Hospital buildings, until the construction of the Cloisters Quadrangle was commenced in 1474.

In 1480–81, towards the end of his life, Waynflete visited the College, installed a new President, and presented new statutes. He also placed the College under the perpetual jurisdiction of the see of Winchester and gave it its endowment. Waynflete died in August 1486, when he was probably over 80. Although he had lived to see the College function as an independent institution, the process of its foundation had occupied virtually all his episcopate of nearly forty years.

The Deed of Foundation is listed as *Chartae Regiae* 81 among the College muniments. The first line has elaborately floriated letters, with the arms of the College and a pot of lilies. The attached seal is of red wax and vesicated, and shows the Bishop kneeling before the patron saints of the see of Winchester.

The first English translation of the charter is given in the Appendix.

GLH

LITERATURE

V. Davis, *William Waynflete, Bishop and Educationalist*, Woodbridge, 1993.

The College's First Statutes

Although Magdalen was founded in 1458, it was not until 1480, over two decades later, that William of Waynflete finally drew up a complete set of statutes for his foundation. They are long and detailed (over 100 pages in modern print), and aim to cover every aspect of Magdalen life, be it the minutiae of College administration, or appropriate and inappropriate recreations for its members. The statutes remained in force — albeit with some clauses being left quietly unenforced, such as the one enjoining members of the College to converse only in Latin — until the mid-1850s, when a Parliamentary Commission prepared new statutes for all Oxford colleges.

At least three copies of the statutes are known to have been made when they were promulgated in 1480, of which this (MS 277) is one. They were produced, it seems, for the use of the President and other senior College officials. This particular copy was made for the Dean of Divinity and is unusual on two counts. First, it has a few notes at the front and back

▶ William of Waynflete's statutes of 1480

which appear to be in Waynflete's own hand. Second, it has been the custom since 1551 to inscribe the name of every Dean of Divinity in its opening pages, usually with the new Dean filling it in himself.

The pages illustrated are emblematic of this double use. On the right-hand page we have the original Introduction to the statutes. This is followed by the first section proper, *De numero scholarium et electione*, which fixes the number of Fellows and Demies (Scholars with half the allowance of Fellows) in the new College and stipulates how its President is to be elected. On the left-hand page we see the names of the most recent Deans of Divinity, ending with that of the College's current Dean, Dr Michael Piret

(b. 1957), who arrived in 1994. Some of his notable predecessors include: Harry Ramsden Bramley (1833–1917), Dean from 1885 to 1889, who, with John Stainer (1840–1901), edited *Christmas Carols Old and New*, the first such anthology to become really popular; Cosmo Gordon Lang (1864–1945), Dean from 1893 to 1896 and Archbishop of Canterbury from 1928 to 1942, who, while at Magdalen, revived the long-defunct practice of preaching the St John's Day sermon in the open-air pulpit in St John's Quadrangle (see p. 81); and, more recently, Dr Jeffrey John (b. 1953), Dean from 1984 to 1991 and Dean of St Alban's Cathedral since 2004.

RHD-S

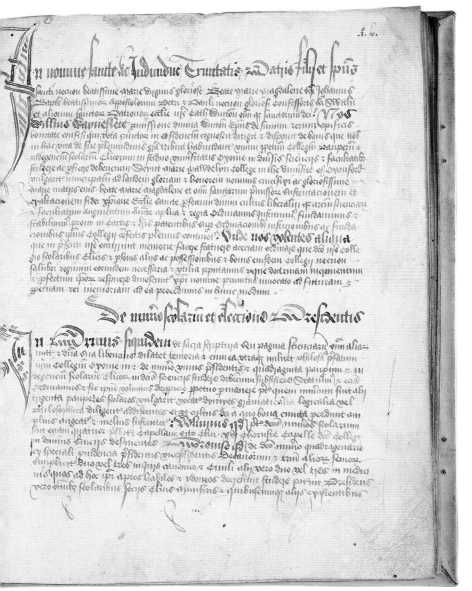

LITERATURE

The statutes are printed in full (although in Latin only) in *Statutes of the Colleges of Oxford: Magdalen College*, Oxford, 1853.

The Cartulary of the Hospital of St John the Baptist

The site of Magdalen College was once occupied by a hospital dedicated to St John the Baptist. It was in existence by the end of the twelfth century, was re-founded by Henry III in 1234, and quickly acquired land in both Oxford and Oxfordshire. Unfortunately, the Hospital gradually fell into decay, and in October 1456 Henry VI granted William of Waynflete the right to close it down and transfer its site and possessions to Magdalen Hall, Waynflete's first Oxford foundation (not to be confused with the later Magdalen Hall which was re-founded as Hertford College in 1874). Two years later, Magdalen Hall was re-founded on the site of the old Hospital as Magdalen College (see p. 7). Most of the latter's buildings were demolished, and the only portions readily visible today are parts of the High Street frontage to the west of the Great Tower and the Old Kitchen. Some old stonework by the Kitchen was exposed during excavations in the 1980s.

Cartularies were books containing copies of title deeds and other important documents which enabled medieval landowners to prove their ownership of lands and privileges. This cartulary was probably created for the Hospital in the late 1270s, and most of it, including this opening, appears to have been written by a professional scribe called Richard of Eppewelle or Epwell who was based in Oxford. Additional entries were made down the centuries. These are arranged topographically, and, as the photograph shows, tags were sewn into the pages to help find the right place.

The illustration shows copies of two deeds that are still in the College's archives. In the first one, dated c. 1220, Walter Cole gives the Hospital some quit rents on properties in the Oxford parish of St Mary Magdalene. In the second, dated 1247/8, Dionisia (or Denise) Blauet gives the Hospital some land in George Street, Oxford. When the Hospital was closed down (see p. 7) — as with the Hospital of St James and St John at Brackley (see p. 12) — all its administrative papers including the cartulary came to Magdalen. So this document has lived on the same site for seven and a half centuries, performing the same duty for the Hospital and the College. Indeed, Magdalen thought it sufficiently useful to have it completely rebound in c. 1500 — probably by an Oxford-based binder called George Chasteilain, who carried out other work for the College.

RHD-S

PROVENANCE

Passed to William of Waynflete on the closure of the Hospital of St John the Baptist in 1457.

LITERATURE

H. E. Salter, ed., *A Cartulary of the Hospital of St. John the Baptist*, 3 vols, Oxford, 1914–17.

▶ A page from the late 13th-century cartulary, with parchment pages and leather binding   28 x 17 cm

beate marie magdalene. Carta Walteri cole.

Sciant p̃sentes ⁊ futuri qd ego Walt' cole concessi dimisi ⁊ relaxaui deo ⁊ hospitali s̃c̃i Johis ex
p̃te oriente Oxon' terras qꝫ Ric' le baleys ⁊ Witts Warinere ⁊ Robt' fil' Aluered
⁊ eadward Aquilri ⁊ Wales kurrel ⁊ Robt' le bere de me tenuerut ex p̃te
Aquilon' Oxon' ⁊ scitum quod Robt' le bere ⁊ Ad' saurer de me tenuerunt
Henend ⁊ tenenda de me ⁊ de heredibz meis in p̃p̃m plen̄ario ⁊ integ̃e cũ oĩbz
p̃tin̄ p̃ quinos sol' ⁊ quatuor den' Annuatim soluend' Ex quibz iiij sol' ⁊ iij d'
p̃d̃m hospit̃ debet redde p me ⁊ p heredibz meis luminari ecc̃e s̃c̃e marie
magd' quatuordecim den' p annu' videlꝫ ad natale dñi Et p oĩbz p̃dc̃as t̃ras
capit̃li dño v d' salu' in die s̃c̃i marci Et p p̃to capit̃li dño ij sol'
videlꝫ in tempe sextõis Et p custodia p̃ti iij d' ⁊ iñ ⁊ heredibz meis v d'
Annuatim videlꝫ ad pasch' Ego ⁊ heredes mei Warantizabim' oĩa p̃dc̃a tene
mentã cũ oĩbz p̃tin' p̃nominato hospit̃ in p̃p̃m cõ oẽs hões in t̃res ⁊ feias
Et p hc̃ concessioe ⁊ dimissioe ⁊ relaxatoe ⁊ Warantizatoe mei p̃dc̃oƿ tenend'
p̃dc̃m hospit̃ debz in inuentur̃ sustinend' victu ⁊ vestitu' q̃m diu vixo. Et
ut oĩ p̃scripta sic p̃dmis̃ sunt in p̃p̃m firma ⁊ stabil' p̃maneant hac mea car
ta notaui ⁊ sigilli mei munimine confirmaui. Hiis testi' Rog̃o penitentiar'
canonico de Oseneǥ. Ric' capt̃o de s̃c̃a maria magd'. Johe de s̃c̃a ella. Ric'
salagod. William fil' eadw̃ni. Robto fil' oem. Ric' fil' henr'. Robto fil' henr' fil'
symon'. Alex' her' Robto fil' aluer. ⁊ c̃.

Sciant p̃ ⁊ f. qd ego diouisia blancur in ligia potestate mea ⁊ in p̃pria viduitate
mea p salute anime mee ⁊ antecessoƿ meoƿ dedi ⁊ cõcessi ⁊ hac p̃senti carta mea
confirmaui deo ⁊ hospit̃ s̃c̃i Johis ex p̃te oriente Oxon' ⁊ fr̃ibz ibid̃ deo s̃uientibz
⁊ s̃uitur' in puram ⁊ p̃pet elemos̃ totam t̃ram mea cũ p̃tin' suis q̃ iacet int
t̃ram Laurentii Rufi ex una p̃te ⁊ t̃ram eiudem laur' ex alt̃a in pochel s̃c̃e
marie magd' ex p̃tin bou' le Oxon'. Henend ⁊ tenend p̃dc̃as t̃ras ibid̃ deo
s̃uientibz ⁊ s̃uitur' libe quiete p̃plen̄e ⁊ integ̃e. Redd' inde Annuatim Abille
de ewistoƿ e duodecim den' ad natale dñi ⁊ Witt le sauuur tres sol' ad quatuor
anni t̃minos. videlꝫ ad Natale dñi ix d' ⁊ ad festu be marie in martio ix
d' ⁊ ad Natiuit' s̃c̃i Johis bapt' ix d' ⁊ ad festu s̃c̃i mich' ix d' p oĩ seruit ⁊ ex
actoe ⁊ demãd̃a. ut q̃ p̃scripta firma ⁊ stabil' sine dolo p̃maneant in p̃p̃m
huic p̃senti scripto sigilla mei apposui. Hiis testi' Hich de stochwell tunc
maiore Oxon'. Alex' durr' Witt le sauuer tunc p̃posit'. Walt' durr' Witt
le sauuer tunc ball'. Witto le taiter. Rad' le plum'. Rob d̃c̃o ⁊ alt'. Aliis.

Sciant p̃ ⁊ f. qd ego Robt' bodin cõcessi ⁊ dedi in pur' ⁊ p̃pet elemos deo

An Old Title Deed

Twelve thousand or so medieval deeds are kept in the Muniment Room (see pp. 28–29) and this particular one (Brackley B. 186) has been selected because of its age and good condition. It tells of a grant made by a certain Hugh de Camvill to Regner the Painter (*Regnerus pictor*) of an acre of land with a meadow in his demesne at 'Godendun', for an annual payment of six pence a year. It also includes some land owned by Hugh's brother Roger that is situated between the house of Eadward and the house of Richard de Estunia. In return for the making of this deed, Regner also agrees to give Hugh a chessboard (*scaccarium*) and his wife some veils (*wimplaria*). The witnesses to this deed are identified as Richard de Camvill, the lady Cristina, Hunfrid the clerk, Alard, Odo son of Regner, and Halimot, who may have written the deed as it ends 'Halimot himself' (or myself: *ipso Halimot*). The seal, showing a mounted Norman knight, is particularly splendid and reads: 'the Seal of Hugh de Canvill' [sic] (*Sigill Hugonis de Canvil*). Although the deed is undated, William Macray suggested from stylistic evidence, when he was cataloguing the College's medieval deeds in the 1860s, that it dates from *c.* 1150–60.

Why has this apparently unrelated document ended up in Magdalen's archives? The reason lies in the situation of 'Godendun', probably Godington, a village in Oxfordshire a few miles away from Brackley, Northamptonshire. There was a hospital at Brackley dedicated to St James and St John, and this foundation acquired or was given property in Brackley and several surrounding towns and villages, including Godington.

Why too should the archives of a college founded in 1458 contain documents that are so much older? The reason lies in English land law, for until 1926, when it became possible to register land, owners of land had to support their claim to their property by producing documents that traced the history of its ownership. So when William of Waynflete was acquiring properties to create Magdalen's endowment, he also acquired all other related deeds and documents.

R H D – S

PROVENANCE

Transferred to William of Waynflete with other documents relating to the Hospital of St James and St John, Brackley, after he acquired the property in 1484.

▶ 12th-century title deed to land in Oxfordshire which was transferred to the College at its foundation in 1458

Hidden
Magdalen

Hugo de camuilla omib9 hominib9 suis godendun 7francis 7anglicis
qui sunt 7qui uenturi sunt sal'. Hotum sit uob qd qndam acram tre
de dominio meo cu prato ad eande tram puinente Regnero pictori
in feudum 7inheredicatem dedi illi 7heredibus suis de me 7heredib9
meis tenadam solidam 7quieta ab omib9 seruicijs sex denarios an
nuatim reddendo 7pcambicione illi terre quam Roger frat nis
ei donauit. Illam scil' acram terre dedi ei que est mt domu eadwardi
7domum Ricardi de estuua. Et sciendum est qd regner9 pp cartam
henda unu scaccariu in 7uxori mee swimplaria qdam donauit. hijs
estib9. Ricardo de camuill'. Dna cristina . hunfrido clico. Alardo. Odon
fit regin. 7ipo halimot'. Val.

13

▲ Letter to William of Waynflete from Cecily, the mother of King Edward IV, late 15th century

A Letter to the Founder from a Grand Lady

Cecily, the widow of Richard Duke of York, the mother of Edward IV and Richard III and the grandmother of Henry VII's Queen, Elizabeth of York, wrote this letter (MS 367 no. 8) to William of Waynflete soon after Magdalen's foundation. It is important because it sheds light on how the new College was viewed by a member of the ruling élite.

The letter is undated, but the fact that Cecily calls herself 'the King's mother' in the first line suggests that it was written in the early 1480s, probably when Edward IV was still alive and just after Magdalen's first set of statutes had been drawn up (see pp. 8–9). Cecily unashamedly plays on her status when asking Waynflete to admit the son of one of her *protégés* to the College as a Demy, for she writes:

> Right reverend Fader in god and Right trusty and Welbeloved We grete you hertly Welle And desyr you to have in knowlage how that our Welbeloved servant William Stephyns hath a son that ye [two words are lost] to be a prest yf that god Wille yeve hyme abbylite and conynge. We tendryng his godly disposicion in that be halve desyr and Right herttely pray you to be so god lord unto hym that he may be admytted one of the number of your Scolers in your noble College that you newly have edified and founded at thuniversyte of Oxford. And the Rather atte thinstance and contemplacion of this our Writing as We may have cause to thanke you hereafter. And ye so doing shalle in our oppynyon do a ryghte meritorious dede. And also cause Us to be your loving lady in any thing We may do for you hereafter as knoweth God Who have you in his kepyng. Yeven under our Signet at our Castell of Berkehampstede the xj day of October.

The name 'Cecilie' can be made out at the bottom of the letter, and as it is in a very different hand it is clearly Cecily's own writing. As a lady of high status, she would have had a secretary to write her letters: nevertheless, she saw fit to append her own signature to this one. This is almost certainly the earliest known example of a woman's handwriting in the College's archives.

Even at this early date Magdalen was clearly thought prestigious enough for Cecily to take an interest in it. But Waynflete was not to be swayed, even by the mother of kings, for no one called Stephens/Stevens was admitted as a Demy in the 1470s or 1480s.

RHD–S

Thomas Wolsey's 'Attendance Register'

At first glance, this document (CP/8/50) is one of the least attractive items in this book, being an opening from an unprepossessing account book from the 1490s and written in a particularly difficult hand. These accounts are called *Books of Names* (*Libri nominum*) because, every week, one of the Fellows used to act as Steward (*Seneschallus*) of Hall and make a note in his own hand of every member of the College who was there that week. It was almost a kind of attendance register.

But if one looks more closely at the top of the left-hand page, one can just about make out the words 'Seneschallus M. Wulsy'. This is none other than Thomas Wolsey (1470/1–1530) — the future Archbishop of York, cardinal, and Lord Chancellor, the chief minister of Henry VIII — who was at this date a Fellow of Magdalen. It is not known exactly when Wolsey came up to Magdalen (it may have been as early as the late 1480s), but he was certainly a Fellow between 1497 and 1502. He also acted briefly as Master of Magdalen College School for part of 1498. At some time in 1497 it fell to the young Wolsey to check off the names and record them in this book. So this is possibly the earliest known example of the handwriting of one of Magdalen's greatest old members.

The arrangement of these lists of names was always the same. On the left-hand page the Steward noted all the members of the Foundation, from the Fellows down to the choristers and servants, who were resident in that particular week. Then, at the top of the right-hand page, he recorded guests who dined in the College during this period. It is a perfectly routine document, but perhaps that makes it more special: at

this date Wolsey was no more than a young Oxford Fellow, still to make his way in the world.

Wolsey went on to serve as one of Magdalen's three Bursars in 1498/9 and 1499/1500, while the College was building its Great Tower. There are legends that he got the College into serious financial trouble over that building, and even that he used force to obtain money from the treasury to continue the work. But they are no more than legends, for the accounts of the time show that the construction of the Tower was overseen by another Fellow. Furthermore, Wolsey then went on to serve as Dean of Divinity in 1500/1, and he remained on good terms with the College for the rest of his life. The College regularly sent him gifts, and in return Wolsey was a generous patron until his fall from power in 1528.

RHD-S

▶ The record of members of the College and guests for a week in 1497, compiled by Thomas Wolsey as Steward

◀ Detail: 'Seneschallus M. Wulsy' heading the list

Hidden
Magdalen

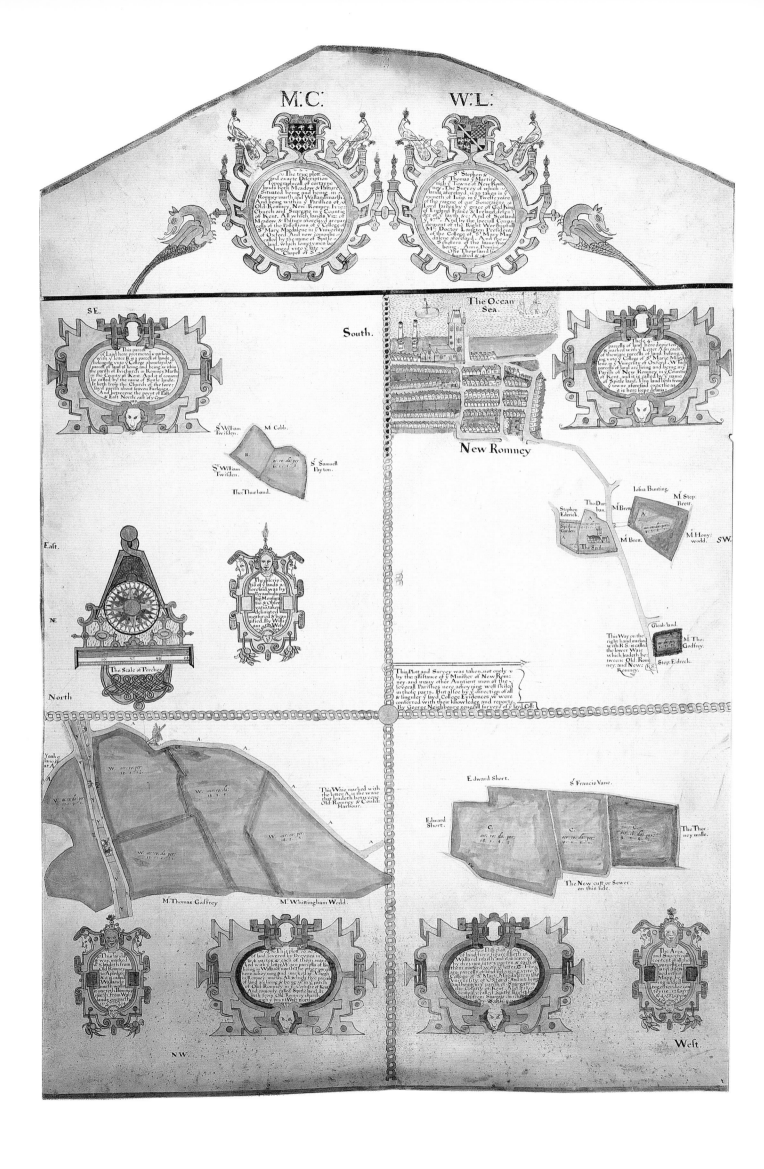

Map of College Estates at Romney

Drawn in 1614 by William Web[b], this is one of the earliest maps of any of Magdalen College's estates (MP/1/24). The College owns three maps drawn by Webb in 1612–14, but this is the most attractive because of its depiction of the town of New Romney, Kent, with its houses, church tower (drawn slightly too large), cannons pointing out towards the 'Ocean Sea', and a couple of ships on the sea. At the top of the map (left) are the arms of Magdalen College, together with those of William Langton (d. 1626), President of Magdalen 1610–26.

The Hospital of St Stephen and St Thomas at Romney was founded in *c.* 1186. William of Waynflete acquired it in 1457 and arranged for its appropriation by the College. The Hospital's lands were in New Romney itself, and also in Old Romney, Ivychurch, and Snargate.

Landowners had begun to commission maps of their estates in the late sixteenth century, partly to help them manage their lands and partly to defend their ownership of them. So most of the older Oxford colleges have maps from this period, mainly of their more distant properties. It made good sense for Magdalen to commission a map of Romney so early for it was one of its remoter properties — the only one of its original estates to be situated in Kent — and the boundaries of the scattered properties needed clear definition.

Until well into the nineteenth century, estate maps tended to depict only those properties belonging to the landowner and not the whole area. Hence the appearance of this map with its disparate pieces of land. As the scattered nature of the College's properties in and around Romney would have required a more complex survey than was usual, the inscription inside one of the cartouches on this map sheds some light on the methods being employed:

This Plott and Survey was taken, not onely by the assistance of the Minister of New Romney, and many other Auntient men of the severall Parishes nere adioyning well stiled in those parts. But also by the direction of all & singular the sayd College Evidences [i.e. title deeds] which were conferred with their knowledge and reported. By George Neighboure generall surveyor of the sayd College.

RHD-S

◀ William Webb's map of 1614
   parchment   97 x 64 cm

PROVENANCE
Commissioned by the College for administrative purposes.

19

Hidden
Magdalen

The Fellows' Scroll

In August 1686 the President and Fellows of Magdalen decided to tighten up the procedures for the admission and resignation of Fellows and created eight new regulations 'out of a deep sense of our duty and most tender regard to the Credit and Reputation of our College as likewise to avoyd all possible Suspicion how groundlesse and undeserved soever'. They also included an undertaking that the Fellows should sign allegiance to the regulations. The changes were approved by the Bishop of Winchester, the Visitor of the College, and then copied, along with the Bishop's formal consent, onto this large parchment scroll (MS 887), with the names of the Fellows of 1686 appended below.

Although nothing explicit is said about this, it seems that every new Fellow was expected to sign the scroll itself to show his acceptance of the College's rules. The Fellows continued this practice for over two hundred years until, in February 1914, the Governing Body voted to stop using the scroll and to transfer it to the archives.

A close-up of some of the signatures sheds light on the variety of Fellows who have passed through Magdalen. One signature is that of the great Edmund Cartwright (see p. 63), credited with inventing the power loom, but two come from other Fellows who are perhaps more typical of their time.

One, John Shaw (1750–1824), was elected Demy in 1764 and Fellow in 1771 and remained in post until his death. He had scholarly ambitions and in 1777 published an edition of the Greek poet Apollonius Rhodius (*fl.* third century BC). It was a failure: the memoirist William Tuckwell (1829–1919) claimed that German scholars, at that time the leaders in classical scholarship, 'had formed their estimate of Oxford from third-rate performances like Dr. Shaw's [which] they treated with contumely'. Rebuffed, Shaw published no more and became, according to another memoirist, George Cox (1786–1875) 'a fine sturdy specimen of the *strong-headed* Fellows, who used to live and die within their College walls'.

The other, James Burton (*c.* 1745–1825), had a happier career. He came to Magdalen as a chorister in 1755, when barely ten years old. He matriculated at Magdalen in 1761, and was then elected Demy in 1762 and Fellow in 1771. Burton had good contacts: in 1771 he also became Rector of Over Worton, Oxfordshire, and in 1775 he felt confident enough financially to marry and resign his Fellowship. His career prospered, and in 1793 he was appointed a Canon of Christ Church, where he died in 1825. He also became a chaplain in ordinary to George III. An obituary in the *Gentleman's Magazine* observed that 'His urbane, kind and hospitable disposition rendered him beloved and respected by a large circle of friends.'

RHD–S

▲ A section from the mid-18th century, showing the names of Edmund Cartwright (**1**), James Burton (**2**), and John Shaw (**3**)

LITERATURE

Bloxam, *Register*, vols 1, pp. 167–68, and 6, pp. 338–39 and 342–45.

G. V. Cox, *Recollections of Oxford*, 2nd edn, London, 1870, p. 111.

W. Tuckwell, *Reminiscences of Oxford*, London, 1900, p. 131.

▲ The beginning of the Fellows' Scroll of 1686
  parchment   82.5 x 85.5 cm

◀ John Shaw (1750–1824)

▼ James Burton (c. 1745–1825)

21

14 . Oct. 1889.

Baptismal and family names in full.	alfred Bruce Douglas (Lord)
Age last birthday; eldest, 2nd, or 3rd son, &c.	eighteen, third son.
Date and place of birth; parish, town, county, &c.	oct: 22d 1870 Ham Hill House, Worcestershire.
Father's names in full, and quality; and present residence.	Marquis of Queensberry, peer, 24 James street Buckingham gate London.
Where educated, and for how long.	Winchester. four years & a term
Demy, Exhibitioner, Clerk, or Commoner.	Commoner.

The matriculation records of ▲ Lord Alfred Douglas,
▼ Edward Prince of Wales, and ▶John Betjeman

October 15th 1912.

Baptismal and family names in full.	Edward, Albert, Christian, George, Andrew, Patrick, David. Prince of Wales.
Age last birthday; eldest, 2nd, or 3rd son, &c.	18. Eldest son.
Date and place of birth; parish, town, county, &c.	June 23rd 1894. White Lodge, Richmond, Surrey.
Father's names in full, and quality; and present residence.	His Majesty King George V.
Where educated, and for how long.	Royal Naval College, Osborne: 2 years. Royal Naval College, Dartmouth: 2 years.
Responsions or Certificate.	
Demy, Exhibitioner, Clerk, or Commoner.	Commoner.

Three Matriculation Forms

Oxford colleges keep their records in very different ways, and this is particularly striking in the way they deal with the admission of new members. Some colleges have long series of detailed registers (University College, for example, has kept such registers since 1674), but others do not bother. For much of its history Magdalen has, unfortunately, been in the latter category. Although the elections of Demies and Fellows were recorded, it was not until the 1850s that any formal attempt was made to collect details of every new member of the College. By the late 1860s, the College had devised these very detailed printed forms for freshmen to fill in. They remained in use until 1928, when the practice ceased.

Three famous old members of Magdalen have been chosen to show how the forms worked. The first is Lord Alfred Douglas (1870–1945), the poet with whom Oscar Wilde, another Magdalen man (see pp. 67–69), fell in love; Douglas came up in 1889. The second is Edward, Prince of Wales (1894–1972; later Edward VIII), who came up in 1912. The third is the future Poet Laureate John Betjeman (1906–84), who came up in 1925.

The first two entries in particular show how such forms did not fit all parties. Alfred Douglas had to remember to include his title, and Prince Edward, when explaining his father's status or profession, had to enter, quite simply and honestly, 'His Majesty King George V'. Apart from the interest to be found in seeing such famous old members of Magdalen at the start of their careers, such books tell us much about the social backgrounds and education of all the College's members.

Only when these three forms had been selected for inclusion did it become apparent that all three men had something in common: none of them got a degree. Prince Edward's situation is the most excusable because of the First World War, but neither Douglas nor Betjeman ever quite managed to pass their exams (in Betjeman's case it did not help that he and his tutor C. S. Lewis (p. 153) did not get on at all well).

RHD-S

Date of Matriculation.	Michaelmas 1925		
Baptismal and family names in full.	John Betjemann		
Age last birthday; eldest, 2nd, or 3rd son, &c.	19 only		
Date and place of birth; parish, town, county, &c.	August 29 / 1906 52 Parliament Hill Mansions Highgate Rd London N.W.		
Father's names in full, and quality; and present residence.	Ernest Edward Betjemann Esq 53 Potter Church Street Chelsea London SW.3		
Where educated, and for how long.	Marlborough 4½ years		
Responsions or Certificate.	Both [2 Credits, Certificate]		
Demy, Exhibitioner, Clerk, or Commoner.	Commoner		

The Buildings

Magdalen College, South Front

The painting shown opposite is one of the oldest known depictions of the College. Only two earlier ones are known: a pen drawing (1566) by John Bereblock (*fl.* 1557–72) and a map of Oxford with a drawing of the College (1578) by Ralph Agas (*c.* 1540–1621). A letter of 15 June 1745 from Dr Richard Rawlinson (1690–1755) to Thomas Rawlins (Bodleian Library, Ballard MS 11, fol. 107) says:

I met with an old painting of Magd. Coll. Oxford at the end of Q. Mary or the beginning of Q. Elizabeth, as appears by the Spanish habits on the bridge. It pleased them so well that they have given it a place in their Hall.

Although the exact date of this painting is unknown, the dress of the men on Magdalen Bridge suggests that it was executed between 1590 and 1630, some forty years after the date suggested by Rawlinson, according to Susan North of the Victoria and Albert Museum. Magdalen's archives hold a pencil drawing of the painting by John Buckler (1770–1851) which bears the caption: 'The picture is painted on panel in AD 1665.' Joseph Skelton (1781/2–1850) published an engraving of the painting in his *Oxonia Antiqua Restaurata* (1823) and dated it to the time of Charles I. A copy of the painting in the illustrated edition of the 'Oxford City Millenary Exhibition Catalogue' (1912) bears the caption: '(*c.* 1620) Magdalen College in the time of James I or Charles I'. If the figures were painted in contemporary dress, then it was executed in 1630 at the latest, or, if Oxford men were fashionable, some years before that.

▲ John Bereblock's pen drawing of 1566

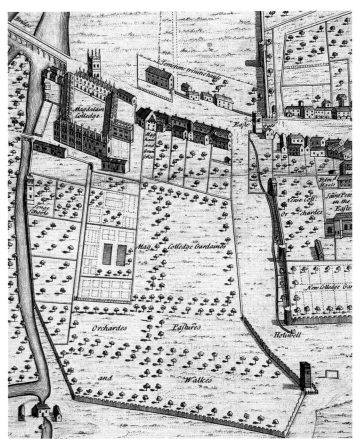

▲ The 1578 map by Ralph Agas

▲ A late 16th- or early 17th-century view of the College
 oil on canvas   87.5 x 179 cm

The painting is a naïve but tolerably accurate representation of the south face of the College. The pale building to the right is different from the remainder of the buildings, which are much closer to the natural colour of the stone. The south wing of the Kitchen Range was built in 1635, i.e. after the likely date of the painting. So if this feature were added later, it would account for the difference in colour.

It is not clear what the figures on the bridge are doing, but they may be 'riding the franchise', a ceremony which was first recorded in 1391/2 and continued until about 1900. At the end of his term of office the Mayor of Oxford would make a circuit of the bounds of the city starting at Magdalen Bridge (*Victoria History*, 4, p. 260).

Dr Richard Rawlinson FRS (1690–1755) was a graduate of St John's College, an antiquarian and collector.

DBR

LITERATURE

Mary Clapinson, 'Rawlinson, Richard', *ODNB*.
The Victoria History of the County of Oxford, 15 vols, vol. 4: *The City of Oxford*, ed. Alan Crossley, London, 1979.

◀ Engraving of the painting from Joseph
 Skelton's *Oxonia Antiqua Restaurata*, 1823

The Muniment Room

William of Waynflete devoted a whole section of the College statutes (see pp. 8–9) to the question of its title deeds, charters and other important documents, ordering that 'at the top of the tower next to the Chapel should be as many chests as are sufficient for the safer keeping of evidences, muniments, and writings'. Consequently, a room in this tower was fitted out in the 1470s to store over 12,000 title deeds

relating to the lands which Waynflete had given to his new College.

Magdalen's so-called Muniment Room is one of the oldest archival storerooms in Great Britain, and one of the few to preserve its original fittings more or less intact. Indeed, this room arguably has the only interior within the College whose appearance has not changed in over five hundred years. It was essential

Hidden
Magdalen

◀ Late 15th-century cupboards containing the boxes, with earlier chests

▲ One of the boxes of deeds

that the College's deeds, some of which date back to the twelfth century (see p. 12), were kept secure and well-organized, because their existence supplied proof of the College's ownership of land against anyone wishing to dispute it. Not for nothing were archives once called 'muniments'.

The Muniment Room is a perfectly functioning example of a late medieval filing system, but at a transitional stage. The muniment room of New College, fitted out in the 1380s, originally stored its archives in large chests. But by the sixteenth century, archives were being stored in cupboards with fitted drawers. At Magdalen, as shown opposite, title deeds were kept in boxes that were loosely stored in cupboards. Each box represents a parish or manor in which the College owned property, and each one is of a unique size, depending on the quantity of deeds it contains. Some of them still bear their original fifteenth-century labels.

The Oxford Dendrochronology Laboratory recently dated the fittings of this room by examining a sample of the boxes in the cupboards and two of the chests. The boxes were all dated to the second half of the fifteenth century, but the two chests proved a surprise. The felling date of the timber used to make a large red chest out of view to the left of the main picture was *c.* 1426–42, while the felling date of the timber used to make the chest with iron straps on the right of the main picture was during the early 1370s, making both chests older than the Muniment Tower itself.

The only way into this room is a spiral staircase which is so narrow that one wonders how the chests were brought up here.

RHD-S

LITERATURE

John Steane, *The Archaeology of Power: England and Northern Europe, AD 800–1600*, Stroud, 2001.

The Medieval West Window
and its Replacement

After the end of the English Civil War, these shattered pieces of late medieval glass in the Chapel vestibule, including a depiction of William of Waynflete, were rescued and gathered together. We know only that the Chapel's main windows were once fully furnished with glass of this age and quality until a visit by Cromwell's troops. According to Antony Wood (1632–95), the Fellows had taken down and hidden the old windows, 'but being unluckily discovered by Cromwell's Troops, they were all demolished by those ignorant fanatics'. Wood does not date the vandalism, but notes elsewhere that Cromwell himself visited the College in 1649. Bloxam, writing over two centuries after the event, says that the Fellows entertained Cromwell for dinner and that the destruction followed afterwards. A College legend recounts that the Roundheads laid out the glass in the Cloisters, rode their horses back and forth across it, and then extracted payment from the College for this service.

A new vast West Window for the Chapel had been made in 1642 by Richard Greenbury (b. before 1600, d. 1670), and it would have been in place and noticed by Cromwell in 1649. But happily, it, and other Greenbury windows around it, escaped destruction on this occasion, perhaps because of their sober colouring.

Some mystery pertains to this episode, for the vandalism of 1649 was not the only Cromwellian attack on Magdalen's precious glass. Macray refers to a pamphlet of 1642 describing an incident which occurred that year, shortly before the King set up residence in Oxford. It reports that some parliamentary soldiers, being prevented from entering the College, 'began to batter the Chappell windowes, whereof one windowe being at the east end of the Chappelle of Darke work which was valued at an hundred pound, which was beaten down to peeces, with many other windowes of thirty pound price'. No other published reference to this affair exists, but the 'Darke work' may well refer to some of Greenbury's

glass, which is now positioned round the West Window in the Antechapel and which may then have been positioned elsewhere in the building.

Although Greenbury's West Window faces the twenty-first century in perfect condition, it has twice suffered from the assaults of history. When made in 1642, it was one of the largest windows in the country and certainly one of the finest examples of 'black-and-white' work (as this form of grisaille was known at the time) in existence. It depicts the Apocalypse, with souls being snatched up into Heaven on one side and despatched down to Hell on the other. Greenbury took the design from an engraving of 1600 by a German artist, Schwartz, who had taken the design from a section of Michelangelo's Sistine Chapel ceiling.

In 1702, a 'great gale' blew the window to shards and it was restored in 1795 by Francis Eginton (1736/7–1805), who subtly tinted the 'Darke work' to create superb effects on summer evenings as light streams into the Antechapel from the west. In the late 1930s, with a European war increasingly imminent, the window was removed and packed into wooden crates, through which, when they were moved, one could hear the splintering of glass. The contents were examined in the 1980s, but the task of restoration and re-erection seemed too daunting. A decade later the matter was raised again and it was resolved to find the money and the craftsmen to restore the window.

An old member, Stuart Lever (matriculated 1944), who was serving as Master of the Worshipful Company of Glaziers, undertook to restore one of the smaller areas above the main window — with spectacular results. Chapel Studio in Kings Langley, Gloucestershire, then agreed to undertake the full restoration, the cost of which was borne by another old member, Professor Jack Richards (Rhodes scholar, matriculated 1951), and his wife, Professor Minnie McMillan, to mark their wedding anniversary. The

task was not easy: one quarter of the entire surface had been irrevocably destroyed and had to be remade. Moreover, no clear and complete likeness had survived — either of the original window or of Eginton's reconstruction — and the nineteenth century had left us only very gloomy photographs taken from the side without full lighting. So the restorers were confronted with a time-consuming and extremely complex jigsaw — thousands of pieces of broken glass with no image to work to. But the completed task — it is universally agreed — is a dazzling success.

ADS

▲ Remnants of medieval glass from the original Chapel West Window, salvaged and made into a window in the Cloisters opposite the Chapel

LITERATURE

Bloxam, *Register*, vol. 2.

Macray, *Register of Members*, vol. 4, pp. 4–5.

Antony Wood, *History and Antiquities of the Colleges and Halls in the University of Oxford*, ed. J. Gutch, 3 vols, Oxford, 1786, vol. 3, p. 351.

Charles I and Henrietta Maria: Glass Portraits

In 1626 Accepted Frewen (1588–1664) was elected President. Although he had formerly been identified with the Puritans who were in the majority in College, his experience as a chaplain to the Madrid embassy and then to Charles I made him ready to embrace the new Laudian ascendancy of the royal court with some enthusiasm. During the 1630s he constructed a grand Baroque gateway to provide a fitting entrance point for solemn processions and visiting dignitaries (see p. 40), and he refitted the Chapel at considerable expense with a new black and white marble floor, new grisaille windows in the Antechapel, and new Laudian furnishings, including the magnificent brass lectern that is still *in situ*.

These remarkable glass portraits of Charles I and his wife Henrietta Maria provide the most eloquent testimony to the way Frewen cultivated and displayed his close royal connections. The portrait of Henrietta Maria is dated 1633 amongst the flowers which frame her head. Drawn with remarkable delicacy and refinement, it is thought to be the work of Richard Greenbury (b. before 1600, d. 1670), who was paid £2 by the College in 1633 (see also pp. 30 and 47). The grand cycle of recently restored grisaille windows in the Antechapel is also ascribed to him, and John Evelyn (1620–1706) went to the Chapel to inspect a 'Greenborrow' depiction of the Last Supper that used a technique of painting on cloth patented by the same artist. Greenbury had attracted royal patronage as early as 1622, when he was commissioned to paint a full-length portrait of James I, and he continued to flourish under Charles I, who appointed him painter to the Queen. On one occasion he was paid the princely sum of £312 10s. for a large body of work. This included new windows in the chapel at St James's and copies of and numerous gilded frames for Charles's new acquisitions by Titian, Leonardo, and other Italian painters.

The glass portraits of Charles and Henrietta used a relatively new technique, with a wide range of enamel colours being painted and then annealed on to the exterior of thin panels of glass. Fine lines were

achieved through the use of a point. The technique allowed much greater elaboration of detail than before and enabled Greenbury to emulate the style of Renaissance oil paintings and contemporary engravings. In fact, these two royal portraits closely follow portraits by Daniel Mytens (1590–1647) which had been engraved by W. J. Delff (1580–1638).

The glass panels were probably originally situated in the President's Lodgings, and moved to the Hall when the Lodgings were remodelled in 1770. In the Lodgings they would have provided tangible evidence of Frewen's close relationship with Charles and Henrietta — a relationship which served the President rather better than it did the College. When Charles was strapped for money in 1643 he wrote to Magdalen and other colleges asking for the loan of their silver plate. Whereas New College evaded the request by claiming that most of its silver was the personal possession of the Warden, Magdalen, under its Royalist President, responded with greater enthusiasm than any other college. It sent off 220 lb of silver plate and 66 lb of gilt to be melted down and added a further loan of £1,000 (half of which came from Frewen himself) as a sign of its special devotion.

The College was left to mourn the loss of its great collection of silver and was soon subject to violent reprisals by Cromwell's victorious troops (see p. 30). In contrast, Frewen's loyalty was handsomely rewarded. In the following year he was consecrated Bishop of Coventry and Lichfield in Magdalen's own chapel (which he had remodelled and adorned at such expense), and at the Restoration he was elevated to the see of York.

JBWN

LITERATURE

L. H. Cust, 'Greenbury, Richard', rev. S. Herring, *ODNB*.

Poole, *Catalogue of Portraits*, vol 2.1, pp. xv–xxiii.

National Portrait Gallery Archive Collection, no. DD19461, engraving of Henrietta Maria by W. J. Delff, after D. Mytens.

◄◄ Glass portraits of Charles I and Henrietta Maria, which probably hung originally in the President's Lodgings. Probably made by Richard Greenbury, 1633

► Detail

▲ Three stalls with seats folded up, showing the misericords and carvings on their undersides

▶ Detail of carving

The Antechapel Stalls and Misericords

The misericords and the stalls to which they belong seem to be all that is left of the fifteenth-century Chapel furnishings. At first they were in the Chapel proper, and Bloxam suggests that they originally numbered forty-two. If this is so, then ten have been lost. Twenty-nine misericords, all with shaped and moulded divisions and arm-rests, are now affixed to the north, south, and west walls of the Antechapel; three others are free-standing. Their overall appearance is currently rather forlorn, especially when one compares their modern situation with the much grander surroundings and fittings they must have had when they stood in the Chapel. At one time, Bloxam says, the stalls were lined and surmounted with canopies and lofty panelling, 'terminating in crocketed arches and handsome tracery, the whole coloured and gilt' and adorned with 'painted figures of saints'.

The ornamental carvings on the misericords become visible when the hinged seats are folded upwards. The word 'misericord' derives from *misericordia*, which in monastic usage signified an indulgence or the relaxation of a rule. When folded upwards, a misericord provided support to someone who was, at least technically, standing during Offices or the Mass.

Magdalen's misericords portray a variety of animals, such as a fox and geese, an owl and mouse, a crouching ape, a swan, a deer, a horse or donkey eating its own foot, and winged monsters. There are also a number of grotesque faces and masks, along with more commonplace devices like the Founder's arms, rich foliage and flowers, and a carving of the pelican in her piety — a traditional symbol of Christ, since the pelican was believed to have fed her young with her own blood.

When Cottingham restored the Chapel in 1829–34, there was some debate over what should become of the original carved seats. One idea was to incorporate them into the new design — but Cottingham believed it would then be necessary to stain all the new wood in the Chapel to match them. It was also suggested that the old wooden furnishings might be given away or sold. If ten stalls are indeed missing, perhaps that was their fate.

MJP

LITERATURE

Bloxam, *Register*, vol. 2, pp. viii–ix, cxcvi, cci–ccii.

The Bells of Magdalen College Tower

Magdalen's bells form a ring of ten, with the heaviest or tenor bell, in the key of E, weighing approximately 965 kg. They are hung for change-ringing and regularly rung for College occasions.

When the Great Tower was nearing completion in 1504/5, five bells were transferred from a previous tower that had formed part of the Hospital buildings (see p. 7). These had been cast by a London bell-founder, William Dawe, alias Founder (*fl. c.* 1393–1418). One of these bells still hangs in the Great Tower and so predates the founding of the College by some fifty years.

In 1602 Joseph Carter of Reading (*fl.* 1600–10) cast a new bell weighing about 318 kg, which increased the ring to six. Two decades later, Ellis Knight of Reading recast two bells, placing his initials, a fleur-de-lys founder's mark, and the date 1623 on each of them. He recast a third bell in 1641, but having inscribed it with 'HONOR THE KINGE', discreetly omitted his initials and founder's marks.

In 1712, Abraham Rudhall of Gloucester (*fl.* 1700–20) cast two new bells to bring the ring up to eight and recast a fourth medieval bell from the Hospital. This augmentation may have caused a degree of rivalry between Magdalen and New College, which had possessed a ring of eight bells since 1655. So it may not be a coincidence that later in that year New College acquired two new bells to bring their ring up to ten.

In 1739/40 Abel Rudhall (*fl.* mid-eighteenth century) cast two more bells for Magdalen to increase its ring to ten. The work was paid for by William Freeman (b. 1702), a member of the College and a keen ringer who, in 1748, also paid for the recasting of the fifth bell. Before the bells assumed their present form, the final recasting was that of the eighth bell by Robert Taylor & Sons of Oxford in 1828.

Accurate weights for the individual bells are not available, but their estimated weights range from 254 kg for the treble or smallest bell to 965 kg for the tenor. Their combined weight is estimated at about 4,270 kg.

For many years the Great Tower had experienced severe oscillation when the bells were rung. In 1963, extensive damage caused by wet rot, dry rot, and deathwatch beetle was found in the timberwork throughout the Tower, and serious defects were discovered in the medieval foundation of the bell frame. So it was resolved to reduce the oscillation by lowering the bells. The Tower's timberwork was also replaced, and the bell frame of *c.* 1912 was given a new steel foundation that was sited much lower in the Tower. The ringing fittings, which had been renewed in 1877, were renovated at the same time.

BJS

◀ A brass rubbing of an inscription on one of the bells

▲ A view of the belfry

▶ The fourth bell

The 'Repton Red Book'

At the end of the eighteenth century, Humphry Repton (1752–1818) was England's most famous garden designer. He developed the tradition of landscape gardening pioneered by William Kent (bap. 1686, d. 1748) and Lancelot 'Capability' Brown (1716–83). Repton was especially famous for his so-called 'Red Books', morocco-bound volumes in which he produced illustrated proposals for potential clients, regularly including 'before' and 'after' views of their estates. He often worked on these projects with architects, first with John Nash (1752–1835), and then, after they quarrelled, with his son John Adey Repton (1775–1860).

Early in 1801 the Reptons produced a Red Book for Magdalen College. This was one of their largest productions and set forth an ambitious scheme. The Reptons proposed that the meadow within Addison's Walk should be partly flooded to create a lake, and that a little temple should be built in its north-east

corner. Within the College, the New Building would be covered with a Gothic veneer, the north range of the Cloisters radically remodelled, and a third range connecting them would create a large, three-sided quadrangle looking out onto the new lake.

As several of these views have often been reproduced, a lesser-known, but no less interesting, pair of views is shown here. The one on p. 39 is the proposed view looking south from beneath the cloister of the New Building, now completely Gothicized. The one above (revealed by lifting a flap) shows the daring plans for the remodelling of the College's medieval buildings after one has walked through this cloister, with the new west range to one's right.

The Reptons were not alone in suggesting plans for the development of Magdalen. From the 1790s until the 1820s President Martin Routh (pp. 60–61) regularly considered how best to complete the New Building and, if possible, unite it with the medieval

Cloisters. Many architects produced designs for his consideration, though none of them, including the Reptons', was ever executed.

Unfortunately, the Red Book is no longer in its original form. At an unknown date it was unbound and its pages were pasted into a large folio volume that contained other drawings. The pages were extracted and reconstituted as a separate volume once again in the 1990s.

RHD-S

PROVENANCE

Presented by the Reptons either to the College or to President Routh.

LITERATURE

H. Colvin, *Unbuilt Oxford*, London, 1983, pp. 78–104.
White and Darwall-Smith, *Architectural Drawings*, pp. 38–43.

◀▲ Two designs by Humphry and John Repton from their Red Book for Magdalen College, 1801

39

The Pugin Gate and its Predecessors

The history of the Pugin gateway (1844), and its precursors is a salutary reminder of how much of Magdalen has been destroyed, whether to meet the changing whims of architectural fashion or to make way for buildings that never materialized.

The carvings depicted here comprise some of the exquisite nineteenth-century carvings from the gateway that are now scattered around College. The Mary Magdalene which topped the outside of the Pugin gateway now graces the north gable of Grove. The statue of Waynflete which, with John the Baptist, stood in elaborate buttress niches on either side, is now in the arcade below. The elaborate intervening armorial panels (Magdalen and the see of Winchester) were reset in the walls of the Cloisters in the 1990s and look as if they were always meant to be there. This Mary, from the Gate's inner face, and the arms of London and Exeter (the latter seemingly a homage to Henry Phillpotts (1778–1869), Magdalen's recent Fellow who had been enthroned as Bishop) are still hidden away in the base of the Great Tower, along with some wonderful fragments of the earlier, seventeenth-century gateway.

The sorry tale of Magdalen's gateways starts with a small Baroque masterpiece of 1633. Variously ascribed to Inigo Jones (1573–1652) and Nicholas Stone (1585–1647), but now identified as the work of the master carvers John (bap. 1599, d. 1654) and Mathias (bap. 1605, d. 1654) Christmas, it was part of the extensive remodelling of the College undertaken by Accepted Frewen (see p. 32). The gate, which is well illustrated in the Loggan engraving of 1675, was at right angles to the High Street so that those entering the College from the city were immediately faced by an imposing spectacle: the Chapel's west façade and great doors, and the adjoining Founder's Tower to the north. Flanked by pairs of Doric pilasters and topped by a broken pediment and cupola with a statue of Waynflete on the exterior and Mary Magdalene on the interior, it was the equal of Stone's grand gateway to the Botanic Garden. But whereas the latter survives,

the sculptural richness of Magdalen's Baroque gate can only be inferred from prints and the quality of the surviving fragments displayed in the Great Tower. The massive brooding presence of the seated (and now headless) Waynflete gives some idea of what has been lost.

The quality of this Baroque gem was lost on the nineteenth century, which considered it (like the New Building) quite inappropriate for a place of learning. As early as 1792, James Wyatt (1746–1813) produced designs to replace it with a more suitable Gothic gateway in the tradition of an entrance lodge to a country estate. In 1828 the College's architect, John Buckler (1770–1851), told President Routh (see pp. 60–61) 'that the old gateway looks more obnoxious than ever; it will be impossible to endure it any length of time'. In 1844 it was demolished in favour of a new gate, by A. W. N. Pugin (1812–52).

Pugin had long harboured designs to build in Oxford, but other commissions came to nought thanks to the furore engendered by his assertive Catholicism. In 1843 his plans to remodel Balliol had been rejected at the last minute and the Magdalen commission was something of a consolation prize. It was dreamed up in considerable secrecy by the influential Fellow and Anglo-Catholic, Dr John Bloxam (see pp. 64–65), with the support of President Routh. The cost of £679 was higher than that incurred by the College when building an entire new church at Tubney according to Pugin's designs in 1846, and testifies to the unusual degree of attention that Pugin lavished on the commission: 'I want to make this little work as perfect as possible & I shall be able to introduce a deal of beautiful detail ... and the carving must be exquisitely done.'

Sadly, none of this stopped the College sweeping away Pugin's gate a mere forty years later in order to make way (as it transpired quite unnecessarily) for George Frederick Bodley's (1827–1907) and Thomas Garner's (1839–1906) St Swithun's Quad. It was replaced by a much weaker design which fronted

▲ Some of the surviving carvings from the
19th-century gateway by Augustus Pugin,
later demolished

directly onto the High Street, thereby destroying
Pugin's only work in Oxford and depriving visitors of
the arresting visual impressions which they had
previously gained when entering the College.
Although the wanton destruction of these two small
architectural masterpieces cannot be righted, it can
only be hoped that one day the College will find a
way to re-enter the Front Quad from the correct
angle.

JBWN

LITERATURE

White and Darwall-Smith, *Architectual Drawings*, pp. xxvii
(Fig. A), nos 59, 383, and 405 (Fig. 80) for the Christmas
Gateway; pp. xlvii–xlviii (Fig. I) and 120ff. for the Pugin
Gateway.

M. Belcher, ed., *The Collected Letters of A. W. N. Pugin*, vols 1
and 2, Oxford, 2001 and 2003 (for Pugin's extensive
correspondence with Bloxam).

H. Colvin, *Unbuilt Oxford*, London, 1983.

L. Litvack, 'An auspicious alliance: Pugin, Bloxam and the
Magdalen commissions', *Journal of the Society of Architectural
Historians* 49 (1990), pp. 154–60.

Hidden
Magdalen

The Great War Memorial Cross

At the end of the First World War the colleges of Oxford, like schools and parishes up and down the country, erected memorials to their dead. Most were content just to erect a list of names of the fallen, but Magdalen was more ambitious and commissioned two tablets of names to go in the passageway leading from

the Chapel to the Cloisters, and also a cross to stand in the middle of St John's Quadrangle. Both memorials were designed by Alfred B. Yeates (1867–1944), whose major work is the Royal Exchange Buildings, London.

The War Memorial was dedicated on 8 February 1921 by the Prince of Wales (later Edward VIII), who had been an undergraduate at Magdalen in 1912–14 and lost several Magdalen friends in the war. A cutting from *The Times* shows him laying a wreath at the base of the cross. Sir Herbert Warren (1853–1930), President of Magdalen from 1885 to 1928, stands behind him.

Some idea of the extent to which the cross dominated its surroundings can be gained from this engraving by Edmund New (1871–1931), an artist who is best known today for his magnificent 'New Loggan' engravings of the Oxford colleges (1907–29).

The cross's life in Magdalen was, however, brief, for it was taken down in 1940. According to contemporary minutes, the College, anxious about the effects of bomb blast on the stone artefacts and cobbles in St John's Quadrangle, ostensibly thought it best to remove as many of them as possible. So most of the Quadrangle was given over to lawns (which were replaced by freshly designed paving in 1999), and the cross was put into storage.

But some sources hint that several Fellows had come to dislike the cross, not so much on religious grounds, but because of what it represented, and the fact that no interest was ever expressed in re-erecting it after the Second World War is very suggestive.

Eventually, in October 1971, the College agreed to loan the cross indefinitely to the Wheatley branch of the Royal British Legion. They erected it in a garden in Wheatley, where it remains to this day. It is not known how the British Legion came to make such an approach, but it has meant that the cross can still be seen, albeit not in its original home.

RHD-S

42

◀ Edmund New's engraving of the Great War Memorial Cross

▼ The dedication ceremony on 8 February 1921, as pictured in *The Times* the following day

▶ The cross in its present position

The People

William of Waynflete and his Buskins

▲ William of Waynflete by an unknown artist, probably late 16th century

▼ Waynflete's embroidered buskins, part of his ceremonial vestments

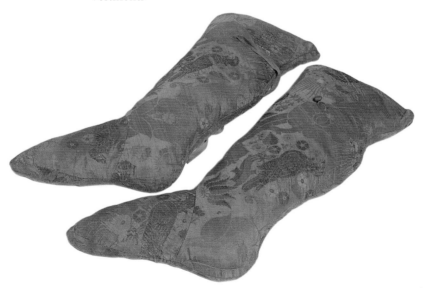

The fashion for painted portraits of founders took hold in the late sixteenth century. Before then the memory of a founder such as William of Waynflete (d. 1486) was kept alive in prayers and manifested in objects such as croziers, copes, and other richly adorned vestments. These offered a visible reminder of the founder's worldly power but also contained an echo of the medieval cult of saints, in which relics such as clothing could be venerated thanks to their physical association with the saint.

Magdalen had a number of such effects, amongst them Waynflete's crozier, which was taken from the College after the Civil War (it may be depicted in Richard Greenbury's portrait of 1638), and a fine, late fifteenth-century damask cope. But Waynflete's richly embroidered lampas silk buskins (ceremonial stockings worn by a bishop during a pontifical mass) and equally splendid velvet ankle boots are the most rare and extraordinary survivals. Probably made in Italy between 1425 and 1450 and preserved because of their direct association with Waynflete, they are already mentioned in a 1495 inventory of Magdalen College Chapel: 'two tunicles of white damask lined with blue tartaroun and a pair of sandals of that set ... a pair of stockings of silk with divers flowers ... a pair of boots of tissue ...'.

The buskins are embroidered in gold with falcons on blue and white cornflowers and squirrels with blue columbines; they are lined with linen and tied with a garter just below the knee. The boots are covered with crimson velvet with silver-gilt weft loops brocaded with silver-gilt bellflowers. Sumptuous items of this kind are likely to have been associated with a great ceremonial occasion, such as Waynflete's installation as Bishop of Winchester in 1448. But recent analysis of the textiles by June Swann and Lisa Monnas has also revealed a quite different aspect to a fifteenth-century bishop's life: one of the buskins' linen linings retains traces of blood, suggestive of a leg ulcer.

It may be overly neat to suggest that the late sixteenth-century vogue for commissioning imagined portraits of founders filled the need which arose once the Reformation had undermined traditional ways of memorializing them. Whatever the case, Magdalen was no exception to the new fashion. In the late sixteenth and early seventeenth centuries two very different portraits of William of Waynflete were produced. Both reflected the religious controversies of the period and provided authoritative images that were widely copied right down to the nineteenth century.

The first portrait illustrated, probably dating from the late sixteenth century, reinvents Waynflete as a good Elizabethan Protestant. He holds a book, the essential marker of Protestant adherence, that is inscribed with the words from the Magnificat which he took as his motto: *fecit mihi magna qui potens est, et sanctum nomen eius*. He is dressed soberly with a black cap and cassock, but also retains some simple items of episcopal attire (a white rochet and fur-lined black chimere) that were rejected by more radical Puritans. This image no doubt reflected the College's cautious but law-abiding Puritan leanings in the late sixteenth and early seventeenth centuries.

The second portrait of Waynflete, which the College paid Richard Greenbury £5 15s. to paint in 1638, was quite different. Waynflete still holds a book in one hand, but his magnificent crozier studded with precious stones, bejewelled mitre, and embroidered cope convey an impression of a very different religious adherence. This may have appealed both to the artist, a Roman Catholic recusant, and to the President, Accepted Frewen (1588–1664), who was at this date busily readorning the Chapel with much finery. With a small picture of Magdalen inset in the top left corner, the portrait closely follows a model that had been established by Sampson Strong (*c.* 1550–1611) when, in the 1590s, he produced portraits of an equally splendid William of Wykeham for Winchester College and New College. Waynflete's buskins and boots evoke Greenbury's portrayal rather than the Protestant bishop of the earlier portrait. But the fact that both portraits continued to be copied and displayed attests to the way these different religious and intellectual dispositions continued to attract adherents in Magdalen over the following centuries.

JBWN

▲ Richard Greenbury's painting of Waynflete, 1638

LITERATURE

M. Campbell, 'Medieval founders' relics: royal and episcopal patronage at Oxford and Cambridge colleges', in P. Coss and M. Keen, eds, *Heraldry, Pageantry and Social Display in Medieval England*, Woodbridge, 2002, pp. 126–42, at 135, plate 22.

R. Marks and P. Williamsom, eds, *Gothic: Art for England*, London, 2003, pp. 370–71, no. 250.

Poole, *Catalogue of Portraits*, vol. 2.1: pp. xi–xxii for Strong and Greenbury; p. 209 f. and plate XXVII for Waynflete; pp. 145 ff. and plate XX for William of Wykeham.

*Hidden
Magdalen*

Waynflete's Tomb: A Wax Model

Perhaps the most curious memorial of the College's cult of its founder is the wax model of his tomb in Winchester Cathedral, made by the sculptor Richard Cockle Lucas (1800–83), who presented it to John Bloxam (see pp. 64–65) in the 1840s. A richly coloured model some 24 inches long by 12 inches high, it has long languished in storage but can now be seen by the doorway into the College's Antechapel.

Lucas had been apprenticed to a Winchester cutler at the age of fourteen, but his autodidact talents were noticed by the Cathedral Dean and in his late twenties he was encouraged to take up sculpture. He secured a place at the Royal Academy, quickly attracted the attention of Frederick Nash (1782–1856), and produced numerous models for Buckingham Palace's chimneypieces and other fittings. Palmerston numbered among those who were attracted by his work and eccentricity (Lucas's albums show him variously dressed as a Druid, necromancer, and poet in classical pose), and he used his position as Prime Minister (1859–65) to obtain an annual civil list pension for Lucas—the first to be awarded to a sculptor rather than a writer.

Models were very much Lucas's *forte* and he produced two 12 foot by 6 foot models of the Parthenon, on commission for the British Museum: one as imagined in its prime and the other as it appeared after the explosion of 1687. He also presented elaborate models of William of Wykeham's chantry chapel to both Winchester College and New College, possibly in the hope of being invited to replace the missing statues in the chantry itself.

The model of Waynflete was much less elaborate and may well have been intended to secure the patronage of Bloxam, whom Pugin had courted so successfully a few years earlier (see p. 64). There is no evidence that Lucas benefited from the gift, but a later description of Bloxam's College rooms by a Magdalen chorister and undergraduate reveals how he displayed it as a veritable shrine to the College's founder: 'the innermost of this set of rooms bore a striking resemblance to a small oratory. From the ceiling there hung a very beautiful and elaborate "corona" designed by Pugin which might have adorned the chancel of a moderately sized church. Under this corona, in the very centre of the room, there stood a richly decorated model of the tomb of the founder of the college.'

JBWN

LITERATURE

E. V. H. Vine Hall, 'Two Oxford rooms fifty years ago', *Oxford Magazine*, 24 (23 May 1906); cited in M. Belcher, ed., *The Collected Letters of A. W. N. Pugin*, 2 vols, Oxford, 2003, vol. 1, p. 379 n. 3.

D. Willows, 'Lucas—Father and Son', *Winchester Cathedral Record* 73 (2004), pp. 56–62; 74 (2005), pp. 49–51; 75 (2006), pp. 58–59.

◀ Wax model of William of Waynflete's tomb, made by Richard Lucas in the 1840s

Cardinal Wolsey by Sampson Strong (attrib.)

Thomas Wolsey (1470/1–1530) graduated from Magdalen with a BA in 1486 at the age of fourteen, before becoming a Fellow (1497), Junior Bursar (1498), Senior Bursar (1499–1500), Master of Magdalen School, and Dean of Divinity (1500). As Bursar, he was responsible for the administration of the College's affairs, including the construction of the Great Tower, which was begun in 1492 but not completed until 1505.

It was not long before Wolsey resigned his Fellowship, but his experience at Magdalen may have helped him on his upward ascent as Royal Almoner, Dean of Lincoln, Hereford, and York, Bishop of Lincoln and Winchester, Archbishop of York, cardinal, Lord Chancellor, papal legate, and founder of Christ Church. Certainly, Magdalen was careful to maintain good relations with him for it sent him frequent gifts of gloves and in 1518 added two hogsheads of Gascon wine, costing 40s. In the same year it entertained him at a cost of £8 11s. 11½d. and paid 12d. for a copy of his arms. By then he was probably already Henry's wealthiest subject with an estimated income of £9,500, and well on the way to becoming the most powerful man in the kingdom.

Wolsey's spectacular fall from power, death, and subsequent vilification possibly dimmed Magdalen's pride in its connection with him for a brief while. But by the early seventeenth century the College was keen to advertise its association again, notwithstanding the strong Protestant currents within the College at the time. Certainly, the College's portrait of Wolsey illustrated here makes no attempt to play down his catholic status for it portrays him in full cardinal's garb. If there were concerns about this, they were presumably outweighed by the cachet gained by reminding viewers that Christ Church (depicted in the inset cameo top left) had been founded by a former student and Fellow of Magdalen.

The portrait is very similar to one painted for Christ Church in 1610–11 by Sampson Strong (c. 1550–1611), who had established the tradition of posthumous founder portraits in Oxford. Both paintings involve an inset picture of Christ Church (a standard hallmark of Strong's founder portraits), and it seems probable that Strong produced the Magdalen picture in much the same way as he produced duplicate portraits of William of Wykeham (c. 1324–1404) for Winchester and New College. This attribution would make it the earliest known portrait to have been painted by a former member of the College. In the register of matriculations Strong is entered by Magdalen in 1589/90 and describes himself as aged 40, from Holland, and the son of a gentleman. He was employed by the College to paint the statues in Magdalen's Cloisters in 1605 and 1610. We also know that Magdalen possessed a picture of Wolsey by 1618, since in this year it paid 5s. to a painter named Louder to improve the picture of Cardinal Wolsey in the President's Lodgings. In 1666 a further £2 was paid to another painter, Taylor, for the restoration of the pictures of the Founder and Cardinal Wolsey — the retouching and reworking of pictures has a long pedigree. The Wolsey portrait still hangs in the President's Lodgings, as does a portrait of Magdalen's only other cardinal, his contemporary, Reginald Pole (1500–58), who fled to Rome, where he became a cardinal, before returning to become Archbishop of Canterbury in the reign of Mary Tudor (1516–58).

JBWN

LITERATURE
P. Gwyn, *The King's Cardinal*, London, 1990.
S. M. Jack, 'Wolsey, Thomas', *ODNB*.
Poole, *Catalogue of Portraits*, vol. 2.1, pp. xi–xii and 211–12.

▶ Thomas Wolsey painted probably by Sampson Strong, early 17th century

50

Hidden
Magdalen

Portrait of John Foxe

The martyrologist John Foxe (1516/17–1587) was one of the founding fathers of the Church of England, along with William Tyndale (*c.* 1494–1536), translator of the Bible, and Thomas Cranmer (1489–1556), author of the Prayer Book. Foxe came from Boston in Lincolnshire. He entered Brasenose in *c.* 1534, took his BA in 1537, and became a Fellow of Magdalen in 1538. Foxe also became a reforming evangelical at about this time, and although one of a like-minded coterie within Magdalen's Fellowship, he found it increasingly difficult to bear the strain of outward conformity. Matters came to a head after he became an MA in 1543 since, according to the College statutes (see pp. 8–9), Fellows had to take holy orders within two years of taking this degree. Because Foxe refused to do so, he had to resign his Fellowship in 1545, just before the religious climate changed in his favour with the accession of Edward VI (*r.* 1547–53).

For most of Edward's short reign Foxe worked as tutor to the Duke of Norfolk's four grandsons. But in 1554, fleeing from the Marian persecution, he escaped to the continent where, with the assistance of other religious exiles, he started to prepare his account of the English Protestant martyrs. The first edition was published as *Actes and Monuments* (known as the Book of Martyrs) in 1563, after Elizabeth I had re-established Protestantism as the national religion. Three further, extended editions appeared in Foxe's lifetime of which the most important was the second (1570). Here Foxe developed the idea that the English were God's chosen people who had valiantly fought through the centuries to keep the true faith alive. The book was a historical and literary milestone, being based on an original mix of oral, archival and secondary material. It was also a masterpiece of English Renaissance prose. From the mid-seventeenth century the work could be consulted in every parish church. Until the nineteenth century, it was the most widely read book in English after the Bible and played a crucial part in the creation of an English national identity.

The Magdalen portrait features a brown-eyed, kindly looking man with a grey, straggly beard who is dressed in a sober black robe trimmed with fur above a white shirt. He wears a black cap and wide-brimmed hat, sports a modest white ruff, and holds a manuscript book in his fine long fingers. It is the portrait of a learned man of the cloth and perfectly captures the martyrologist's reputation for charitable deeds. The portrait is incontestably of Foxe, for the artist has painted the words JHON and FOX on either side of the subject's hat. Whether it was painted from life or from a contemporary or slightly later copy we shall never know. Only two other purported paintings of Foxe exist. The portrait owned by Queen's College, Oxford, cannot be authenticated and resembles the Magdalen portrait only superficially. But the painting in the National Portrait Gallery is almost identical with Magdalen's, except that the subject is reversed, the face is more pinched, the ruff is less evident, the fur trimming is more prominent, and only the book's cover is visible. The age of the sitter is given on the canvas and reveals that the portrait was painted in the last years of Foxe's life. But if this is so, it is odd that his beard and moustache, in contrast to the Magdalen likeness, are brown and well kept.

During Elizabeth's reign Foxe maintained close relations with his Alma Mater and in 1563 he gave the College a copy of the first edition of his book. He was a long-standing friend of Magdalen's first Protestant President, Laurence Humphrey (1527–90), who was installed in 1561 after the ejection of the Catholic Thomas Coveney (d. 1571), and in 1574 Foxe entrusted his son, Samuel (1560–1630), to Humphrey's care. Samuel Foxe in turn became a Fellow in 1579 but suffered the indignity of being expelled, albeit temporarily, two years later, when he fell out with the religious radicals in the College who were pushing for further reform. Foxe junior, though, seems not to have borne a grudge. He inherited his father's collection of books and manuscripts, and when his

IHON   FOX

own son, Thomas (1592–1662), graduated as MA from Magdalen in 1614, he presented the College with fourteen of the manuscripts.

The martyrologist was Magdalen's most prestigious sixteenth-century Fellow apart from Wolsey. As one of those who helped to create and stabilize English as a written language, it was only fitting that his likeness should have been purchased in 1934 during the Presidency of George Gordon (1881–1942), a former Professor of English Literature.

Foxe's *Book of Martyrs*

The title page of *Actes and Monuments*, illustrated overleaf, consists of an engraving of the two sides of the religious divide, split into three panels. On the left of the pair of bottom panels a Protestant pastor addresses the faithful; on the right a Catholic priest seeks to control his flock. On the left of the pair of middle panels, the Protestant martyrs blow trumpets heavenwards as they succumb to the flames; on the

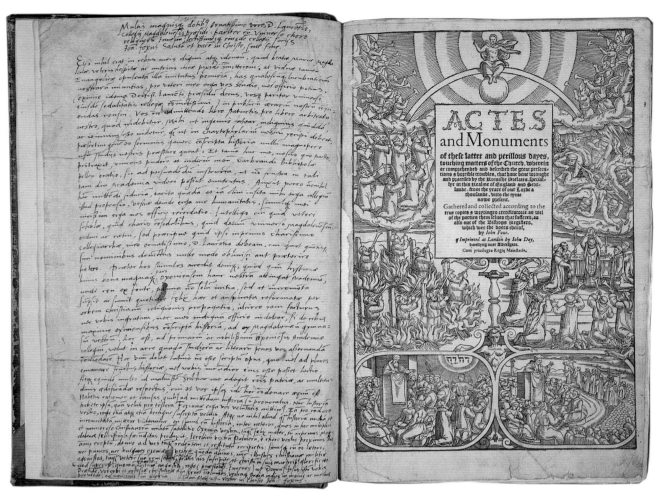

▲ The title page of Foxe's *Book of Martyrs*, with his letter to
President Humphrey on the left-hand page

right, the celebrants at mass blow their trumpets
heavenwards as the priest elevates the host. On the left
of the pair of top panels, the crowned martyrs point
their trumpets at the Deity; on the right, devils blow
theirs downwards. In the single uppermost panel the
Deity is celebrated by trumpeting angels on both sides.

Foxe wrote a letter in Latin to President Humphrey,
which was later tipped in to face the title page. Here
Foxe explains that he had initially been reluctant to
donate such a book to his old college because it was
written in English and of little use to scholars. He had,
however, been persuaded to change his mind by the
London bookseller Garbrand (*fl.* 1539–90) and by his
recollection of how much he owed to Magdalen.
Moreover, as the book contained the histories of many
Oxford men, including Magdalen's own Marian
martyr, Julins [sic] Palmer (1531/2–1556), Foxe

believed that the gift was also a way of returning the
University's lost sons to their Alma Mater.

Palmer was born in Coventry, attended Magdalen
College School, and became a Fellow in 1549. At first
a religious conservative, he seems to have been
converted in 1555 on witnessing the burning of
Latimer and Ridley in Oxford. Early in the next year
he resigned his Fellowship and became a schoolmaster
in Reading. Unable to keep his views to himself, he
was eventually denounced, tried for heresy, and
executed at Newbury. The first edition of the *Actes
and Monuments* provides only a short account of
Palmer's life (pp. 1539–41), but the second contains a
lengthy and well-researched biography and a
harrowing account of his last moments.

L W B B

PROVENANCE
Portrait purchased from Mr A. D. Kettle in 1934; cost: £10.

Portrait of John Hampden

John Hampden (1593–1643), known as 'the Patriot', was the son of William Hampden, a Buckinghamshire gentleman, and Elizabeth Cromwell, a relative of Oliver. His father died before he was two and tradition has it that John went to Thame Grammar School before matriculating at Magdalen on 30 March 1610. The Hampdens were strong Calvinists and doubtless found the 1559 Elizabethan Settlement of the Church too 'Catholic'. It is possible that John was sent to Magdalen because the then President, John Harding DD (c. 1555–1610), elected in 1608, belonged to the Puritan camp. But Harding died in November 1610 and Hampden may not have found his successor, the conformist William Langton (1574–1626), so congenial. Hampden may also have moved next door to Magdalen Hall, whose Principal was the Puritan, John Wilkinson (c. 1570–1650). Hampden's stay is not mentioned in Magdalen's archives and he can only have been in residence for a couple of years before moving to London in order, like many other young gentlemen, to finish his education at the Inns of Court.

Although Hampden was an MP from the 1620s, he gained national fame only in 1637/8 when he was taken to court for refusing to pay 'ship money', a tax levied by Charles I in the mid-1630s to finance a navy for defence against Barbary pirates. When levied on the sea-board counties it was accepted; but when extended to inland counties it met greater resistance, and in 1637 Hampden, one of the more prominent refuseniks, was called before the Court of the Exchequer to explain his behaviour. So effectively did his counsel, Oliver St John, make the case for the illegality of the tax that the judges, hand-picked by the King, only found seven to five in Charles's favour.

Charles called a Parliament again in 1640, when he needed to raise money to put down the rebellion that had broken out against his religious policies in Scotland two years earlier. Hampden sat in both the Short and Long Parliaments of that year and played an important role in the subsequent attack on Charles's policies of the previous eleven years. When Parliament

▲ John Hampden, probably a 19th-century copy of an earlier portrait by an unknown artist
oil on canvas   75 cm x 60 cm

split in 1642 over how far reform should go, Hampden sided with Pym and the radicals. He became a soldier during the Civil War and was killed at Chalgrove Field, Oxfordshire, in 1643. No authentic contemporary portraits exist of John Hampden, and the colours, tone, brushwork and flat unfinished quality of Magdalen's portrait suggest that it is a copy that was painted in haste in the second half of the nineteenth century, or even later. According to Mrs R. L. Poole it is a copy of a painting in the possession of the Earl of St Germans. It was presented to Magdalen by C. R. L. Fletcher (1857–1934), Fellow 1891–1906 and a long-serving Modern History Tutor.

LWBB

LITERATURE
Poole, *Catalogue of Portraits*, vol. 2, p. 217.

The Expulsion of the Fellows by Joseph Tonneau

In March 1687 Magdalen's President died, and the subsequent events thrust an unwilling College into the limelight. The Fellows elected John Hough (1651–1743) as their new President, but James II wished to impose his own candidate. Fearful of a Catholic monarch who had imposed a Catholic Dean on Christ Church, the Fellows refused to accept his choice and the King offered a second nominee. Again the Fellows refused, and were fiercely reprimanded by the King when he visited Oxford in September 1687. In the following month, James ordered a visitation of the College. Hough was expelled from Magdalen, but not before he had boldly declared to the King's Commissioners:

> I do hereby Protest against all your Proceedings, and against all that you have done, or hereafter shall do, in prejudice of me and my Right, as illegal, unjust and null, and therefore I appeal to my Sovereign Lord the King in his Courts of Justice. (Bloxam, p. 136)

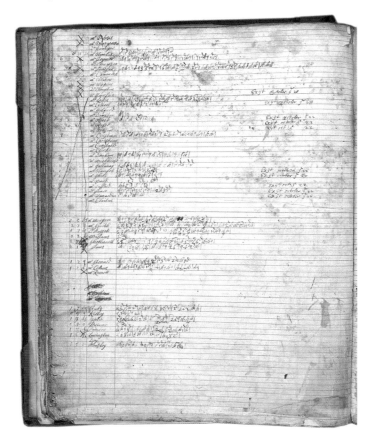

The Fellows then offered to submit to the Commissioners 'so far as is lawful and agreeable to the Statutes', but this was insufficient for James, who ordered their expulsion in November and filled the College with new Fellows. The incident was quickly held up as an example of James's unjust rule, and a subscription was even set up to help the extruded Fellows. But eventually even James accepted his error and in October 1688, shortly before his deposition, he reversed his decision. The Bishop of Winchester, Peter Mews (1619–1706), who was also the College's Visitor, reinstated the extruded Fellows, and with his own hand deleted the names of the intruded Fellows from the College's Buttery Book. That page is reproduced here.

The main illustration depicts a later recreation of the act of expulsion and is the work of Joseph Tonneau (d. 1891), a Belgian artist who had settled in Britain. Having painted several Fellows, he was commissioned in 1880 to paint Frederick Bulley (1811–85), who was Magdalen's President from 1855 to 1885. Delighted with the result, the College, according to an advertising brochure of March 1884, commissioned Tonneau to recreate Magdalen's finest hour. His painting depicts 'The moment of Bishop Hough's leaving the Hall, after his appearance before the King's Commissioners and his protest against their illegal act in depriving him of the office of President.'

Tonneau tried to get as many details correct as he could, be it of academic dress or the possible appearance of the Hall in the 1680s, and John Bloxam (pp. 64–65) helped him locate portraits of the leading characters. But Tonneau made one major error: as Bloxam himself said in a letter of February 1884 to his friend General Rigaud, 'It is a pity that [the painting] is historically incorrect and misleading, the Protest having taken place in the [Senior] Common Room.' Setting the scene in the much larger Hall, however, made for a better picture.

RHD-S

▲ *The Expulsion of the Fellows*   Joseph Tonneau,
painted 1884
oil on canvas   100 x 150 cm

LITERATURE

J. R. Bloxam, *Magdalen College and King James II 1686–88*,
Oxford, 1886.

L. Brockliss, G. Harriss, and A. Macintyre, *Magdalen College
and the Crown: Essays for the Tercentenary of the Restoration of the
College 1688*, Oxford, 1988.

◀ The Buttery Book showing the deleted names of
James II's intruded Fellows

Dr Henry Sacheverell by Thomas Gibson

Henry Sacheverell DD was born in 1674 at Marlborough, where his father was Rector. He became a Demy in the 'Golden Election' of 1689, as did Addison (see p. 144), with whom he may have shared a room and who dedicated to him his 'Account of the Greatest English Poets'. Sacheverell was ordained priest in 1697 and became a Fellow of Magdalen in 1701. Like Addison, but from a very different standpoint, he was one of the most prominent controversialists of his time, defending Tory High Church interests against Dissenters and Whigs. He condemned his opponents with relentless vigour, in the hard-hitting political language that was common at the time. His sermons were very popular and those that were published sold in large numbers, as did his pamphlets. Indeed, phrases from them became watchwords for his faction ('hang out the bloody flag and banner of defiance!').

On 5 November 1709 he preached at St Paul's Cathedral, but instead of giving a disquisition on Guy Fawkes he attacked Dissenters and Occasional Conformists. His sermon was a vehement defence of the established order in Church and State and a condemnation of 'the utter *Illegality* of *Resistance*' to the Sovereign. Speedily published, the sermon sold massively. Because the Whig ministry chose to construe it as a seditious attack on the 1689 Settlement and Queen Anne's right to the throne, Sacheverell was impeached by the Commons — but the mob repeatedly rioted in his favour, burning the meeting houses of Dissenters. Tried before the Lords in 1710, he was found guilty, but sentenced only to a three-year ban on preaching. The ministry had to resign, and the general election of 1710 was won by the Tories, partly as a result of popular enthusiasm for Sacheverell in many parts of the country. He was rewarded with the living of St Andrew's Holborn, one of the richest in England, though this meant resigning his Fellowship (1713). He married in 1716 and died in 1724, leaving £200 to Magdalen in his will.

He composed the inscription for the memorial to Thomas Collins, long-term Master of Magdalen College School, that is to be found in the Antechapel.

Sacheverell has had limited sympathy from historians. That may be partly because his enemies had blackened him viciously, and Bloxam (see pp. 64–65) could be right to suggest that many of the stories about him were 'groundless calumnies, circulated only by the spirit of party'. Thomas Gibson (*c.* 1680–1751) was a portrait painter and a founder director of Kneller's Academy in London. He executed this portrait in about 1710.

RCSW

PROVENANCE

Bequeathed in 1799 by William Clements (Demy 1728), son of Henry Clements, Sacheverell's publisher.

LITERATURE

Bloxam, *Register*, vol. 6, p. 99.

G. Holmes, *The Trial of Doctor Sacheverell*, London, 1973.

▶ Henry Sacheverell painted by Thomas Gibson, *c.* 1710 oil on canvas 71 x 61 cm

59

President Routh

Martin Joseph Routh (1755–1854) is one of Magdalen's most legendary figures. Having matriculated from Queen's College in 1770, he was elected Demy at Magdalen in 1771, and then Fellow in 1775. He became President in 1791 and remained

in post until his death sixty-three years later, having been a member of the College for over eight decades.

In his extreme old age Routh fascinated his contemporaries. He had long been much respected for his piety and he had won an international reputation for his scholarship. But the remarkable retention of his faculties to the end (he published a new book in the year before he died) meant that he also came to be seen as a precious link with the past. As a result, many were eager to obtain an audience with the aged President, who continued to wear the wig and knee-breeches which had been the fashion of his youth.

Two of the objects illustrated reflect this interest in Routh. According to Bloxam (see pp. 64–65), the daguerreotype above was taken on Routh's ninety-ninth birthday (19 September 1854), just three months before his death. Unfortunately, as Bloxam himself observed, the photographer failed to prop Routh high enough up in his seat for him to be able to look directly at the camera. Nevertheless, we should be grateful for this precious image of the President, wig and all, since very few other photographic images exist of people who were born in the 1750s.

The second object reflects on the symbolic nature of Routh's wig. In his later years, Routh stood firm against attempts to meddle with Oxford's traditional ways. Even in the early 1850s, when a Parliamentary Commission was set up to investigate the reform of Oxford, Routh remained unmoved. One of Magdalen's more progressive Fellows of this time was the scientist Charles Daubeny (see p. 203), and although Daubeny liked Routh personally, he was frustrated at his refusal to accept change. So on Routh's death, Daubeny dipped one of Routh's famous wigs into a stream near Matlock whose water was famed for its high mineral content. The wig became petrified and now stands in a glass case in the Old Library, as a monument, certainly, but also as a comment and a warning.

RHD–S

PROVENANCE

The daguerreotype has presumably always been in the College's possession; the wig was given by Charles Daubeny.

LITERATURE

Bloxam, *Register*, vol. 7, pp. 1–37.

J. W. Burgon, *Lives of Twelve Good Men*, 2 vols, London, 1888, vol. 1, pp. 1–115.

C. Daubeny, *A Biographical Sketch of Rev. Dr. Routh*, Oxford, [*c.* 1855].

R. D. Middleton, *Dr. Routh*, Oxford, 1938.

◀ (ABOVE)   President Routh at 99
   daguerreotype   12 x 9.5 cm   1854

◀ (BELOW)   Portrait of Routh by Karl Hartmann, painted in
   1850

▲ Routh's petrified wig

*Hidden
Magdalen*

Edmund Cartwright

ENGRAVED BY J. OLDHAM BARLOW, FROM THE ORIGINAL PICTURE BY ROBERT FULTON.

LENT TO Mr B. WOODCROFT, GREAT SEAL PATENT OFFICE.

Artist's Proof.

62

Hidden
Magdalen

Edmund Cartwright by Thomas Barlow, after Robert Fulton

Edmund Cartwright (1743–1823), an undergraduate at University College, was elected Demy at Magdalen in 1762 and Fellow in 1764. He relinquished his Fellowship in 1775 on his marriage to Alice Whitaker. While at Magdalen he started to publish poetry, and Sir Walter Scott thought highly of *Armine and Elvira* (1770). Cartwright's brother John (1740–1824) was a political activist who advocated parliamentary reform and deplored the war in America. Edmund shared his brother's views and this is reflected in *Prince of Peace* (1779), his most important literary work.

Cartwright became a rural clergyman in 1772 and, by accident, an inventor and major influence on the Industrial Revolution. One of his first inventions was the power loom, supposedly in response to the imminent expiry of the patent on Arkwright's 'spinning jenny' and the concomitant over-production of yarn. According to an oft-repeated but apocryphal story, Cartwright was inspired to invent the power loom after seeing the Mechanical Turk in action. This automaton allegedly played chess and was very popular in Europe at the turn of the eighteenth–nineteenth centuries. But in spite of its wheels and cogs, the player was human. It is, however, possible that Cartwright heard of the Turk and felt that if a machine could be made to play chess then it must be possible to construct one which could perform the simpler task of weaving cloth. While Cartwright's original loom and later modifications were not an unqualified success, he was influential in demonstrating that mechanical looms were possible. He later invented a rope-making machine and a wool-combing machine which, together with his mechanical loom, aroused opposition from cottage industries. Cartwright was responsible for many other inventions, and because of his interest in farming he devised agricultural machinery and compiled a study of the use of manure.

Cartwright also collaborated with Robert Fulton (1765–1815), the inventor who is credited with the first commercial steamboat, and the two of them worked on the application of power to drive steamboats. Fulton was originally an artist, and on his first visit to England had studied under Benjamin West, PRA (1738–1820). It is Fulton's portrait of Cartwright as engraved by Thomas Oldham Barlow (1824–89) that is illustrated here.

DBR

LITERATURE
D. Hunt, 'Cartwright, Edmund', *ODNB*.

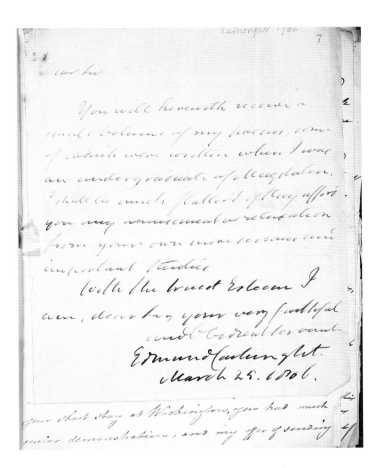

▲ A letter from Cartwright to President Routh

◄ Edmund Cartwright, engraved by Thomas Barlow, 1862, from a painting by Robert Fulton
mezzotint 33 x 27 cm

John Bloxam and his Friends

John Rouse Bloxam (1807–91) was the first great historian of Magdalen. He matriculated at Worcester College in 1826, and was elected Demy at Magdalen in 1830. He became a Fellow in 1835 but resigned his Fellowship in 1863, a year after obtaining a College living at Upper Beeding, Sussex.

Bloxam adored the history and traditions of Magdalen. He re-created May Morning in its modern form; in the 1840s he had the choir sing carols around a tree at Christmas time when this was still a novelty; and he compiled an eight-volume biographical register of the choir, organists, schoolmasters and Demies of Magdalen. He also started the library's collection of Magdalen authors.

Unsurprisingly, Bloxam kept many letters from his friends, of whom two are represented here: John Henry Newman (1801–90), the future cardinal, and the architect Augustus Pugin (1812–52) (see p. 40). In the 1830s, when Newman still belonged to the Church of England, Bloxam became his curate at Littlemore. The two men became great friends, and their friendship survived Newman's conversion to Roman Catholicism. The end of one of Newman's letters to Bloxam is reproduced here.

Bloxam first met Augustus Pugin in 1840. By then, Pugin was a Roman Catholic, but once again this did not prevent a close friendship from developing, for Bloxam shared many of Pugin's architectural ideals and

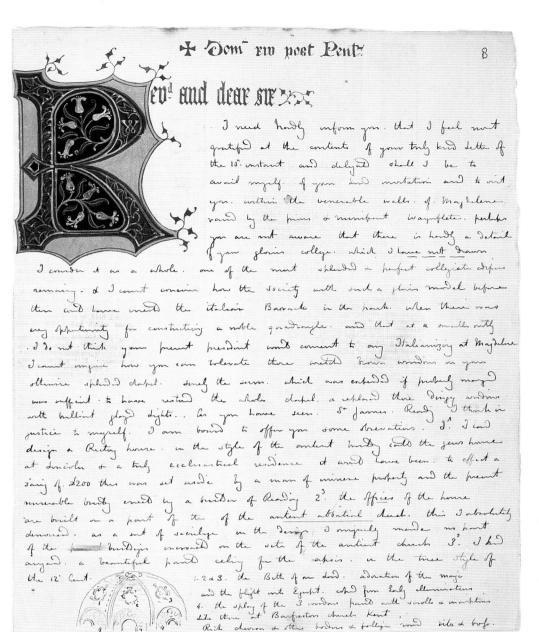

I consider it as a whole. one of the most splendid & perfect collegiate edifices remaining. & I cannot conceive how the society with such a glorious model before them could have erected the italian Barrack in the park. when there was every opportunity for constructing a noble quadrangle. and that at a small outlay.

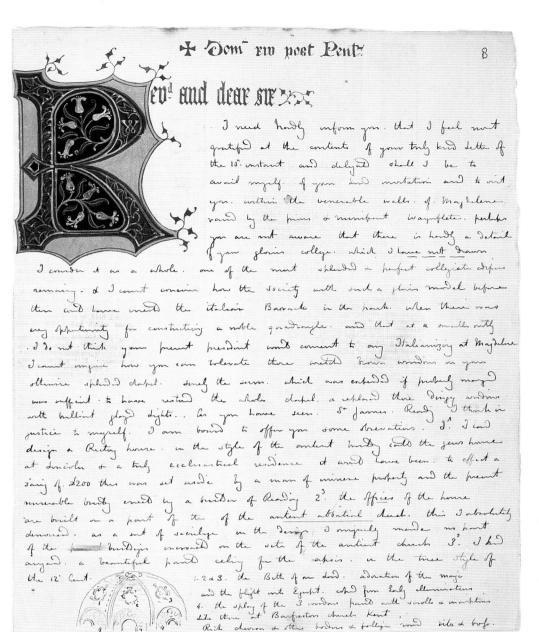

The end of a letter to Bloxam from John Henry Newman

Letter from Augustus Pugin, from the year in which he and Bloxam first met

love of ritual. Pugin wrote frequently to his 'Reverend and dear Dr. Bloxam', and even decorated Bloxam's rooms in College. Pugin often drew little sketches on his letters, but on this one (MS 528/8), dated 13 September 1840, he painted a grand illuminated initial for his friend. In a passage which starts just below the illuminated letter R, Pugin expresses — with his customary vehemence (and idiosyncratic spelling) — his affection for the Gothic Cloisters, and his dislike of the classical (and in his eyes foreign) New Building:

> I consider it [Magdalen] as a whole — one of the most splendid & perfect collegiate edifices remaining — & I cannot conceive how the society with such a glorio[u]s model before them could have errected the italian

Barrack in the park when there was every opportunity for constructing a noble quadrangle—and that at a small outl[a]y. I do not think your present president would consent to any Italianizing at Magdalene.

RHD-S

PROVENANCE

The letters from Newman to Bloxam were given to the College by Bloxam himself; Pugin's letters were first given to Pugin's widow and she gave them to the College in 1908.

LITERATURE

M. Belcher, ed., *The Collected Letters of A. W. N. Pugin*, 2 vols, Oxford, 2001, vol. 1 (1830–42), p. 142.

R. D. Middleton, *Newman and Bloxam: An Oxford Friendship*, Oxford, 1947.

Hidden
Magdalen

Oscar Wilde

Writing in February 1891 to the theatre producer George Alexander (1858–1918) about *Lady Windermere's Fan*, his first society comedy, Oscar Wilde (1854–1900) worried that his celebrated wit was deserting him just when he needed it most: 'I am not satisfied with myself or my work. I can't get a grip of the play yet.' The surviving drafts of this play show how hard Wilde worked to ensure that he got a grip of his material in a way that would also grip his audience.

Magdalen's copy is the second draft of Acts I and II, with many pencilled cuts and revisions in Wilde's hand, all of which aim to make his dialogue sound both elegantly crafted and effortless. Individual speeches are pared down to suggest how much is being left unsaid. Key words are lightly touched on in order to set up shock waves later in the play (Lady Windermere's reference to 'good friends', for example, will turn out to be part of a much wider enquiry into what is meant by 'good' in a play which, at this stage, still had the working title *A Good Woman*). Individual phrases are polished until they have the glitter of epigrams: 'I can resist everything except temptation'; 'In this world there are only two tragedies. One is not getting what one wants, and the other is getting it'; 'we are all in the gutter, but some of us are looking at the stars.'

The College is a natural home for this draft, because it was during his time as a Magdalen undergraduate that Wilde perfected the personal and literary style upon which he would play a set of elegant variations for the rest of his career. He later remarked: 'What is true in a man's life is not what he does, but the legend which grows up around him', and after matriculating in October 1874 he quickly set about providing enough material to keep the local gossips busy for years. Stories about him rippled enquiringly around Oxford: about how he was dragged by some hearties to the top of a hill, after which he dusted himself off and observed coolly 'The view from this hill is really very charming'; how he furnished his rooms with blue

▲ Letter from Wilde to Ward

◀ Bronze bust of Wilde by Melanie le Brocquy

67

▲ Wilde's etching of William Ward on the window of his room

vases full of heavily scented lilies, lamenting that 'I find it harder and harder every day to live up to my china'; how he made his scout wear felt slippers because of the 'agony' caused by hearing his shoes creak.

Many of these stories tangle together fact and fiction in a way that is impossible to unpick, but there are also some solid pieces of evidence about Wilde's time at Magdalen. In his final year, for example, he occupied the three-room set of Kitchen Stairs, I Pair Left, the site of the present Oscar Wilde Room, and on one of the window panes he scratched a cartoon of 'Little Mr Bouncer'. 'Bouncer' was William Ward (1854–1932), who had occupied the rooms before

Wilde and was his 'most intimate' friend at Magdalen. His nickname derived from a character in the illustrated comic novels of 'Cuthbert Bede' (Revd Edward Bradley, 1827–89), beginning with *The Adventures of Mr. Verdant Green, An Oxford Freshman* (1853) and ending with *Little Mr. Bouncer and His Friend, Verdant Green* (1873).

Like the affectionately teasing tone of his letter to 'My Dear Bouncer', with its knowing joke about successfully emerging from 'the clutches of those barbarous Irish' (Wilde himself had carefully removed all traces of his Irish accent when he arrived in Oxford), Wilde's caricature of Ward hints at a world of male friendships and playful banter that he often tried to recapture in his later life. Just as he returned regularly to Magdalen to visit Lord Alfred Douglas (see pp. 22–23), so his writing repeatedly finds itself describing the sort of encounters between men that could be seen either as innocent fun or edged with longing.

The pleasures of hindsight make it tempting to examine Wilde's time at Magdalen for further hints and glimpses of his later career. There was his flirtation with Freemasonry, with its stress on all-male society and secret rituals. There was his willingness to read lessons in the Chapel 'with an air of scepticism', if not outright mockery, suggesting his refusal to commit himself to an idea without recognizing that its opposite might be equally true. But above all, there was his eloquence and the risk that it could become merely a pleasure in the sound of his own voice: 'You have a phrase for everything', Walter Pater once told him reprovingly.

Similar hints can be seen in the extract from *Lady Windermere's Fan*. The rhythm of writing, in which Wilde would add and remove lines until he achieved the right balance of self-expression and self-restraint, looks forward not only to the completed play, with its plot about concealment and revelation, but also to the world of secrets that was increasingly taking over Wilde's own life. At the play's first night, 20 February 1892, Wilde encouraged some of his actors and his closest friends to wear green carnations, a sign suggesting that a secret brotherhood existed both

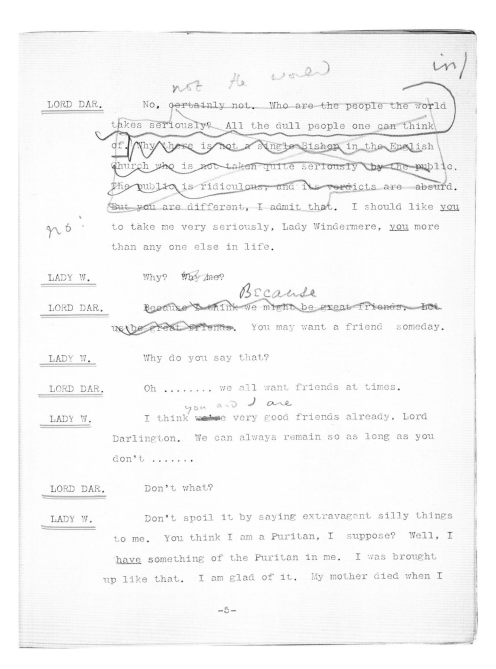

handwritten annotations: "not the world", "in/", "no.", "Because", "you and I are"

LORD DAR.   No, certainly not. Who are the people the world
takes seriously? All the dull people one can think
of. Why there is not a single Bishop in the English
Church who is not taken quite seriously by the public.
The public is ridiculous, and its verdicts are absurd.
But you are different, I admit that. I should like you
to take me very seriously, Lady Windermere, you more
than any one else in life.

LADY W.   Why? Why me?

LORD DAR.   Because I think we might be great friends. Let
us be great friends. You may want a friend someday.

LADY W.   Why do you say that?

LORD DAR.   Oh .... we all want friends at times.

LADY W.   I think we are very good friends already, Lord
Darlington. We can always remain so as long as you
don't ....

LORD DAR.   Don't what?

LADY W.   Don't spoil it by saying extravagant silly things
to me. You think I am a Puritan, I suppose? Well, I
have something of the Puritan in me. I was brought
up like that. I am glad of it. My mother died when I

-5-

◄ A page from the second draft of
Lady Windermere's Fan

inside and alongside mainstream society. That night he took Edward Shelley, a clerk at the Bodley Head, to bed at the Albemarle Hotel. Perhaps he could still hear faint echoes of one of Mrs Erlynne's speeches in the play:

> You don't know what it is to fall into the pit, to be despised, mocked, abandoned, sneered at — to be an outcast! To find the door shut against one, to have to creep in by hideous byways, afraid every moment lest the mask should be stripped from one's face, and all the while to hear the laughter, the horrible laughter of the world, a thing more tragic than all the tears the world has ever shed.

Masks were important to Wilde, whose work often plays in the gap between what people think in private and what they say in public. He might have especially enjoyed the fact that his weightiest presence in Magdalen is now in the form of a bronze bust by Melanie le Brocquy (b. 1919)—a three-dimensional mask that is even more impassive than the sort of society figures he so enjoyed mocking. But in *Lady Windermere's Fan* we can already see the mask starting to slip and the line between art and life starting to blur. The day when Wilde would find out who his 'good friends' were was getting closer.

R J D – F

69

Portrait of Robert Robinson

Sir Robert Robinson FRS (1886–1975) was the ninth of the thirteen children of William Robinson, a textile manufacturer in Chesterfield, Derbyshire. As William hoped that Robert would enter the family firm, which had close ties with the dye-stuffs industry, he persuaded him to study Chemistry at Manchester Victoria University. Robert graduated top of his year group in 1905.

Robinson stayed at Manchester to study with Professor W. H. Perkin (1860–1929), who gave him his life-long interest in alkaloid and pigment chemistry. When his doctorate was awarded in 1910 Robinson had already published thirty research papers, an extraordinary output even by modern standards. Appointments followed to Chairs in Sydney, Liverpool, St Andrews and Manchester. By 1920, aged only thirty-four, he had been awarded a Fellowship of the Royal Society — British science's most prestigious distinction.

In 1929 Robinson was appointed Waynflete Professor of Chemistry at Oxford, a post that is always associated with a Fellowship at Magdalen. Soon after

his arrival he remarked that since the only better place to be was heaven, he intended to stay in Oxford. This he did for twenty-five years, during which time he published 400 research papers.

Robinson is renowned for his work on naturally occurring, biologically active molecules, including the sex hormones and penicillin. He was awarded the Nobel Prize for his work on alkaloids — compounds that have striking, sometimes spectacular physiological effects. Among the most familiar are quinine, cocaine, atropine and morphine, all of which have important medicinal qualities, as well as strychnine — a very potent poison. These are large, complex molecules and today's chemists possess sophisticated tools that make it easy to determine their chemical make-up. But in Robinson's day it was necessary to break up a natural product into small, readily identifiable fragments so that the original structure could be established by using an unambiguous pathway of chemical reconstruction. This laborious process involved great experimental skill, creativity and keen logic. Robinson was the acknowledged master of this technique, but he

Hidden
Magdalen

Robert Robinson drawn by James Arden Grant
(1885–1976) pastel

Replica of Robinson's Nobel Prize Medal for Chemistry,
awarded 1947

also went further, establishing that his synthetic
pathways could reveal how these compounds were
synthesized in Nature itself.

On one side the medal displays a portrait of Alfred
Nobel and the years of his birth (1833) and death
(1896) in Latin. The other side portrays Nature as the
goddess Isis, holding a cornucopia: her veil is being
lifted by the Genius of Science. The inscription reads:
Inventas vitam juvat excoluisse per artes ('Inventions
enhance life which is beautified through art').

Sir Robert Robinson received the 23-carat gold
medal from the Royal Swedish Academy of Sciences
in 1947, together with a gilded brass replica which was
given to Magdalen.

RGD

71

72

*Hidden
Magdalen*

Erwin Schrödinger by Peter Edwards

Professor Erwin Schrödinger (1887–1961), a theoretical physicist and one of the great scientists of the twentieth century, was a Fellow of Magdalen from 1933 to 1938. In a remarkable scientific paper of 1926 he published the Schrödinger wave equation, which enables the energies and properties of molecules and materials to be accurately predicted. The paper also forms the basis for understanding many twenty-first-century fields of science such as chemistry, materials science, semi-conductors, nano-technology and molecular biology. It is likely that many modern devices—such as lasers, computers and mobile phones—would not have been developed without Schrödinger's fundamental contribution.

Schrödinger published nearly all his papers on his own and held appointments in several European countries. He had the Chair in Berlin that had previously been occupied by Max Planck (1858–1947), the founder of quantum theory. But when Hitler came to power Schrödinger left Berlin and came to a Fellowship at Magdalen that had been arranged by Professor Frederick Lindemann (Viscount Cherwell) (1886–1957) and President George Gordon (1881–1942). Schrödinger was admitted as a Fellow on 9 November 1933 in the President's Lodgings, and just minutes later the phone rang to inform him that he had been awarded the Nobel Prize, together with Paul Dirac (1902–84). On the same evening, he signed the Fellows' Weights Book (see p. 89).

Schrödinger did not settle well at Magdalen. But in 1935 he did publish his ideas on particle entanglement that have recently become very influential on research aiming to produce a new type of quantum computer. He also proposed the 'Schrödinger's cat' thought experiment. In 1936 he was tempted back to his home country, Austria. After the *Anschluss* of 1938 President Gordon wrote to the Foreign Secretary, Lord Halifax, expressing his concern that Schrödinger, still a Magdalen Fellow, might have been arrested. Halifax consulted the German Foreign Minister, Joachim von Ribbentrop, who said that 'Schrödinger has proceeded to busy himself as a fanatical opponent of National Socialism'. At the same time, W. J. M. Mackenzie (1909–96), a Magdalen Fellow who was visiting Austria, reported that he had met Schrödinger, who told him that 'they ought logically to promote me or put me in a concentration camp'. Schrödinger escaped from Austria and took refuge in the Vatican, where he was already a Member of the Pontifical Academy of Sciences.

He then moved to Dublin at the personal invitation of the *Taoiseach*, Éamon De Valera. There he spent the war and wrote an article, 'What is Life?', that influenced many physical scientists, including Francis Crick (1916–2004), to work on biological problems. Schrödinger returned to live in Austria, where he died in 1961. His grave is in Alpbach, where his daughter Ruth, who was baptized in Magdalen Chapel in 1934, still lives.

Although Schrödinger was widely photographed and his face adorned the Austrian 1,000 Schilling banknote before Austria joined the Euro, no good portrait of him exists. But in 2006, Peter Edwards (b. 1955) — who also did the College's portrait of another Magdalen Nobel Laureate, Seamus Heaney (b. 1939) — executed this fine drawing. It is on display in the President's office, where Schrödinger heard he had won the Nobel Prize and Magdalen undergraduates now have tutorials on his wave mechanics.

DCC

◀ Erwin Schrödinger drawn by Peter Edwards, 2006
charcoal on paper 73 x 52.5 cm

Senior Common Room and Summer Common Room by Alan Sorrell

In 1952 Magdalen's Senior Common Room commissioned Alan Sorrell (1904–74) to paint two conversation pieces for £100 each. The College also owns the many preparatory sketches that Sorrell made of the individuals and items to be featured in the paintings. Sorrell was a pupil of Sir William Rothenstein (1872–1945) — who had also painted Fellows of the College — and joined him on the staff of the Royal College of Art from 1931 to 1948. Sorrell is best known for painting reconstructions of archaeological sites (including Stonehenge and Avebury), and he also recorded the riverside temples and villages in Nubia before they were drowned by Lake Nasser.

Both paintings depict a group of Fellows at dessert after dinner in Hall. The Senior Common Room is used for dessert during Michaelmas and Hilary Terms and the Summer Common Room is used in Trinity Term. In the first painting the Port Railway (pp. 86–87) can be seen across the fireplace. The Vice-President, Colin Hardie (second from left), presides at dessert with President Boase (fifth from left) as a guest. The most senior Fellow present, Godfrey Driver, sits to the left of the fireplace and the next most senior, Clive Lewis, sits to the right. The most junior Fellow, Alan Raitt, sits across the table from the Vice-President. In the second painting the Vice-President, Brian Lloyd, sits at the head of the table: there are no other fixed places.

DBR

▶ *Senior Common Room* and *Summer Common Room*
Alan Sorrell, 1954 and 1967   oil on canvas
Senior: 57 x 68.5 cm   Summer: 61 x 71 cm

Group in Senior Common Room

1   Alan William Raitt (1930–2006), Fellow and Tutor in French 1966–97

2   Colin Graham Hardie (1906–88), Fellow and Tutor in Classics 1936–73, Vice-President 1953–54

3   Arthur White Adams (1912–97), Fellow 1949–79, Dean of Divinity 1949–75

4   Gilbert Ryle (1900–76), Fellow and Waynflete Professor of Metaphysical Philosophy 1945–68

5   Thomas Sherrer Ross Boase (1898–1974), President 1947–68

6   Godfrey Rolles Driver (1892–1975), Fellow 1919–62, Tutor in Classics 1919–28

7   Jack Arthur Walter Bennett (1911–81), Fellow and Tutor in English 1947–64

8   James Howard Eagle Griffiths (1908–81), Fellow and Tutor in Physics 1934–68, President 1968–79

9   Clive Staples Lewis (1898–1963), Fellow and Tutor in English 1925–54

Group in Summer Common Room

1   Patrick Johnson (1904–96), Fellow 1928–47

2   Colin Arthur Cooke (1903–2001), Fellow and Senior Bursar 1944–70

3   Alan William Raitt (1930–2006)

4   Cecil Grayson (1920–28), Fellow and Serena Professor of Italian Studies 1958–87

5   Colin Graham Hardie (1906–88)

6   Robert Spenser Stanier (1907–80), Master MCS 1944–67

7   Hugh Macdonald Sinclair (1910–90), Fellow and Tutor in Biochemistry 1937–80

8   Gerald Norman Cullen Crawford (b. 1919), Fellow and Tutor in Anatomy 1964–73

9   Brian Beynon Lloyd (b. 1920), Fellow and Tutor in Physiology 1952–70, Vice-President 1967–68

The Visit of Khrushchev and Bulganin

The SCR photograph album contains an interesting document of one of Magdalen's encounters with the wider world. The black-and-white picture reproduced on p. 77 was taken on 21 April 1956 and captures the visit to the College of Nikita Khrushchev (1894–1971), then Chairman of the Communist Party of the Soviet Union, and Nikolai Bulganin (1895–1975), then Soviet Prime Minister.

The image, which uncharacteristically for photos of that period is a snapshot with all the protagonists in motion, shows not only the primacy of Khrushchev over Bulganin, the nominal leader of the delegation, but also the studied detachment of the students. The young men and women, one or two of whom sport dark glasses and have cigarettes dangling from their lips in parody of the stereotypical secret agent, contrasted greatly with what Khrushchev was used to in Russia, where universities habitually presented their most ideologically reliable students to visiting dignitaries.

Khrushchev was generally very nervous about his reception by the British public, especially after someone had explained to him the meaning of 'boo' — to which, from then on, he responded in kind. At Magdalen, he was visibly apprehensive when a sole trumpet played the Last Post and strains of the spiritual *Poor Old Joe*, a reference to his recent denunciation of 'Joe' Stalin, were heard in St Swithun's Quad. Unused to British humour, the Soviet leaders missed the irony behind the chant.

In Broad Street, an unidentified object had been thrown in front of the delegation's car, and a Magdalen Fellow inadvertently caused a second security scare. C. E. (Tom Brown) Stevens (see p. 186) suddenly emerged from behind a bush opposite Magdalen's famous plane tree to greet his old school friend, Sir William Hayter (1906–95), the British Ambassador to Moscow (1953–57). Being large, of ruddy countenance, and, as usual, 'unimmaculately dressed', he was thought to be an assassin.

The image is doubly interesting because it captures a forgotten episode in Khrushchev's life. He said nothing about Oxford in his memoirs and complained that he had been herded around too many English towns and cities. According to his son Sergei, the statue of Lazarus in New College Chapel persistently haunted his dreams, but Magdalen left no comparable impression. Nevertheless, Khrushchev did behave himself in Magdalen, unlike in New College, where he burst into students' collections and sat down next to a terrified undergraduate. He also made only one biting remark about the apolitical nature of Magdalen's May Day celebrations.

Although Khrushchev's visit to Britain was overshadowed by his 1959 journey to the USA, it was his first trip to the West and he himself regarded it as pivotal. Certainly, its timing was most interesting. News about Khrushchev's sensational February speech denouncing Stalin's cult of personality had recently emerged, and the tensions of the Suez and Hungarian crises were still ahead. A few months later Oxford students would be demonstrating against the Anglo-French invasion of Egypt and Khrushchev would become known as the ruthless enforcer of Soviet power within the Eastern bloc. But in April 1956 the head of the Soviet Union was still a mystery and the only real scandal occurred when members of the Labour Party confronted him with a list of missing Eastern European Socialists.

In 1956, Khrushchev faced much more serious domestic problems. Emboldened by the February speech, restless Soviet students exacerbated his long-standing tense relationship with the intelligentsia. Khrushchev's encounter with the boisterous Oxford students might well have influenced his dealings with students at home, for in 1957 there was a severe clampdown on critical voices in Soviet universities.

JCAF

▲ Magdalen students in 1956 greeted the Russian delegation
with ironic detachment
SCR photograph album

KEY

1   Karl Leyser (1920–92), Fellow and Tutor in History
    (1948–84)

2   Nikolai Bulganin

3   Selwyn Lloyd (1904–78), Foreign Secretary (1955–60)

4   Nikita Khruschev

5   Sir William Hayter

6   T. S. R. Boase (1898–1974), President of Magdalen
    (1947–68)

The Artefacts

The College Seal

For many centuries and in many cultures seals have been used to authenticate documents. From ancient Egypt, where seals in the form of pharonic signet rings have been found, to China, where seal engraving is a form of calligraphy, to early Christian Europe, sealing a document has testified to its validity. One of the letters of St Augustine (354–430) refers to his use of a seal; by the ninth century it was normal for bishops and others in authority to issue letters under seal. Initially, the seal was attached to cords which fastened the letter shut and protected its confidentiality, but the seal was later used as a sign of the letter's authenticity.

The oldest document in Magdalen's archives to which the College seal is attached dates from 20 July 1477, predating the statutes (see pp. 8–9). It grants power of attorney to three people, allowing them to represent the College in receiving seisin of the manor of Multon Hall, Lincolnshire, about 20 miles south of Wainflete, the founder's birthplace.

The photographs show the press which the College now uses to seal legal documents (usually those related

to transactions in property) and also the seal itself. These were supplied in the second half of the nineteenth century by Thomas Moring (1819–84) of 44 High Holborn, London. Moring was an engraver and heraldic artist whose business was the provision of 'ecclesiastical, corporate, official and private seals' and he received a gold medal for his engraving. He probably engraved the College seal himself but bought in the press from another source. The seal depicts St Mary Magdalene flanked by St Peter and St Paul: the smaller figure beneath her feet is William of Waynflete, accompanied by his coat of arms.

Before a document is sealed, a circular red patch is stuck to it at the point where the seal is to be placed. The paper is then inserted between the upper and lower faces of the seal; the screw of the press is turned and a relief image is formed on the red patch. The Bursar (whose responsibilities under the bylaws include 'the safe custody of the College Seal') and the President or Vice-President then witness the document by signing next to the seal. Every use of the seal is reported to a College Meeting.

CGY

◄▲ Thomas Moring's 19th-century seal and press, still in use, with its impression

The Pulpit Cloth

This is used for two services during the academic year, both in the Trinity Term, when the College hosts a University Sermon. The first takes place on the Sunday in Full Term nearest to St Mark's Day (25 April); the second takes place on the Sunday nearest to St John Baptist's Day (24 June), unless that happens to be the Sunday before *Encaenia*, in which case the sermon is preached on the following Sunday.

When the weather permits the sermon for St John Baptist's Day to be preached outdoors, the cloth is hung from the stone pulpit in St John's Quadrangle. The tradition of holding this service outdoors is an ancient one, and was restored in 1896 after more than a century of neglect, when the preacher was the Dean of Divinity, Cosmo Gordon Lang (1864–1945), later Archbishop of Canterbury. When the University Sermon takes place in Chapel — which the St Mark's Day sermon always does, and the St John's Day sermon does in inclement weather — the cloth is draped over the front of the preacher's stall.

Bloxam (see pp. 64–65) seems confident that the cloth was made specially for the outdoor pulpit and given to the College as a present. Its transport in the year of its arrival (1617) cost 1s. 6d. Bloxam describes the cloth as

> an Antependium of green velvet, embroidered with the Founder's arms enclosed within the garter and surmounted by a mitre. Above the armorial bearings is the date 1617, and beneath them the Founder's initials, W.W. The whole is surrounded by a very elegant border of white lilies and a gold fringe. The embroidery consists for the most part of satin of various colours laid upon the velvet, and enriched with gold and silver thread.

The year 1617 features with such prominence in the embroidery that it looks as if it has particular significance for the history of the College. But it would seem to be nothing more than the year in which the cloth was presented.

MJP

LITERATURE
R. H. Darwall-Smith, 'The Stone Pulpit and the St John's Day Sermon', *Magdalen College Record* (2003), pp. 104–12.

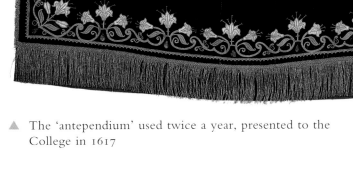

▲ The 'antependium' used twice a year, presented to the College in 1617

The Bursar's Guns

The College owns six pistols and a blunderbuss, all probably dating from the mid-eighteenth century. Two of the pistols, shown in the lower half of the photograph, are similar in design but not a matched pair even though they both have an engraved escutcheon bearing the Magdalen crest behind their firing mechanisms. Their barrels were originally supported by full stocks, which at some point were cut back to half stocks, perhaps to make them easier to draw. The result is a slightly unbalanced appearance that is emphasized by the abbreviated decoration on the stocks. As the pistols take a single ball and are fired by a flint, they had to be reloaded after each shot by ramming gunpowder and a new ball down the barrel, a slow process which meant that the accuracy of each shot was critical. Cleaning and polishing has worn down the stocks and barrels of the pistols, but the relatively undamaged surface of their firing mechanisms suggests that they were not often used. The pistols may have been carried by the Bursar, or the College's designated rent collector, for protection against highwaymen and other robbers.

Like the pistols, the blunderbuss, also called a musketeer, dates from *c.*1730 and was loaded in the same slow way using the ramrod that is stored beneath the stock. It takes a handful of shot rather than a single ball, and its barrel is shaped to scatter the shot in a wide arc. As it is better suited to crowd control than self-defence, it could have been used to deter unruly students from getting out of hand. Like the pistols, it shows more signs of constant cleaning and polishing than it does of real use, so perhaps its appearance alone was enough to fulfil its function.

The blunderbuss is marked with the name of James Walker, an Oxford firearms dealer, and a bill from Walker dated 1729 is in the College archives. Here Walker charges Magdalen £7 10*s.* for three pairs of pistols, £1 11*s.* for another pair of pistols, and various lesser sums for cleaning guns and for powder and flints. Although there is no verifiable link between this invoice and the pistols in the photograph, enough circumstantial evidence exists to suggest they are connected.

CGY

▲ Blunderbuss and two pistols, mid-18th century

The Chancellor's Chair

This highly ornate item of furniture is used only once a year and then, despite its fragility, in the open air. On the Sunday morning closest to St John's Day (see p. 81) it is carefully carried from the Lodgings into St John's Quadrangle. Here it is placed under the stone pulpit in the far corner of the quad, with a pair of capacious seventeenth-century oak armchairs on either side of it and many rows of chairs behind them. The Chancellor (or his Vice-Chancellor or a Pro-Vice-Chancellor) and the macebearers process from the Lodgings, together with the Proctors, President, Dean of Divinity and lastly the preacher, who is led into the building and up into the pulpit. The University Sermon for St John's Day is preached at ten in the morning and often attended by hundreds of worshippers. The sermon is now part of the Oxford University Calendar of sermons, most of which are normally given at the University Church. In recent times both Chancellor Roy Jenkins (1920–2003) and Chancellor Chris Patten (b. 1944) have participated in the event.

The Chair was constructed in the 1820s from the wood of the Magdalen Oak that stood in the area behind the New Building — where some of its scions continue to flourish. The diary of Dean Richard Paget for 29 June 1789 records:

> St. Peter's Day, between 3 and 4 in the morning the great oak fell down in the meadow, *nulli quam mihi*. The principal roots were entirely rotted off, so that twas a wonder it stood so long. Many hundred of people came for several days to view it.

A month later the Governing Body voted £20 for the construction of a chair to be used by the President and designed by Paget himself; a year later the diary records that work was about to begin. But it was to be thirty years before the work, with its decoration of acorns and oak leaves topped by the lilies of Magdalen, was completed.

The tree was believed to be over six centuries old when it collapsed, for it was celebrated as the 'Great Oak' even when William of Waynflete acquired the

▲ The chair used for the annual St John Baptist's Day outdoor service, made in the 1820s

land on which the College stands. *Nichols' Literary Anecdotes* records that 'the people used to divert themselves in crowding in numbers in the inside of the trunk'.

A D S

LITERATURE
Nichols' Literary Anecdotes, London, 1812–15.

Dr Routh's Dish

Silver gilt and circular, with a gadrooned edge and a wide border decorated with laurel leaves and six oval panels of symbols of the Arts and Sciences. In the centre is a large Russian Imperial Eagle.

Routh's dish testifies to a rather unexpected meeting. Magdalen has often featured on the itinerary of eminent visitors to Oxford (e.g. Khrushchev and Bulganin, see pp. 76–77), but perhaps the most remarkable such visit occurred in June 1814. After the defeat of Napoleon in that year, the Prince Regent invited Tsar Alexander I of Russia and King Frederick William III of Prussia to England. During their stay he brought them to Oxford, where they were shown round Magdalen. The Vice-President that year recorded in his Register that the College's royal guests 'deigned to express themselves delighted with what they saw' (*prospiciendo laetos se praedicare dignati sunt*).

President Martin Routh (pp. 60–61) had his own way of marking the great event. As the first volume of his life's work, the *Reliquiae Sacrae* (an edition of the fragments of early Christian writers), had just come out, he presented a copy to each of the royal visitors.

It is not clear what the visitors really made of their learned presents, but Tsar Alexander at least was prepared to express his gratitude in a generous spirit some years later, for, as Routh wrote to his friend Samuel Parr on 11 April 1821:

> I have had the magnificent present of a Silver Dish from the Emperor of Russia in return for the *Reliquiae Sacrae*, which I was urged to present to him, and to the other great Princes, when they visited Oxford about six years since. (MS 462 no. 61)

The hallmark dates the dish to 1820/1 and shows that the Tsar had not sent over a piece that had been made in Russia, but had commissioned it from a London silversmith, Philip Rundell (1746–1827). The dish was a personal present for Routh, but in June 1854, just a few months before his death, he gave it to the College for safe-keeping, as the inscription below (probably the work of Routh himself, who was praised for his inscriptions and epitaphs) so elegantly put it.

RHD-S/DBR

LITERATURE

E. Jones, *Catalogue of the Plate of Magdalen College, Oxford*, Oxford, 1940.

Inscription

UT IMPERATORIO DONO SIT SEMPER HONOS
COMMISSUM FIDEI EST MAGDALENENSIUM
SALVUM CONSERVANDUM A RAPACIBUS ET FURIBUS TUTUM

(So that an imperial gift may be honoured in perpetuity,
it was given into the trust of the members of Magdalen
to be preserved safe and sound from robbers and thieves.)

▲ President Routh's present from Tsar Alexander I, made in London
1820–21 by Philip Rundell
diameter 55 cm

The Port Railway

Magdalen's Port Railway is used for dessert in the Senior Common Room after dinner in Hall and saves the Fellows from having to stand up when passing decanters across the open fireplace, which in winter holds a brightly burning fire (see the painting on p. 75). For medium-sized gatherings, the Butler places small tables and chairs in a horseshoe round the fireplace, with a table containing port, Madeira, Sauternes, claret, fruit, biscuits and chocolates opposite the fireplace. The Port Railway goes in front of the fireplace. The Vice-President sits with the drinks table on his right-hand side. He passes the decanters round the horseshoe to his left until they reach the most senior Fellow by the fireplace, at the head of the Port Railway. After due warning, the decanters are dispatched down the inclined plane of the railway to the second most senior Fellow at the other side of the fireplace. He or she then continues the decanters' circuit to the left, until they reach the most junior Fellow on the opposite side of the drinks table from the Vice-President. Three circuits of all the decanters is normal practice, though this has recently been reduced to two except on Guest Nights. For small numbers in Common Room a single table is used; for large numbers six tables are required. The Port Railway is used only for medium-sized gatherings, but this is the norm for most Guest Nights in Michaelmas and Hilary Terms.

Magdalen's Port Railway is believed to be a copy of the railway in New College, which was invented by Philip Shuttleworth (Warden 1822–40) and lives in the Panelled Room in the SCR. Shuttleworth, who had allegedly seen railways in the collieries of his native Durham, designed a mahogany ramp with a coaster at each end. The ramp slopes gently and the two coasters, running in parallel tracks, are linked by a rope passing through a pulley wheel at the top of the ramp. When a decanter is placed in the coaster at the top of the ramp, it descends under gravity, while pulling the empty coaster to the top.

Like its New College predecessor, Magdalen's Port Railway is made of mahogany. It is 2.5 m long and 457 mm wide. Each coaster consists of a decanter holder whose inside diameter is 159 mm, with a pair of brass wheels at its lower end (diameter 127 mm, width 6.4 mm) and a single wheel at its upper end (diameter 50.8 mm, width 3.2 mm). The track for the large wheels is 197 mm wide, with each wheel running on a brass rail; the small wheel runs in a mahogany groove 6.4 mm wide. The ramp is set at an angle of 5.8 degrees, with a drop of 216 mm over a run of 2.13 m.

The Railway was refurbished by F. H. Bellhouse in the early 1980s and by J. F. Gregg in 2004. Even though a coaster with a half-full decanter can descend under its own weight, heavy-handed Fellows have caused some notable crashes and derailments, hence the need for an experienced and sober catcher at the bottom of the ramp.

BJB

▲   The Port Railway

Hidden
Magdalen

The Smoking Room Scales and Weights Book

Frederic Bulley Jr presented the scales to Magdalen's SCR in 1899. He was born on 10 February 1857, two years after his father had been elected President and so, unlike the other Fellows, was allowed to marry. Frederic Jr was a chorister at Magdalen when John Stainer was its Informator (Master of the Choristers), and then went to Eton before returning to Magdalen as an undergraduate (1875–79). Although he only got a pass degree, he was a demon oarsman, rowing in the First Eight in 1877–79, 1881 and 1883, and in the University Trial Eights for 1880. In 1884–97 he served as Magdalen's Home Bursar, although he was never a Fellow. He then seems to have lived the life of a country gentleman, living in Gloucestershire and serving as a JP. He married a baronet's daughter in 1887 and died on 3 August 1940.

The scales are in frequent use on Guest Nights after dinner and dessert (see the painting on p. 75), when it is the custom for Fellows and their guests to weigh themselves and enter their names and weights in a special book. A sample of some interesting names in early books are T. E. Lawrence (signing on 21 December 1912 and 2 August 1914), J. R. R. Tolkein (12 July 1925), E. Schrödinger (11 November 1934 and 1 October 1938; see pp. 72–73), Howard Florey (20 October 1935) and Theodor W. Adorno and John Eccles (24 November 1935).

The scales consist of a four-legged frame from which a padded seat is suspended. The weight of the person sitting on the seat with their feet off the floor is linked mechanically to a brass lever on the left-hand side of the weighing chair. This is arranged with its fulcrum towards the back of the chair and movable brass weights towards the front. The weighing arm is 368 mm long in front of the fulcrum and 127 mm towards the back. The weight of the person (considerably more than the brass weights) is linked to a point 38 mm behind the fulcrum.

The chair stands 584 mm high, and its seat is 451 mm wide and 406 mm deep. The large brass weight is moved to a position where the lever just moves upwards and the fine adjustment is made with a smaller brass weight. Positions for each weight are marked by transverse slots in the weighing arm. As the large weight measures 0–25 stone and the smaller weight 0–14 lb, a person would need to be heavier than 26 stone (364 lb) to defeat the machine.

BJB

◀ The scales with their weighing mechanism

▲ Page of the Weights Book from autumn 1935, signed by, among others, Theodor W. Adorno and John Eccles

The Bequests

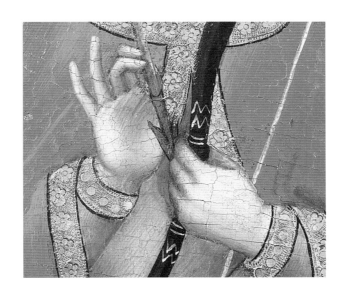

John Brocklebank by Augustus John

John Ralph Auckland Brocklebank (1919–43) was the son of Richard Hugh Royds Brocklebank (1881–1957), both of whom studied at Magdalen. John read Modern Languages for a year before enlisting in the Grenadier Guards, and in April 1943, just before his son was posted to Egypt, Richard commissioned Augustus John to draw this portrait. John Brocklebank was killed in action in Italy on 8 November 1943 during the attack on Monte Camino. The portrait and John's medals form part of the College's Brocklebank Collection.

Richard Brocklebank studied at Magdalen from 1899 to 1901, when he left for the Boer War. He did not return to take a degree and became a professional soldier. He served in the First World War, finishing as a Lieutenant-Colonel in the 9th Queen's Royal Lancers. Like his own father, he was a connoisseur and mainly collected paintings, prints and Iznik pottery (see pp. 118–21). When Richard died, he left around fifty paintings, over a hundred prints, and a very significant collection of Iznik pottery to Magdalen. Some of these items feature in this book as part of the Brocklebank Bequest — the most significant art bequest in the College's history.

Richard also left a privately published commentary on his paintings entitled *A Turn or Two I'll Walk to Still my Beating Mind* (Cresset Press, London, 1955). Here, Richard justifies collecting with a quotation from Percy Gardner's essay 'The Lamps of Greek Art', a contribution to R. W. Livingstone's *The Legacy of Greece* (1921):

> We seek out works of art not to foster pessimism but to inspire optimism. Not to show us the world of nature on its repulsive side, but to reveal to us how much underlying beauty is to be found in it.

He then explains his somewhat idiosyncratic view of his collection as follows:

> These essays are my personal reflections. If I am accused, not without reason, of being diffuse—well, one thought leads to another; and though others, no doubt, would have conceived quite different ideas, these have been my thoughts as I stood before each picture, entering the realms of fancy every now and then, as the spirit moved me, and returning again suddenly to earth. My book does not aim at being a professional catalogue.

DBR

PROVENANCE
Brocklebank Bequest.

LITERATURE
R. Hutchins and R. W. Sheppard, *The Undone Years: Magdalen College Roll of Honour 1939–1947 and Roll of Service 1939–1945 and Vietnam*, Oxford, 2004, pp. 41–45.

▶ *John Brocklebank*   Augustus John OM, RA, painted 1943
red and black crayon   45.75 cm x 31.75 cm

93

*Hidden
Magdalen*

Madonna and Child, with two Angels
attrib. Ambrogio Lorenzetti

The attribution of this exquisite and oft-exhibited panel has shifted back and forth between the two Lorenzetti brothers: Pietro (*c.* 1280–1348) and Ambrogio (*c.* 1290–1348). Along with Simone Martini (*c.* 1280–1344), they were the most important painters in Siena in the second quarter of the fourteenth century after the death of Duccio (*fl.* 1278–1318), and before the depredations of the Black Death of 1348–49.

When the panel was exhibited in 1934 at the Burlington Fine Arts Club it was attributed to a follower of Ambrogio; but in the Royal Academy's exhibition of 1960, 'Italian Art in Britain', it was attributed to Pietro. This latter attribution was endorsed when the panel was exhibited at Wildenstein's, London, in 1965. But when reviewing these exhibitions, scholars judged that the panel resembles more the work of Ambrogio than that of Pietro (see particularly Longhi 1960). Bernard Berenson was also unconvinced by the attribution to Ambrogio and regarded the work as by a close follower of the Lorenzetti. More recently, Professor Miklós Boskovits, too, has expressed some doubt about the full attribution to Ambrogio (see Boskovits 1968, and private communication 24 February 2007).

Nevertheless, on the last occasion that the panel was exhibited, at the Matthiesen Gallery, London, in 1983, the catalogue ascribed it to Ambrogio in full. It is presented here with a qualified attribution to Ambrogio Lorenzetti. But whatever its autograph status, there is no doubt about its high quality and refined execution, which form the hallmarks of Sienese painting at its high point in the early fourteenth century.

The Lorenzetti brothers were born in Siena, and although nothing is known of their upbringing and training, they became the dominant painters in a city that had, since the time of Duccio, been the only artistic centre that could rival nearby Florence. But while upholding the Sienese tradition, the brothers were far from oblivious to outside influences, most notably the work of the Florentine Giotto (*c.* 1267–1337). Ambrogio in particular is known to have undertaken a number of commisions in Florence in the 1320s. Once back in Siena, he collaborated with his brother on the frescoes on the façade of Santa Maria della Scala in 1335, and further public commissions came his way, particularly after the departure of the painter Simone Martini (*c.* 1280–1344) to the Papal Court in Avignon in 1336. These commissions culminated in the frescoes that Ambrogio executed for the Palazzo Publico (1337–39). Still *in situ*, they are known as the *Allegories of Good and Bad Government* and reckoned among the greatest achievements of fourteenth-century art in Italy.

Magdalen's small devotional work, possibly part of a diptych or the central panel of a triptych, is painted with jewel-like precision and delicacy. The curly-haired Christ Child holds what appear to be two oranges or apples, one of which he offers to his mother in a poignant gesture; the Virgin, with a beautiful yet impassive face, returns his gaze. Her blue mantel and gilt-decorated robe are now somewhat abraded, but the tooling of her halo is in remarkably good condition. The pair are flanked by two apparently female figures wearing garlands of red and white roses and richly embroidered robes with blue collars highlighted in gold. They have been variously interpreted as angels or the Saints Valerian and Cecilia (they were first identified as such in the 1934–35 exhibition; see also the catalogue of the 1965 exhibition, 'The Art of Painting in Florence and Siena from 1250–1500'). St Cecilia is the patron saint of music and is normally depicted playing an instrument, while Valerian, her husband, is more usually shown wearing a centurion's armour. It seems that the main reason for the identification with these saints is their attire, which has been interpreted as implying marriage or betrothal. But the lack of attributes and the feminine appearance of both figures make it more likely that they are angels, even if their wings are not visible and lie outside the picture frame.

I am grateful to Professor Boskovits for his kind assistance in cataloguing this work.

TJH

PROVENANCE
Sterbini Collection, Rome;
Thomas B. Brocklebank (1841–1919), Wateringbury Place, Kent, purchased in Rome in 1894, and by descent to:
Lieutenant-Colonel R. H. R. Brocklebank, purchased from his executors in 1937;
Brocklebank Bequest.

EXHIBITED
London, Burlington Fine Arts Club, 'Winter Exhibition' 1934–35, no. 11, as Follower of Ambrogio Lorenzetti *c.* 1350.
London, Royal Academy, 'Italian Art in Britain', 1960, no. 264, as Pietro Lorenzetti.
London, Wildenstein, 'The Art of Painting in Florence and Siena from 1250–1500', 24 February–10 April 1965, catalogue by St John Gore, p. 48, cat. no. 83, pp. 47–8, fig. 76, as Pietro Lorenzetti.
London, Matthiesen Fine Art, 'Early Italian Paintings and Works of Art 1300–1480', 1983, cat. no. 12, as Ambrogio Lorenzetti, *c.* 1340.

LITERATURE
B. Berenson, *Italian Pictures of the Renaissance: Central Italian and North Italian Schools*, 3 vols, New York, 1968, vol. 1, p. 221, as follower of Lorenzetti.
M. Boskovits, exhibition review, *Acta Historiae Artium* 14 (1968), p. 109, as difficult to reconcile with Ambrogio.
R. Longhi, 'Uno sguardo alle fotografie della mostra', *Paragone* 125 (1960), p. 60, as 'Più giusto ... l'avvicinamento ad Ambrogio'.

◀ *Madonna and Child, with two Angels,* attributed to Ambrogio Lorenzetti (*fl. c.* 1317–48) egg tempera on gold ground panel   28.2 x 18.4 cm

Saint Ursula by Taddeo di Bartolo

Taddeo di Bartolo (1362/3–after 1422) was the most important Sienese painter during the first two decades of the fifteenth century: he ran a successful workshop and executed a number of altarpieces for churches throughout southern Tuscany. Some evidence suggests that he had travelled further afield during the early part of his career. Giorgio Vasari (1511–74) states that he was invited to Padua by Francesco da Carrara, but none of the Paduan works survive, and two documented polyptychs of 1393 that were commissioned by the Spinola family for the church of St Luca in Genoa are also untraced. By 1399 Taddeo had returned to Siena, where he quickly gained important commissions, including a series of frescoes for the *Duomo* (now destroyed). While heavily influenced by the earlier generation of Sienese artists such as the Lorenzetti brothers (see p. 94) and Simone Martini (c. 1280–1344), Taddeo's style had developed with his travels and consequent exposure to the work of such artists as Barnaba da Modena (c. 1330–86) and Piero di Puccio (fl. c. 1355–1400). Taddeo's mature work displays a preference for clear-cut, robust figures softened by careful modelling.

Judging from the integral arched frame, this remarkably well-preserved panel, depicting St Ursula (with the bow and arrow of her martyrdom), most probably formed the upper part of a polyptych altarpiece. It corresponds closely to another panel of identical format depicting St Agnes (private collection, USA; see Symeonides 1965, plate XLVIb), which Bernard Berenson first suggested was a pendant to the present work (Berenson 1968, p. 423). Stylistically, these two works are also similar to five other panels depicting saints in three-quarter length (four were formerly in the Loew-Beer collection, Frankfurt, and one was in the Liechtenstein collection). But the different dimensions and the fact that the Liechtenstein picture is of St Agnes indicate that these various panels are remnants from two different commissions.

Symeonides dates the present work to c. 1395–1400, but Solberg prefers a date of 1415–20, which would make it contemporary with two of Taddeo's rare dated panels (one of 1418 in the Fogg Art Museum, Cambridge, Mass.; the other of 1420 in the Museo Diocesano, Orte; see Solberg 1991, vol. 1, pp. 36–38 and 572–82 respectively). I am grateful to Professor Miklós Boskovits for his assistance in cataloguing this work.

TJH

PROVENANCE

With Colnaghi's, London, *Paintings by Old Masters*, 1–31 March 1950, no. 14, from whom purchased by:
Lieutenant-Colonel R. H. R. Brocklebank;
Brocklebank Bequest.

LITERATURE

Bernard Berenson, *Italian Pictures of the Renaissance: Central Italian and North Italian Schools*, 3 vols, London and New York, 1968, vol. 1, p. 419.
G. E. Solberg, 'Taddeo di Bartolo: His Life and Work', unpublished Ph.D. dissertation, 3 vols., New York University, 1991; see esp. vol. 2, pp. 583–85, fig. 269, dated to c. 1415–20.
S. Symeonides, *Taddeo di Bartolo*, Siena, 1965, p. 218, pl. XLVIb, dated to c. 1395–1400.

▶ *Saint Ursula*   Taddeo di Bartolo, probably painted 1395–1420
egg tempera on gold ground panel, in engaged gilt frame with arched top and twisted colonettes   39.5 x 27.5 cm

*Hidden
Magdalen*

97

Hidden
Magdalen

Saint Giles and Saint Romuald
by Mariotto di Nardo

Two monastic saints are depicted on this striking panel: St Giles (d. *c.*710; on the left with his attribute, a deer) and St Romuald of Ravenna (d. 1027). The work has been variously attributed to the Florentine artists Jacopo di Cione (*c.*1325–*c.*1400), Lorenzo Monaco (*c.*1370–*c.*1427), and Ambrogio di Baldese (1352–1429), although none of these suggestions has commanded universal scholarly acceptance. Professor Miklós Boskovits, for whose assistance in cataloguing this work I am grateful, had formerly suggested an attribution to Ambrogio di Baldese (Boskovits 1975). But he now regards it as an early work by Mariotto di Nardo (private communication, 24 February 2007).

Mariotto di Nardo (*fl.* 1394–1424) was the son of the sculptor Nardo di Cione (*c.* 1320–1365/6), who probably oversaw his early training. He became a highly sought-after painter in Florence around the

turn of the fifteenth century and numerous documents attest to his public and private commissions. From 1394 to 1404 he executed a large number of paintings for the *Duomo*, only a few of which survive today, and from *c.* 1400 he was employed on the fresco decorations of two of Florence's most important churches: Santa Maria Maggiore and Orsanmichele. Only fragments of these frescoes remain *in situ*. Mariotto's versatility is demonstrated by the fact that he also executed polyptych altarpieces and even manuscript illuminations.

Mariotto's success stemmed partly from the appeal of his distinctive late Gothic style, with its use of oblique perspective and rocky landscapes and the nervous tension to be found in his somewhat statuesque figures. The present panel is part of a predella, from an as yet unidentified altarpiece, and its subject matter suggests that it was intended for a monastic church. The raised gilt decoration separating the two saints and framing the panel is similar, though not identical, to another predella panel by Mariotto, formerly in the collection of Erwin Rosenthal, Munich (see Berenson 1963, vol. 1, fig. 522).

TJH

PROVENANCE
M. Marignane;
with Percy Moore Turner (d. 1952);
with Colnaghi's, London, from whom purchased in October 1952 by:
Lieutenant-Colonel R. H. R. Brocklebank;
Brocklebank Bequest.

EXHIBITED
London, Royal Academy, 'Italian Art in Britain', 1960, no. 281.

LITERATURE
B. Berenson, *Italian Pictures of the Renaissance: Florentine School*, 2 vols, London, 1963, vol. 1.

M. Boskovits, *Pittura fiorentina alla vigilia del Rinascimento 1370–1400*, Florence, 1975, p. 275, fig. 370, as Ambrogio di Baldese.

G. Kaftal, *Iconography of the Saints in Tuscan Painting*, Florence, 1952, pp. 451–55, no. 135 (c), fig. 533 (detail), under St Giles, as Jacopo di Cione.

▲ *Saint Giles and Saint Romuald of Ravenna*
Mariotto di Nardo (*fl.* 1394–1424)
egg tempera on gold ground panel, in integral gilt frame
38 x 48.5 cm

◀ Detail: St Giles

Hidden
Magdalen

Jeanne d'Halluin by a Follower of Clouet

Jeanne d'Halluin (b. *c.* 1540) was one of six surviving children of a prominent member of the French aristocracy, Antoine d'Halluin, *Grand Louvetier de France*, who was killed at Thérouanne in 1553 fighting against Emperor Charles V. Jeanne was initially engaged to the eldest son of the Constable of France, Anne de Montmorency, but eventually married Florimond Robertit, Baron d'Alluye, the Governor of Orléans and Secretary of State in the 1560s under François II and Charles IX. During his short life — he died in 1569 at the age of 36 — Florimond was entrusted with a number of delicate diplomatic negotiations. In 1563, he was appointed ambassador extraordinary to England, and he and his young wife presumably spent several months at the Court of Elizabeth I. Jeanne's death date is unknown and the couple were probably childless.

The half-length portrait depicts a young woman, probably in her twenties, wearing a black velvet dress trimmed with galloon (a kind of braid), with pink sleeves and a white under-dress. On her head she sports a bejewelled cap, and round her neck she wears a pearl necklace on a fine thread that hangs down the front of her dress. There is a calm, demure dignity in the sitter's pose, for Jeanne is very much the obedient wife, caparisoned in her husband's wealth. This is certainly a portrait of Jeanne d'Halluin, since two other likenesses exist. The first, a half-length drawing (1563), is in the collection of portraits of sixteenth-century French courtiers in the Musée Condé at Chantilly. Although the sitter here faces in the opposite direction and her dress is not the same, there is no mistaking the serene, round face, the quiet eyes and the full lips. Besides which, the sitter's name (though with a birth date of 1530) is given on its mounting. The second, a portrait in oils in private hands, appears to be a copy of the 1563 drawing and was originally thought to be a likeness of Catherine de Medici (d. 1589), the mother of François II and Charles IX and the power behind the French throne for some three decades. It was Catherine who commissioned the collection of drawings that are now in the Musée Condé.

Magdalen's portrait and the two other likenesses are all attributed to the school of François Clouet (1522–72). Born at Tours, Clouet was the son of Jean Clouet (*c.* 1486–1540), court painter to François I (d. 1547). Nicknamed Janet, François was the leading portrait painter at the French court in the middle decades of the sixteenth century. His portraits differ from his father's in providing more naturalistic detail and they also reveal an awareness of Florentine portraiture. His most famous painting, now in the National Gallery, Washington, is of a woman in her bath (*c.* 1570), thought to be Charles IX's mistress, Marie Touchet. But because it is notoriously difficult to ascribe sixteenth-century French portraits to a specific artist, it will never be known who really painted Magdalen's Jeanne d'Halluin.

LWBB

PROVENANCE
Sir George Donaldson;
Ralph Brocklebank, his sale, Christie's 7 July 1922, lot 70 (bought by Agnew, 115 guineas);
Brocklebank Bequest.

▶ *Jeanne d'Halluin*
   oil on panel   33 x 24 cm   painted mid-16th century

Hidden
Magdalen

101

Hidden
Magdalen

Margaret of Lorraine attrib. Catharina van Hemessen

Margaret of Lorraine (1564–1625) was the daughter of Nicolas de Lorraine, Duc de Mercoeur and Comte de Bar. Her elder sister Louise (1553–1601) married King Henri III of France in 1575. Margaret married the King's favourite, Anne, Duc de Joyeuse, in 1581, and then, after his early death, François de Luxembourg, Duc de Piney, in 1599, by whom she had children.

The Magdalen portrait is three-quarters length and depicts a young, thin-faced woman in her early twenties in a pearl-studded cap wearing a black velvet dress covered in gold studs, with a cream satin under-dress. She holds gloves in her left hand while her right hand fingers a gold girdle. Around her neck is a gold chain encrusted with gems. She is self-assured, and the smile on her face is not enigmatic, but playful and slightly cruel, for it is the look of a woman who enjoys the fact that she is powerful and dangerous to cross. This is not the conventional portrait of a sixteenth-century French noblewoman.

Whether it is a portrait of Margaret of Lorraine is another question. One of the two other extant likenesses of Margaret is in the Musée National du Château et des Trianons at Versailles and is not a portrait but part of a painting of the ball given by Henri III in honour of her wedding. She is at the centre of a crowded composition, dancing with either her new husband or the King. She is painted as a thin woman, as tall as her partner, but it is hard to make out her features. The other likeness is a half-length drawing in the collection of portraits of French courtiers at the Musée Chantilly and depicts a woman looking to her right with a slightly fuller face than the Magdalen sitter. She wears an expansive ruff and the smile on her face is enigmatic rather than feisty. On the mounting it is named and dated to *c.* 1584, roughly the date of Magdalen's painting. The one feature of Magdalen's portrait that lends credence to the ascription is the sitter's wasp waist. Tight corsets and farthingales were only just coming into fashion in the sixteenth century, and Margaret, along with Henri III, was a trendsetter. The most striking feature of Margaret in the ball portrait is her wasp waist exactly on the line which cuts the painting in two.

If Magdalen's portrait is of Margaret of Lorraine, then it cannot be by Catharina van Hemessen (1528–*c.*1590) as labelled. Catharina was the daughter of the Antwerp painter Jan Sanders van Hemessen (*c.*1500–66), and although her portraits are strong, naturalistic representations of mid-sixteenth century women, the subjects are not courtiers. Moreover, to have painted Margaret, Catharina would have had to have spent time at the French court, and there is no evidence that she ever visited France. It would seem, too, that she gave up painting in 1554 when she married Antwerp's organ master, Christian de Moryn. Who did paint the Magdalen portrait is a mystery. Although it was sold as a Clouet at Christie's in 1922, François Clouet, the French court painter, died in 1572. It could also be by a pupil of his, but if this is so, then he or she had eschewed their master's style, for Clouet's female sitters were portrayed as demure and obedient, not as women of spirit (see the entry on Jeanne d'Halluin, p. 100).

LWBB

PROVENANCE

Agnews, London, acquired by them in Holland, purchased by Ralph Brocklebank, 1906;

Ralph Brocklebank, his sale, Christie's 7 July 1922, lot 77, as by Clouet (bought by Agnew, £210);

Brocklebank Bequest.

▶ *Margaret of Lorraine*
oil on panel   51 x 42 cm   painted late 16th century

103

Hidden
Magdalen

A Forest Scene by Roelandt Savery

Born in Flanders, Roelandt Savery (1576–1639) emigrated to the Netherlands with his family in about 1585. He settled first in Haarlem, but by 1602 he was in Amsterdam with his elder brother Jacob, a painter of still lifes and landscapes who may have been his earliest teacher. At this early date Roelandt seems to have painted mainly flower still lifes and village scenes in the manner of Hans Bol (1534–93). By 1604 Roelandt was sufficiently well known to be invited to the Prague court of Emperor Rudolf II, one of the greatest patrons of the age. He remained until the Emperor's death in 1613 as part of the select group of international artists whom the Emperor had gathered around him. This group included the painters Bartholomeus Spranger (1546–1611), Hans Hoffman (1545/50–1591/2), Matthaus Gundelach (c. 1566–1653/4), and Joris Hoefnagel (1542–1601), the sculptor Adriaen de Vries (c. 1545–1626), and the silversmith Paulus van Vianen (1570–1613), as well as important composers and architects. Roelandt must have been highly stimulated by this cultivated environment, since both his style and repertoire evolved in exciting and novel ways during this period.

In c. 1606/7 the Emperor commissioned Roelandt to make a series of sketches of scenes from the Tyrol. The resulting studies of alpine scenery, with its craggy peaks, dense forests, and dramatic waterfalls, are among the earliest interpretations of such natural phenomena in Western art. The sketches then formed the bases for numerous works in which Roelandt populated the exuberant landscapes with beautifully painted animals and birds. Indeed, the sketches served as reference material throughout his career, since his preoccupation with the accurate transcription of Nature persisted even after he had left Prague. Roelandt then returned to Amsterdam, where he lived until 1619. In that year he moved to Utrecht with his nephew Hans Savery II (1589–1654), who became part of his extended studio. Despite Roelandt's originality and the prestige he had gained from serving at Rudolf's court, his later years were marked by declining output, financial insecurity, and eventual madness.

Magdalen's beautiful and delicately painted hunting scene is one of a number of works from the 1620s that draw on the artist's earlier Tyrolean sketches. The carefully rendered woodland landscape is brought to life with animals running in all directions. A terrified stag tries to escape his pursuers in the bottom left. A fox emerges from behind a rock and a wild boar has been caught by hounds. Two figures can be seen: the one in the middle ground is a shepherd and the other, on a distant hill, is possibly a huntsman blowing his horn. Some of the motifs can be found in other works by Savery: the escaping stag, for example can be seen in a landscape of 1620 in the Rijksmuseum, Amsterdam (inv. C/447; see Müllenmeister 1988, no. 75).

TJH

PROVENANCE

M. Heriard-Dubrenil, Cognac;

Henry G. Bohn, his posthumous sale, Christie's, London, 19 March 1885, as R. Savery (4 guineas to Thomas Brocklebank);

Thomas B. Brocklebank, Wateringbury Place, Kent, and by descent to:

Lieutenant-Colonel R. H. R. Brocklebank, purchased from his executors;

Brocklebank Bequest.

LITERATURE

K. J. Müllenmeister, *Roeland[t] Savery: Die Gemälde mit kritischem Oeuvrekatalog*, Düsseldorf, 1988, no. 85, p. 234, illustrated.

▲ *A Forest Scene*   Roelandt Savery
signed and dated 1622 (lower right on a rock)
oil on panel   15 x 22 cm

Study for a Warrior by Guercino

Giovanni Francesco Barbieri, 'Il Guercino' ('The Squinter'; 1591–1666), was the leading painter in Bologna in the mid-seventeenth century and one of the greatest draughtsmen of the Italian Baroque. Most of Guercino's drawings were preparatory studies for major paintings, and he would frequently make numerous sketches in chalk, pen, ink and wash for each composition. Critics have frequently remarked on

the freshness and vitality of Guercino's sketches, for they show the immense fecundity of his artistic imagination. They quickly became collectable in their own right, as can be seen from the distinguished provenance of this particular sketch.

In style and execution Magdalen's drawing is similar to another study of a warrior (Courtauld Institute Galleries, London, Witt Collection inv. no. 1368) that has generally been regarded as a sketch for the figure of Tatius on the right of Guercino's painting, *Hersilia Separating Romulus and Tatius* (Musée du Louvre, Paris, S, 1988, no. 226; see Turner and Plazzotta 1991, no. 141, p. 171). Magdalen's drawing may be a study for Romulus, the figure on the left of the same picture, since the position of the right hand, with the sword held horizontally, is close to the pose in the painting. However, as the raised left arm has no parallel in the finished composition, this identification remains doubtful. Turner and Plazzotta make the alternative suggestion that the drawing relates to a lost work entitled *Cupid Restraining the Enraged Mars*, for which a sketch exists (Courtauld Institute Galleries, London, Witt Collection inv. no. 1349), although the absence of Cupid and the lack of tension in the pose of the warrior also make this identification unlikely.

A hitherto unconsidered possibility is that this drawing is a preliminary sketch for the figure of *Mars as a Warrior* in the Wellington Museum (Apsley House, London) that is also illustrated here. This Mars stands in a similar pose to the warrior in the drawing, with his lowered right arm holding the sword and his other arm raised. Although the Apsley House picture uses antique armour and shows a bearded Mars turning his head to look at the viewer, this picture provides us with the closest parallel, in which case Magdalen's drawing would date from *c.* 1634.

The provenance of Magdalen's drawing is also interesting because it stretches back to the artist himself. After Guercino's death, many of his graphic works passed to his nephews, the Gennari brothers, who had them bound into eight large volumes. These

106

remained in Bologna until 1719, when some of the volumes began to appear on the art market. In the 1750s and 1760s a large number were purchased by Richard Dalton for King George III. They are still in the Royal Collection at Windsor Castle and form the largest collection of Guercino's drawings anywhere in the world. In 1742 the English collector John Bouverie purchased one of the above volumes when he passed through Florence during his Grand Tour. He probably purchased more drawings on subsequent trips to Italy, for his collection of works by Guercino was second only to that of the King. This impressive collection then passed by descent to the Earls of Gainsborough, who began selling individual drawings from as early as 1859, mainly at Christie's. At the beginning of the twentieth century Sir Robert Witt built up another distinguished collection of Guercino drawings, many of which came from subsequent sales of the Gainsborough collection. While most of Sir Robert's drawings were bequeathed to the Courtauld Institute, he generously presented *Study of a Warrior* to his friend, the art historian Thomas Boase, who was Director of the Courtauld Institute from 1937 to 1947 and then President of Magdalen from 1947 to 1968.

TJH

PROVENANCE

By descent in the artist's family to his nephews Carlo and Benedetto Gennari, Bologna, until at least 1719;

John Bouverie (c. 1722–50), probably purchased in 1742 through Abbé Bonducci in Florence while on the Grand Tour, and by descent through his sister;

Anne Bouverie (d. 1757), to her son (?);

Christopher Hervey (d. 1768), to his aunt;

Elizabeth Bouverie (d. 1798), the surviving sister of John Bouverie, by whom bequeathed to:

Sir Charles Middleton, later 1st Baron Barham (1726–1813), husband of Elizabeth Bouverie's childhood friend Margaret Gambier, and by descent through his son-in-law;

Sir Gerard Noel Noel, 2nd Baron Barham (1759–1838), to his son;

Sir Charles Noel, 3rd Baron Barham and later 1st Earl of Gainsborough (1781–1866);

(possibly) Christie's, London, 26 February 1937, lot 2 (2½ guineas to Wheeler);

Sir Robert Witt (1872–1952), by whom given to:

Thomas S. R. Boase (1898–1974);

President Boase's Bequest.

▲ *Mars as a Warrior*
(Wellington Museum, Apsley House, London)
Guercino (Giovanni Francesco Barbieri; 1591–1666)
oil on canvas
© V&A Images, Victoria & Albert Museum

LITERATURE

N. Turner and C. Plazzotta, *Drawings by Guercino from British Collections*, London, 1991, no. 134, pp. 161–65, illustrated.

◄ *Study for a warrior*, half-length, in profile to the right and holding a sword in his right hand
Guercino
stamped with ownership stamp 'B' (lower right)
pen, point of the brush, and brown wash   25.4 x 15.9 cm

Hidden
Magdalen

Cilgerran Castle by Richard Wilson

Richard Wilson (1712/13–1782) was the son of John Wilson, a graduate of Wadham College and Rector of Penegoes, Montgomeryshire. Richard was apprenticed as a portraitist for six years and executed his first commissioned portrait in 1738. He also started to paint landscapes and cityscapes, including *The Hall of the Inner Temple after the Fire of 4 January 1737* (now in the Tate Collection, London). In the mid-1740s he painted his first Welsh view, *Caernarvon Castle* (Yale Center for British Art) and in the early 1750s he spent five years in Italy, where he continued to develop his landscape painting. His major influences were Nicholas Poussin (1594–1665) and Claude Lorrain (1604/05–1682). Wilson was also influenced by the work of Marco Ricci (1676–1730), and we are able to compare the College's Wilson landscapes with its landscape attributed to an unknown follower of Ricci.

Wilson was a founder member of the Royal Academy of Arts and is depicted in Johann Zoffany's well-known painting of the founders (1772). In the late 1760s he started on a series of paintings in Wales, of which this picture is one. His work influenced both J. M. W. Turner (1775–1851), who also painted Cilgerran Castle, and John Constable (1776–1837). In later life Wilson became impoverished through drink, but was rescued by his appointment as Librarian of the Royal Academy at an annual salary of £50.

William Elliott (1727–66) prepared an engraving of this painting, which was coloured by hand and published by John Boydell (1720–1804) in 1775.

The remains of Cilgerran Castle are administered by the National Trust and stand high above the River Teifi at its tidal limit, where it passes through Cilgerran Gorge on its way to Cardigan Bay some three miles downstream. The first castle on this site was built in *c.* 1100 and the present castle was built between 1220 and 1230. It was not always successful in keeping the Welsh under control and changed hands several times, even as late as 1405 during Owain Glyndwr's abortive war of independence. It was occupied until the seventeenth century, when it began to fall into the ruin seen today. The reminders of the past include the coracle races that are held on the Teifi below the castle in August. The castle was an early tourist attraction; Victorian visitors came upriver by boat from Cardigan.

DBR

PROVENANCE

Painted for Sir Robert Howell Vaughn of Nannau and Hengwrt;

Joseph Gillot, his sale, Christie's 19 and 26 April and 3 May 1872, lot 228 (bought W. Cox £53 11*d*.);

John Chesshire, Rothes Park, Birmingham;

Canon R. S. P. Chesshire of Areley Kings near Stourport, Worcestershire;

Purchased by Lieutenant-Colonel [Richard] Hugh [Royds] Brocklebank, June 1934;

Brocklebank Bequest.

▲ *Cilgerran Castle*   Richard Wilson RA
painted 1760s–1770s
oil on canvas   51 x 74 cm

*Hidden
Magdalen*

The Embarkation of St Ursula by Richard Earlom, after Lorrain

Claude Gellée (1604/5–82), born in Lorraine, was one of the great landscape painters of the seventeenth century. His contemporary Nicolas Poussin (1594–1665), another great landscape painter, was also French, but both men did most of their work in Italy. As Claude's success was so great that other artists were trying to pass off their work as his, from 1635 he kept a book of drawings of all the paintings that left his studio. This book, the *Liber Veritatis (Book of Truth)*, was then used to authenticate his works: in the eighteenth century it was owned by the Duke of Devonshire and acquired by the British Museum in 1957.

Richard Earlom (1743–1822) was an English print-maker best known for his mezzotints (a method of engraving to produce tones and half-tones). By 1777 he had published drawings from Claude's *Liber Veritatis* in two volumes of etchings and mezzotints. These, also known as *Liber Veritatis*, were then published by John Boydell (1720–1804), a major print-seller and publisher who had trained as an engraver. He was an Alderman, Sheriff, and finally Lord Mayor of London (1790–91).

J. M. W. Turner (1775–1851) was greatly influenced by the work of Claude, and it has been argued that his *Liber Studiorum* (see p. 114) was inspired by Earlom's prints of Claude's *Liber Veritatis*. This may be so, but in his history of the *Liber Studiorum* Finberg is particularly scathing of Earlom's prints of Claude's drawings: 'he libelled Claude's originals outrageously'. You can judge for yourself by comparing the print reproduced here with Claude's original drawing in the British Museum.

The original of Magdalen's print, an oil painting on canvas (113 x 149 cm), is in London's National Gallery. It was painted in 1641 and is entitled *Port Scene with the Embarkation of St Ursula*, a British princess who was martyred in Cologne with her 11,000 virgin companions on her return from a pilgrimage to Rome.

DBR

PROVENANCE
Brocklebank Bequest.

LITERATURE
J. Finberg, *The History of Turner's Liber Studiorum*, with a New Catalogue Raisonné, London, 1924.

▶ *The Embarkation of St Ursula*   Richard Earlom, after a 1641 painting by Claude Lorrain
mezzotint   20.3 x 25.4 cm

III

———

Hidden
Magdalen

Rio de Janeiro by Henry Chamberlain

This fine early view of Rio de Janeiro (*c.* 1820) looks over the city (now downtown Rio) and bay from the Morro de Santa Teresa.

> Morro do San Antonio lies in the middle, above the head of the slave with pink shirt, topped with its church. Ponto da Calhabouco is the point running out into the harbour: Morro do Castello is the hill above the point—it was here that the original town was founded: to the left and slightly above San Antonio is Morro da Conceicao: Morro do Convento is the hill to the left again, surmounted with buildings and with the escarpment which Morro da Favela is on the extreme left and behind the palm tree. Campo [Square] de Santa Anna is behind the palm tree and the road.
> (Brocklebank, p. 23)

Following the arrival of the exiled Portuguese royal family, court, and government in 1808, Rio de Janeiro was quickly transformed from a sleepy colonial backwater into an imperial city, which a Brazilian, Paulo Fernando Viana, was appointed to improve by paving streets, clearing squares, and draining marshes.

> Rio was changing rapidly, spurred on not just by court-imposed city works, but by a deeper sense of its own importance on the international stage. With the court's tacit decision to stay on, more embassies were set up and foreigners poured into the capital. Diplomats and their teams created new demands, bringing traders and their luxury goods from post-war Europe. Rich travellers spent weeks, months, sometimes even years sampling the delights of a city that was fast becoming one of the New World's foremost attractions.
> (Wilcken, p. 176)

This panorama by Lieutenant Henry Chamberlain (1796–1843) depicts the city in the final years of the Portuguese court's residence: Dom João returned to Lisbon in 1821 and his son, Dom Pedro, declared an independent Brazil in 1822.

The artist was the eldest son of Sir Henry Chamberlain (1773–1829), who held the posts of Consul General and *chargé d'affaires* in Rio from 1815 to 1829. He is best known as the author of the rare album *Views and costumes of the city and neighbourhood of*

Rio de Janeiro, Brazil, from drawings taken by Lieutenant Chamberlain, Royal Artillery, during the Years 1819–1820, with descriptive explanations (London, 1822). This has been described as 'the finest English colour plate book on Brazil' (Tooley 1954) and 'one of the most beautiful, and also one of the rarest, books published about Brazil in the nineteenth century' (Borba de Moraes 1983). Chamberlain was primarily a watercolourist, and Ferrez recorded just four other oils in 2000 (pp. 198–99, nos. 1048–50 and 1055). These included one other large unsigned panorama of Rio taken from Niteroi (the opposite viewpoint), now in the Museu de Arte de São Paulo.

N L

PROVENANCE
Anonymous sale, Christie's, London, 22 February 1935, lot 114, as 'F. Post' (16 guineas to S. Hartveld) to: Lieutenant-Colonel [Richard] Hugh [Royds] Brocklebank; Brocklebank Bequest.

LITERATURE
R. Borba de Moraes, *Bibliografia Brasiliana*, Los Angeles and Rio, 1983.

R. H. R. Brocklebank, *A Turn or Two I'll Walk, to Still my Beating Mind*, London, 1955, pp. 23–25.

H. Chamberlain, *Vistas e Costumes da Ciudade e arredores do Rio de Janeiro em 1819–1820 segundo desenhos feitos pelo Tte. Chamberlain, da artilharia Real, com descricoes*, ed. and trans. R. Borba de Moraes, Rio and São Paulo, 1943, illustrated.

G. Ferrez, *Iconografia do Rio de Janeiro 1530–1890 Catalogo Analitico*, Rio, 2000, vol. 1, p. 196, no. 1033 (as collection Hugh Brocklebank, and incorrectly described as a watercolour measuring 90 x 160 cm).

R. V. Tooley, *English Books with Coloured Plates, 1790–1860*, London, 1954.

P. Wilcken, *Empire Adrift: The Portuguese Court in Rio de Janeiro 1808–1821*, London, 2004, p. 176.

Hidden
Magdalen

▲ *A Panoramic View of the City of Rio de Janeiro from Santa Teresa* Lieutenant Henry Chamberlain, painted 1815–21
oil on canvas 64 x 129 cm ▼ Detail

Hedging and Ditching by J. M. W. Turner

The *Liber Studiorum* of J. M. W. Turner (1775–1851) comprises a series of engravings and was published between 1807 and 1819 in parts of five engravings. The *Liber Veritatis* of Claude Lorrain consisted of sketches of his published paintings: it was engraved in 1777 by Richard Earlom and published by John Boydell (see p. 110). Some see Earlom's engravings of the *Liber Veritatis* as the inspiration for Turner's *Liber Studiorum*, but the two books differ considerably. Whereas the *Liber Veritatis* consisted of paintings already published, Turner's *Liber Studiorum* sought to produce each print from an unpublished work. Moreover, whilst Turner kept strict control over the production process, Claude had no influence on Boydell's publication, since Earlom's engravings were made long after his death.

Turner's prospectus for the *Liber Studiorum* describes it as an attempt to classify various styles of landscape into Pastoral, Marine, Mountainous, Historical and EP (possibly Elevated Pastoral), though others have suggested meanings that go beyond the mere classification of landscapes. Turner had intended to produce 100 plates, but only a frontispiece and 70 plates were published: a further 20 plates were executed but never published. Although the drawings and nearly all the etchings were by Turner himself, most of the mezzotint engravings were by other engravers working under Turner's supervision. Only in a few cases were they executed by Turner himself.

The pastoral *Hedging and Ditching* was published on 23 May 1812 and is the second plate of Part X, whose first plate was the frontispiece. The pen and sepia drawing was sketched in 1807 during a journey from Portsmouth and is in Turner's *Spithead Sketchbook*. Although the etching is also by Turner, the engraving is by J. C. Easling (*fl.* 1788–after 1815). John Ruskin (1819–1900) commended this plate as one of *Liber Studiorum*'s 'most desirable' subjects. In addition to the etching, engraver's proofs and various states of printing, each recognizable by subtle changes, were sold.

The College owns 147 prints from the *Liber Studiorum*, including examples of 58 of the published and six of the unpublished plates. Most of these are etchings and the remainder are engravings, with some duplicates. It is estimated that no more than 170 prints were published for each motif.

DBR

PROVENANCE
Brocklebank Bequest.

LITERATURE
A. Finberg, *The History of Turner's Liber Studiorum*, London, 1924.

▲ *Hedging and Ditching* from *Liber Studiorum*
Joseph Mallord William Turner RA
plate mark 21 x 29 cm   engraved surface   19 x 26 cm
published 1812

Hidden
Magdalen

Italian Street Scene by John Ruskin

John Ruskin (1819–1900), the most influential art critic of the nineteenth century, entered Christ Church as a gentleman commoner in January 1837 — not an obvious choice for a sensitive youth who was still accompanied everywhere by his mother. One of his contemporaries recalled the chief amusements of Christ Church undergraduates at the time as 'tandem-driving, hack-riding, long walks, rat-killing, cock-fighting, prize-fighting, otter-hunting, badger-baiting, boating', and Ruskin later confessed that he had 'expected some ridicule'. But his artistic talent attracted some respect, since a letter written by Dean Liddell in 1837 describes 'a very wonderful gentleman-commoner here who draws wonderfully'. Indeed, Ruskin spent much of his time at Oxford producing sketches and watercolours which reflected his sense of wonder at the world, especially those parts of it which time had softened into suitably picturesque shapes.

From the start, Ruskin's interest in art had been bound up with his parallel interest in travel. His first drawings, dating from 1827, were detailed little maps made to teach himself geography. But the event which 'determined the main tenor of my life' was his thirteenth birthday gift of Samuel Rogers's book *Italy* (1830), which included vignette illustrations by J. M. W. Turner (1775–1851). Responding to his attempts to imitate the styles of Turner and Samuel Prout (1783–1852), Ruskin's parents sent him for lessons with A. V. Copley Fielding (1787–1855) of the Society of Painters in Watercolours. These lasted five years, leaving Ruskin a skilled and versatile artist who was particularly interested in capturing the details and spirit of different architectural styles.

A rhyming letter sent to his father from Oxford declares:

> I cannot bear to paint in oil,
> C. Fielding's tints alone for me!

and the watercolours from his numerous later trips to Italy show Fielding's continued influence, in addition to elements of Prout and Turner.

At their best, Ruskin's Italian pictures offer tantalizing glimpses of a world which, according to his diaries, haunted him by its combination of the enchanting and the shabby:

> the old clothes hanging out of a marble architrave, that architrave smashed at one side and built into a piece of the Roman frieze, which moulders away the next instant into a patch of broken brickwork ... but all to be studied closely before it can be felt or even seen.

This particular street scene, with its careful composition of details that are both practical and picturesque (cracked walls, carelessly strung lines of washing, sun-bleached colours), shows how closely Ruskin studied what was before his eyes. Like all his best work, it also shows how much he felt about what he saw.

RJD-F

PROVENANCE
Brocklebank Bequest.

▲ *Italian Street Scene* John Ruskin
watercolour over pencil heightened with white on canvas
30.5 x 43 cm

117

*Hidden
Magdalen*

Iznik and Kütahyan Pottery

A remarkable collection of Iznik pottery, particularly the Kütahyan items, forms part of the Brocklebank Bequest (see p. 92). There are over 180 pieces in all, more even than in the superb British Museum collection, which contains some spectacularly large and rare items. Three generations of the Brocklebank family collected the pottery between the 1870s and the late 1950s, searching for items all over Europe and noting in an exercise book the price paid and the dealer's name. As the family sold as well as bought and sometimes bought items for a second time, Magdalen's Iznik is also fascinating as a documented example of Victorian collecting.

In the late nineteenth century this kind of pottery was generally known as Rhodian ware because of the prevailing belief that it emanated from Rhodes. But when it became clear that Iznik in Anatolia was its birthplace, the pottery became the object of a collecting enthusiasm, though it remained relatively inexpensive until the 1970s, when its value started to rocket.

Iznik is a highly decorated ceramic and was made in a town in western Anatolia in the second half of the sixteenth century. Using fritware, comprising silica, glass, white clay, lead and soda, the potters often adapted forms found in Chinese porcelain, which they were unable to make. Because the material could not be easily worked on a wheel, the vessels were seldom thrown in one piece and were moulded or turned instead.

The great discovery made by the Iznik potters was how to coat the ware with white slip before decorating the underglaze using a stencil. Seven colours can be identified although many items contain only four: blue (cobalt oxide), purple (manganese), red (silica and iron oxide), green (copper oxide), turquoise, grey, and black. The Iznik craftsmen made many different kinds of vessel for display or use: jugs, hanging lamps, cups, bowls, hookahs, rose-water sprinklers, candleholders, and dishes.

The most important items in the Brocklebank Bequest are the two curious lime presses, whose use was re-discovered only when they were cleaned: the juice passes through the bowl by means of a siphon and into a bowl below. No other examples are known to exist.

The impetus for creating these wares came from Süleyman the Magnificent (1494–1566), his wife Hürrem Roxelana (1510–58), and the Grand Vizier Rüstem Pasha (d. 1561), when they commissioned a huge building programme which demanded large quantities of tiles: the Blue Mosque alone, for example, contains 20,000 tiles. As Ottoman power declined, so did the making of Iznik ware and by the middle of the seventeenth century the necessary knowledge had disappeared.

But at Kütahya (the birthplace of Aesop), an ancient town on the Porsuk river 200 miles south of Istanbul, potters continued to make decorated fritware even after the demise of Iznik, and the craft still flourishes there today with one fifth of the town's population engaged in making pottery. Kütahya had been a centre of pottery making from early times and was part of the kingdom of Phrygia until captured by the Crusaders in 1095. But the Seljuks wrested it back within a century, and in 1514 Sultan Selim I (1465–1520) decided to settle tile workers from Tabriz and Iznik there. Its ware, whose colouring is softer and more subtle than that of Iznik, rapidly began to find its way all over the Middle East for the decoration of mosques, churches, and official buildings. Many of Magdalen's pieces come from Kütahya, and the Brocklebank Bequest contains several items of great rarity.

ADS

PROVENANCE
Brocklebank Bequest.

LITERATURE
Nurhan Atasoy and Julian Raby, *Iznik: The Pottery of Ottoman Turkey*, London, 1989.

118

▲▲ Iznik jugs and lime presses

▲ Iznik dishes

119

Four Iznik Tiles

The Brocklebank Collection includes these exquisite, repeating-pattern tiles which date from the mid-sixteenth century. This period was the golden age of Iznik tiles, when Turkish craftsmen had perfected polychrome underglaze painting and developed large-scale decorative schemes for the palaces and mosques of Süleyman the Magnificent (1494–1566) and his officials. New colours — turquoise, pale green, and purple — had been added to the traditional cobalt blue in the 1530s, with emerald green and brilliant red following in the 1560s. Although the feathery saz leaves, prunus blossom, tulips, and carnations decorating these tiles had long been part of Iznik's repertoire, the use of dark green — a precursor of emerald green — indicates that they were made in the mid-1560s (possibly, even, as late as the mid-1580s).

It is traditionally thought that these tiles came from the shrine and mosque complex at Eyüp on the Golden Horn, where the first mosque was constructed after the Ottoman conquest of Constantinople (1453). If this is so, then they connect two great religious institutions founded in 1458. But this neat link — spanning a whole continent, different cultures, and two religions — is more problematic than it seems.

Thanks to earthquakes, war, the redecoration of Istanbul's mosques and palaces with tiles from elsewhere, the surplus production of Iznik tiles, and the appetites of nineteenth- and twentieth-century collectors, it is notoriously hard to trace the provenance of such tiles. The Eyüp shrine was extensively remodelled in 1592, when the interior was decorated with the wonderful Iznik panels that are still *in situ*. Two centuries later, after the 1766 earthquake, the adjoining mosque was demolished and rebuilt. After the great earthquake of 1894 the shrine's exterior wall was decorated with a *pasticcio* of broken shards and tiles that are identical with Magdalen's. So these could have come either from another part of the Eyüp complex or from a quite different site. Walter Denny

has recently suggested that the mosque of Mihrimah Sultan (1522–78), the daughter of Süleyman, may have provided a source for these and other tiles between 1592 and 1894 since, unlike almost all of the other important buildings designed by the architect Sinan (1489–1588), it is now devoid of tile decoration.

Brocklebank does not mention these tiles in his meticulously detailed catalogue of his other Iznik acquisitions (where he even included photographs showing how he displayed all the other items in his collection). But panels of eight or more tiles of the same pattern are in the Benaki Museum (Athens), the Gulbenkian Museum (Lisbon), the Louvre, and the Victoria and Albert Museum (acquired in 1900). Other, smaller groups are in the Ashmolean, the David Collection (Copenhagen), the Rijksmuseum, the Los Angeles County Museum of Art, the Museum of Islamic Art (Cairo), and the Cinili Kosk (Istanbul). More widely dispersed in museum collections than any other Iznik tile pattern, they testify to the voraciousness of Western collectors. Although their diffusion because of war, earthquakes and the decline of Ottoman authority can be regretted, it has played an important part in ensuring widespread recognition for these masterpieces of Turkish art.

J B W N

PROVENANCE
Brocklebank Bequest.

LITERATURE
N. Atasoy and J. Raby, *Iznik: The Pottery of Ottoman Turkey*, London, 1989.
W. Denny, 'Dispersed Ottoman Repeating-Pattern Iznik Tiles', in A. Parzymies, ed., *Studies in Oriental Art and Culture in Honour of Professor Tadeusz Majda*, Warsaw, 2006, pp. 169–90. I am indebted to Professor Denny for his advice on these tiles.
A. Lane, *Later Islamic Pottery*, London, 1971.

▶ Iznik tiles from the mid-16th century

121

Portrait of Queen Elizabeth I

Elizabeth I, Queen of England (1533–1603), remains alive in the national psyche for establishing the Protestant religion, fighting off Spanish invasion, and presiding over the age of Shakespeare. She was extremely conscious of her public image and, as a woman in a man's world who felt constantly under threat, she deliberately hid her feelings behind a mask of make-up and always dressed to impress and make a political statement. Elizabeth also expected the great and good of her realm to display her likeness in their houses as a sign of loyalty and deference, thus creating a growing demand for her picture. But as she was an unwilling sitter and seldom had her likeness drawn, only a handful of her many portraits were taken from life. Rather, these were copies of an original 'head' to which artists added a body and clothing with the help of pattern books and manuals of iconography. Because many such portraits were poorly and swiftly executed, she ordered, seven years before her death, that inferior likenesses should be sought out and burnt. In his 1963 catalogue Sir Roy Strong lists only 101 surviving images of Elizabeth.

Magdalen's portrait is among the forty or so surviving likenesses based on the anonymous 'Darnley' portrait in the National Portrait Gallery (c. 1575). Here, Elizabeth is presented as a majestic, elegant, oval-faced woman in the prime of life, with auburn hair and beautiful hands (of which she was notoriously vain). Magdalen's portrait belongs to a sub-group of three 'Darnley' heads, called the 'Brocket' portraits after the likeness in Brocket Hall (Hertfordshire). Although Strong offers no further explanation for this categorization, the Magdalen painting is clearly a close relative of the Brocket portrait. Both depict Elizabeth wearing a low-cut, tight dress over a farthingale, with a ruff that leaves her chest exposed and shows off a swan's neck (the more so in the Magdalen painting, where both ruff and wired veil are transparent). The Queen's dress is studded with pearls (symbolizing humility, constancy, and purity), and she wears a pearl necklace with the same pendant jewel (probably a ruby). Her left hand holds a fan of ostrich feathers, while her right rests on a desk or table.

The two portraits are not, however, identical. Although the dresses are of the same style, they are decorated differently. The dominant design of the Magdalen image is a geometric pattern of a square edged by four circles suggesting a monogram, whilst the Brocket dress has a fussier, catherine-wheel design, and its breast region bears a symbol which invites the viewer to see Elizabeth as the sun and moon. The Magdalen portrait has a more imposing background, for Elizabeth stands in front of a russet hanging festooned with large pearls, jewels and possibly sapphires. Strong dated the Brocket paintings to the 1590s by the triangular shape of the Queen's dress above the waist. If he is right, then the Magdalen portrait is a perfect illustration of Gloriana's wish in later life to be depicted as frozen in time, forever the perfect embodiment of regal beauty and distance.

LWBB

PROVENANCE
Gift of Robert Coe of Wyoming (Magdalen College, 1923–26); acquired 1987.

LITERATURE
R. C. Strong, *Portraits of Queen Elizabeth I*, Oxford, 1963.

▶ Portrait of Elizabeth I by an unknown artist
oil on panel   109 x 81 cm   painted c. 1595

123

Hidden
Magdalen

Sunsets by William Gilpin

William Gilpin (1724–1804) was a clergyman and schoolteacher who claimed in his memoirs that he might be remembered for 'his mode of managing his school at Cheam ... & his mode of endowing his parish-school at Boldre, from the profits of his amusements'. Instead, he is best known for his comments on painting and the picturesque which anticipate the aesthetics of Romanticism.

Whilst the term 'picturesque' had been used in English from the beginning of the eighteenth century, and much earlier than that in Italian, Gilpin defined it in 1768 as 'a term expressive of that peculiar kind of beauty, which is agreeable in a picture'. He developed this definition in a series of books entitled *Observations on several parts of England: particularly the mountains and lakes of [Cumberland and Westmorland]; relative chiefly to picturesque beauty, made in the year 1772 by William Gilpin*, with, among others, *Highlands of Scotland* appearing in 1776 and *Isle of White* in 1798. These books were essentially for tourists and amateur painters, and they indicated from which locations an artist could get the most picturesque effect. A typical Gilpin picture would consist of three distances: the foreground (with trees framing the picture), the middle ground (with the main subject such as a castle, ruined tower, waterfall, or river), and the background (a range of hills or mountains). Sometimes figures or animals were introduced in the foreground to bring life to the picture. In reply to the accusation that his portrayal of familiar scenes was unfaithful, he replied: 'I am so attached to my picturesque rules, that if nature gets it wrong, I cannot help putting it right.'

In 1955 Magdalen's President Boase bought Gilpin's sketchbook entitled *Sunsets* in Bicester for 10s. 6d. (the equivalent of about £9 today). It contains five pages of manuscript text and seventeen of the original twenty-four drawings. In the notebook Gilpin writes: 'Now among the various modes of producing a picturesque effect, none is equal in point of splendo[u]r to a sunset'; and with reference to the actual drawings: 'A dark subject against a glowing light may often have a good effect; as the towers in I II III IV. A tree also in shadow may show a light through its leaves and branches, to advantage as in V.'

DBR

Hidden
Magdalen

PROVENANCE

'These sunsets were drawn by the Revd. William Gilpin (1724–1804), M. A., Vicar of Boldre, Hampshire, Prebendary of Sarum';
President Boase's Bequest.

◀ *Sunset IV*   William Gilpin
watercolour   26 x 37 cm

▲ *Sunsets* X and *XVII*

LITERATURE

C. P. Barbier, *William Gilpin: His Drawings, Teaching, and Theory of the Picturesque*, Oxford, 1963.

The Gifts

Hidden
Magdalen

The Assyrian Relief

Magdalen's relief is made of grey alabaster and comes from the palace at Nimrud (modern-day Kalhu) that was built by Ashurnasirpal II, King of Assyria from 883 to 859 BC. Reliefs from this period are agreed to be among the finest examples of Assyrian art. During the excavations carried out at Nimrud in 1845–47 by Austen Henry Layard (1817–94), the relief depicted here was discovered in a large L-shaped room that was probably used for ceremonial purposes. The room was lavishly decorated with two levels of relief sculptures, the upper one of which was based on the motif of two figures kneeling either side of a sacred tree. There were about fifty of these figures, which are held in museums all over the world.

Magdalen was given this relief by Hormuzd Rassam (1826–1910), who had worked as Layard's assistant at Nimrud. Born into a wealthy Christian family in Mosul, he later became an archaeologist himself. In 1847 Rassam came to England with Layard and studied at Oxford for about fifteen months. He hoped to study at Magdalen, but in 1849 Layard insisted that he return to the excavations, which he reluctantly did, and never formally matriculated. But Rassam came to know and like Magdalen and its President, Martin Routh (see p. 60), and in July 1849, just before leaving for Mesopotamia, he wrote to Routh. He thanked him warmly 'for the kindness I have received from you first, and also for the indulgence with which the College generally has treated me, and that hospitality I hope never to forget' and declared 'that I am not forgetful of the many kind offices performed to me by the benevolent Mrs. Routh' (MS 464 no. 304). The relief is evidently a more tangible expression of Rassam's gratitude for the hospitality and, although we do not know precisely when he made the donation, Macray dates it to 1848 or 1849. As Macray was an academical clerk at Magdalen at that time, his testimony seems reliable.

Rassam maintained his links with Magdalen, since the College also possesses two much smaller Assyrian reliefs, one depicting two human figures, the other an ox's head. To judge from notes on the back of them, these originate from Layard's and Rassam's dig at Nineveh in 1849–51 and were given by Rassam to individual Fellows who subsequently presented them to the College.

RHD–S

LITERATURE

Macray, *Register of Members*, vol. 7, p. 17.

◄ Wall decoration from the palace at Nimrud
alabaster relief   75 x 63 cm   9th century BC

The Magdalen Papyrus 17

Three tiny fragments of papyrus, no bigger than postage stamps, catalogued as Magdalen P17 (Gregory-Aland P64), have generated more excitement and controversy in recent years than any other of the College's possessions. They were given to the College in 1901 by a Magdalen alumnus and keen papyrologist, Charles Huleatt (1863–1908), who was serving as a chaplain at Luxor and who rightly identified them as important fragments from an early codex of St Matthew's Gospel. But the gift provoked so little interest that Huleatt had to write again two months later to check whether the College had received it. Any further information that Huleatt may have had about the find was lost when he, his wife, and four children perished in the Messina earthquake of 1908. We can, however, speculate that the fragments' content made him decide that Magdalen was their proper home, for two of them contain passages from the verses in which Mary Magdalene anoints Jesus (Matthew 26: 7–8 and 10).

The fragments have text on both sides and so are from a codex rather than a scroll (which would have had writing on one side only). It was traditionally assumed that biblical codices emerged only in the third and fourth centuries. Huleatt thought the fragments might date from the third century, but the leading papyrologist of the day and former Magdalen Demy, Arthur Hunt (1871–1934), suggested a fourth century date. This late dating assigned the fragments to obscurity for half a century until the discovery of codex fragments among the Dead Sea Scrolls established that biblical codices could have been produced at a much earlier date.

In 1953 the papyrologist Colin Roberts (1909–90) argued that Magdalen's fragments involved an early precursor of the biblical uncial script which emerged around the end of the second century. Although this re-dating to AD *c.* 200 was widely accepted and gave the Magdalen papyrus a good claim to be the earliest surviving fragments of St Matthew's Gospel, interest remained confined to scholarly circles. Indeed, they continued to be displayed in a cabinet of curiosities alongside Joseph Addison's shoe buckles and a ring that Oscar Wilde gave to Lord Alfred Douglas.

This all changed when the New Testament scholar and papyrologist Carsten Thiede (1952–2004) re-dated the fragments to the first century AD on palaeographic grounds. His thesis was unleashed on the world with huge publicity: *The Times* broke the story on its front page on Christmas Eve 1994 with the claim that Thiede had discovered in an Oxford college 'the first material evidence that the gospel according to St Matthew is an eyewitness account written by contemporaries of Christ'. The implications were momentous and the rest of the media quickly joined in. But other papyrologists and biblical scholars were not so easily convinced and ten years on, Thiede's thesis has found few supporters. The consensus remains for a late second-century date, although the slender basis for dating biblical papyri leaves plenty of room for further turns to the debate. Nevertheless: even a second-century date still leaves the College in possession of the earliest extant object in which Mary Magdalene makes her appearance. Even a college with a 550-year pedigree may be tempted to feel that such an association adds a certain lustre to its name.

JBWN

LITERATURE

P. M. Head, 'The date of the Magdalen Papyrus of Matthew: A response to C. P. Thiede', *Tyndale Bulletin* 46 (1995), pp. 251–85.

C. P. Thiede, 'Papyrus Magdalen Greek 17 (Gregory-Aland P64): a reappraisal', *Zeitschrift für Papyrologie und Epigraphik* 105 (1995), pp. 13–20.

C. P. Thiede and M. D'Ancona, *The Jesus Papyrus*, London, 1996.

▶ Possibly the earliest surviving fragments of St Matthew's Gospel (magnified)

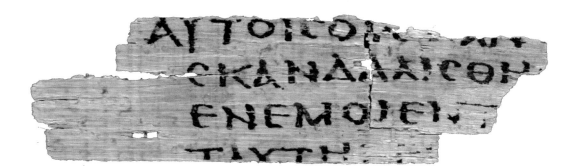

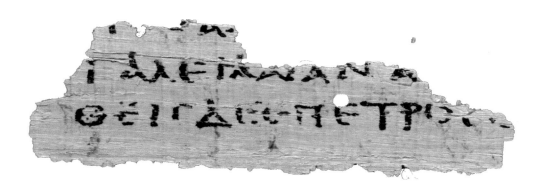

131

Hidden
Magdalen

The Catherine and Arthur Betrothal Tapestries

Magdalen's most famous possessions are probably four tapestries from the early sixteenth century, which are among the few surviving items of furnishing that indisputably date back to the College's earliest years. We know very little of their origin, purpose, or provenance, but much College legend surrounds them, every element of which has been challenged at some point by one expert or another.

The legend proceeds thus: the tapestries were acquired by President Mayew (or Mayhew; 1439/40–1516), the first appointed President of

Magdalen. In 1490, Mayew was sent to Spain by Henry VII to negotiate a marriage between Catherine of Aragon (daughter of the joint monarchs Ferdinand and Isabella) and Prince Arthur, heir to the throne of England and four years old at the time. The planned marriage comprised one section of a treaty which aimed to bring lasting peace between the two countries. So, from infancy, Catherine was taught that her future husband was the reincarnation of the great Arthur of ancient European legend. In England, too, the marriage was regarded as the expression of a

▶ One of the tapestries supposedly celebrating the marriage of Prince Arthur to Catherine of Aragon in 1501 254 x 582 cm

▶▶ Detail

renewal of Arthurian glory and the final reconciliation between the warring Houses of York and Lancaster. The bridal couple exchanged letters (in Latin) throughout their childhood. Arthur made a couple of visits to Magdalen as a child. In 1501 the marriage took place in London, amid much public rejoicing when the couple arrived at St Paul's Cathedral. But it lasted only a few months for when, as Prince and Princess of Wales, the couple paid a visit to the Principality, Arthur contracted a fearsome disease at Ludlow and died. Catherine then lingered in London for nine lonely years before marrying Henry VIII, her husband's younger brother, in 1509.

According to Macray, the tapestries depict scenes from the marriage ceremony: as Almoner to the King, Mayew was presented with them after the ceremony and bore them back to the President's Lodgings at Magdalen, of which he was the first occupant. In 1504 Mayew become Bishop of Hereford and three years later he retired from the College. Mayew left many things to Magdalen, but as his will makes no mention of the tapestries, it has been surmised that he already regarded them as College property and left them there. Later inventories of the Lodgings duly list the tapestries as part of the furnishings — in 1554, 1589, 1661 and 1667. But thereafter no reference is made to them until the nineteenth century, when we hear of more than the currently known four pieces — so since then, one or more has evidently disappeared.

The tapestries have excited historians and aroused scepticism among textile experts for a century or more. Sir Herbert Warren (1853–1930), President from 1885 to 1928, believed that they depict the betrothal, Catherine's arrival at Cheapside in London, and other scenes from the marriage. Antonia Fraser is moved by the depiction of the child bride and groom. But most tapestry restorers and experts think that the scenes, or some of them, relate to the biblical story of King David and Bathsheba, which formed the subject of many sets of tapestries circulating around the Holy Roman Empire in the early sixteenth century. Others argue that the characters' clothing suggests a later (post-1510) date of manufacture. As many crucial figures have been cut from the tapestries and one or

two inserted at later dates, it is very hard to determine the nature of the drama being narrated, and one can only speculate about its subject. So we are left with scenes from a marriage which may be from the Bible, and with the last surviving possessions of a President who had been promoted and was even possibly dead before the tapestries existed. On the other hand, pomegranates, the symbol of the Kingdom of Aragon, have been woven around the edges (which are judged to be authentic and original) and into some of the main designs. For some experts, this guarantees the Catherine connection, while others point out that pomegranates appear in other tapestries of the time that have no connection with Spain.

But wherever they come from and whatever they depict, these tapestries have adorned the walls of Magdalen's President's Lodgings for around five hundred years.

ADS

LITERATURE
Macray, *Register of Members.*

133

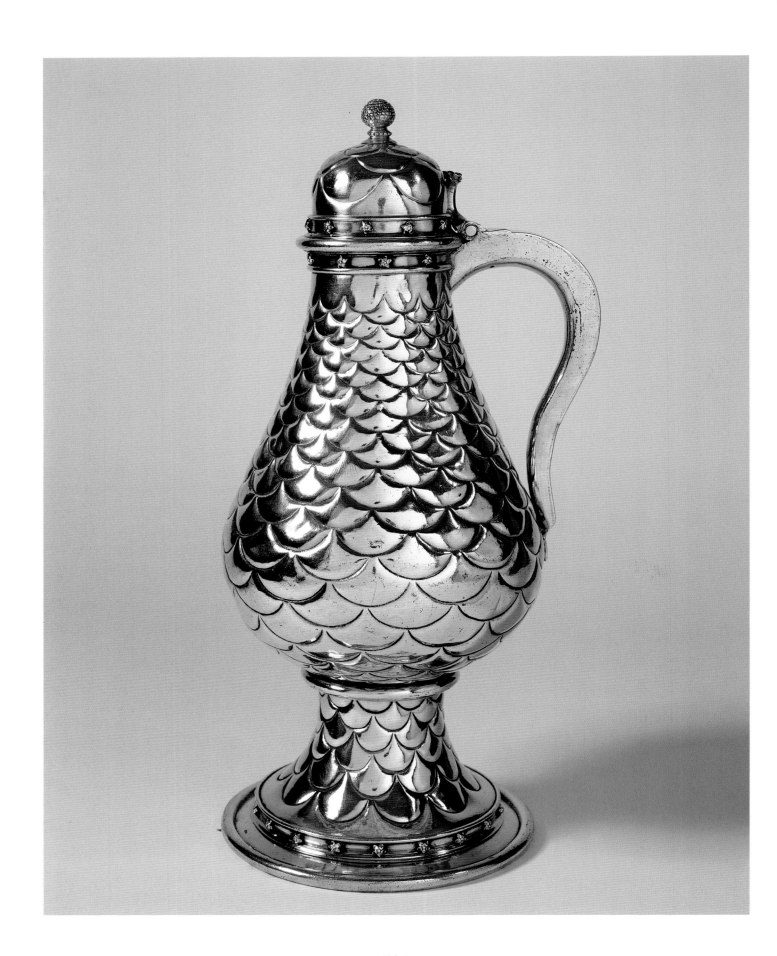

134

Hidden
Magdalen

The Magdalen Pot

Silver gilt, with a pear-shaped body and domed cover surmounted by a seeded berry; the whole is decorated with graduated scales.

This pot or 'potte', once thought to be German, was researched by the late John Hayward (1916–83), who tells an interesting story. It is one of the two pieces of College silver (the other being the Founder's Cup) to have survived the English Civil War (see pp. 33 and 140).

The 'potte', a bellied vessel for liquids, was the most frequently mentioned vessel in the 1574 inventory of Queen Elizabeth I's plate. None survives, but a pewter vessel of similar shape and style was recovered from the wreck of the *Mary Rose*. So Magdalen's pot may well be the only surviving example of a Tudor 'potte' in precious metal. When new royal plate was made after the Restoration, the Tudor form was revived, and a large 'buffet' example from 1664, for show rather than use, has scalloping similar to that on the Magdalen pot.

An inventory of the College silver from 1580/1 described this pot as follows: 'long potts of silver with scales and covers gilted'. It is not recorded in the inventory of 1495, but as this document listed Chapel plate only, the pot, intended for secular use, would not have been included in any case. Although this pot is probably unique, features of its designs occur on English silver vessels of the late fifteenth and early sixteenth centuries. The domed lid is unusual and

replicated only in a piece of silver in Wells Cathedral dating from 1572–73. So the Magdalen pot probably dates from the early sixteenth century.

How did the Magdalen pot survive? Hayward conjectures that it was saved from King Charles by inclusion in the Chapel plate. But after the fall of Oxford in 1646 some Popish effects belonging to the Chapel were removed by a Parliamentary official: the Magdalen pot was not among these. According to William Browne (the College Manciple), it was sent in 1648 to the house of his father John Browne in St Mary's parish as part of the attempt to safeguard what was left of the Chapel plate. William's brother, who lived with their father, remembered 'a guilt ewer that came with them'. Three years later these items were sent to Dr John Dale (b. *c*. 1620), a Fellow of the College who lived in London, and in a letter of 5 December 1661 to Dr Henry Yerbury (1627–86) at Magdalen, Dale explains why he has not returned a 'Cristall Salt': it had been taken by his landlord to pay his rent. But Dale's letter also implies that the Magdalen pot had been returned to the College in early December 1661, having escaped the predations of both Royalists and Puritans.

DBR

LITERATURE

J. Hayward, 'The Tudor plate of Magdalen College, Oxford', *Burlington Magazine* 125 (1983), pp. 260–65.

◀ The only known surviving Tudor silver 'potte'
total height 35.6 cm   diameter of the mouth 7.6 cm, of the foot 14 cm

The Founder's Cup

Standing cup and cover, silver gilt, melon-shaped, engraved with sprays of arabesques, supported on a fluted baluster stem. This cup has long been known as the 'Founder's Cup', as though it were linked in some way to William of Waynflete. But the true story is more complex.

As the cup bears a hallmark that dates it to 1601/2, it was made long after Waynflete's day. An inventory of the President's plate from the early seventeenth century (CS/1/9) alludes to a 'cup with Marie Magdalene on the Cover thereof', which must be this one. But the little figure of St Mary Magdalene is stylistically earlier than the rest of the cup, and an even earlier inventory of the President's plate (1580/1; CS/1/1) mentions 'one pece wth a cover gilt haveing the Image of Marie Magdalen called ye Magdalen boxe'. It has been suggested that this 'image' was the figure of the saint and that, at some point between 1580 and 1601, the 'Magdalen boxe' — which does not appear in the later inventory — was disposed of, save for the figure of the saint which was transferred to this newly-made cup. Such cavalier treatment of old silver plate was not unusual at the time.

During the English Civil War, when Charles I set up court in Oxford (1642–46), the colleges donated their silver for melting down as a contribution to his cause. As a result, few Oxford colleges own pre-1642 silver plate. Although the Founder's Cup, together with the rest of the College's silver, went to the Royal Mint, the President of the day, Accepted Frewen (1588–1664), had second thoughts about this particular object, which he referred to as the 'Mag[dalen] Bole', and donated the money himself to have it returned to the College. It cost him £11 11s. 6d. (CS/1/3 and 8). Thanks to Frewen's generosity, a significant early piece of College silver was preserved for posterity.

DBR/RHD-S

LITERATURE

E. A. Jones, *Catalogue of the Plate of Magdalen College Oxford*, Oxford, 1940.

J. Hayward, 'The Tudor plate of Magdalen College, Oxford,' *The Burlington Magazine* 125 (1983), pp. 260–65.

▶ A rare pre-Civil War silver cup with a figure of Mary Magdalene on its cover.
London 1601–02; maker's mark an animal head erased between the initials WI   total height 15½ in. original weight marked 42 oz. 10 dwt.

◀◀ Detail

*Hidden
Magdalen*

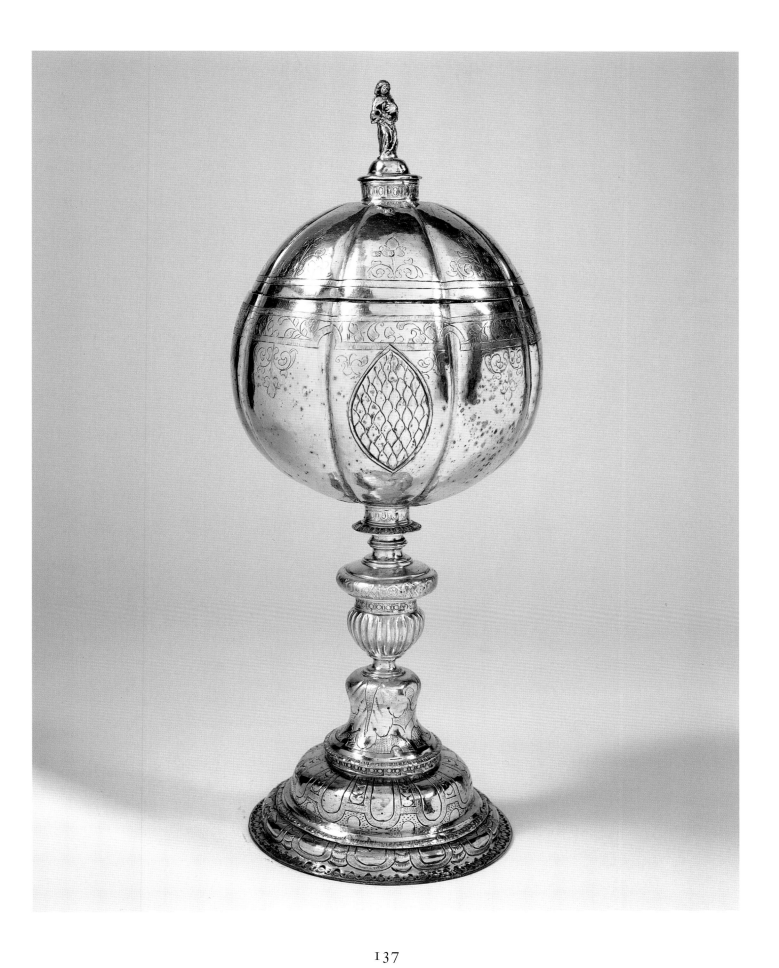

137

*Hidden
Magdalen*

The Cup of the Restored Fellows

Standing cup, silver gilt, tapering bowl on a circular foot, with a tall pointed cover. Engraved with the royal coat of arms within the garter under a crown and 'CR' (*Carolus Rex*), and in a medallion the Magdalen coat of arms.

In 1648, after the final defeat of the Royalist cause in the English Civil War, Parliament carried out a thorough visitation of Oxford University in order to weed out members still loyal to Charles I. Magdalen suffered particularly badly, for its President and well over half of its Fellows and Demies were ejected by the Visitors and replaced by men who were more to the Parliamentarians' taste. Inevitably, on the restoration of the monarchy in 1660, a second visitation took place, during which those Fellows who were unable to accept the new order were expelled and those Fellows of 1648 who were still willing or eligible were reinstated in their old posts, along with the former President. This cup commemorates their restoration.

DBR/RHD-S

LITERATURE

E. Jones, *Catalogue of the Plate of Magdalen College, Oxford*, Oxford, 1940.

Inscription

DONO DEDERVNT

ABRAHAM FORMAN, *S: Theol: Bac: Vicepreses*, HEN.
YERBVRY. *med: Dr.* EDM: DIGGLE. *S. Theol: Bac:*
ALLEXANDER IENNINGS: IOHS: TAYLER: EDW: ROGERS
GVL. COX: GEO: LANGTON: NATH: CHYLES. *Art: M*
Socij Coll: Magd: Oxon:
Pars non minima Eorum
Qui cum per duodecim continuos annos exulassent
Eo quod turbatis rebus Parti Regiae studerunt
REGNANTE CARLO PRIMO
In monumentum perenne
Ipsorum Restitutionis postliminio factae
Anno 1660
AVSPICIIS CAROLI SECUNDI

(Abraham Forman, Bachelor of Theology and Vice-President, Henry Yerbury, Doctor of Medicine, Edmund Diggle, Bachelor of Theology, Alexander Jennings, John Tayler, Edward Rogers, William Cox, George Langton, and Nathaniel Chyles, MAs and Fellows of Magdalen College, Oxford, not the least part of those who had been in exile for twelve unbroken years because, in times of strife, when Charles I was King, they had favoured the King's side, have presented this as a gift in everlasting memory of their restoration back home again made in the year 1660, under the auspices of Charles II.)

Engraving on the cover

CAROLI RESTITVTORI SACRVM

(sacred to Charles the Restorer)

138

◄ A cup commemorating the reinstatement of Royalist
Fellows following the Restoration
London 1660–61; maker's mark an orb and flame in a
plain shield
original weight 57 oz. 10 dwt.   total height 46.4 cm
diameter of mouth 15.5 cm, of foot 16.5 cm

Magdalen Tankard and Tun

In his catalogue of Magdalen's plate, Jones notes, with reference to Magdalen and three other colleges, 'the lamentable losses of their early plate at the Reformation, the Civil War, and in more recent times'. Magdalen's losses included a robbery on 25 February 1786, for which one of the robbers, Miles Ward, was hanged. Magdalen's only other pieces of pre-Civil War silver are an early sixteenth-century chalice and paten (presented by Sir John Noble (1855–1938) in 1936), the Founder's Cup (see pp. 136–37), and the Magdalen Pot (p. 135). The tankard and tun are representative of early acquisitions of silver in Magdalen's present collection.

Tankard

Small and plain, with a flat-topped cover pointed in front, and a thumb-piece composed of hollow lobes.

The discrepancy between the maker's date and the date in the inscription suggests that it was made from or exchanged for an earlier tankard, whose donor had matriculated in 1657 and been admitted to the Middle Temple in 1658. An inventory of 1678 mentions this piece as being in the President's Lodgings.

Inscription

College arms within scrolled feathers.

Coll: Mag.
Ex dono Manselli Stradling Edvardi Stradling
Equitis et Baronetti filij natu minimi de St Donato
In Comitatu Glamorgan hujus Coll: Comensalis 1657

Donor's arms with foliated scrolls.

▲ Silver tankard
London 1672–73; maker's mark: FL, with a bird between two pellets, below in a shaped punch
original weight marked 24 oz. 6 dwt.   height 14.5 cm
diameter of mouth 10.8 cm, of base 12 cm

Tun

The OED defines a tun as 'a kind of cup or small drinking vessel. [The name is still applied at Magdalen College, Oxford, to silver drinking cups, holding a third of a quart, some of which are dated 1657 and 1663.]' The College has nearly fifty tuns, the earliest dated 1657 and the last 1888/9. Recent examples have been made, with the latest being presented to President Smith on his retirement in 2005.

The one depicted here is the earliest and has a 'bellied' shape and two small ring handles. Although the Thomson of the inscription matriculated in 1657, the hallmark dates the tun to 1718/19, suggesting that it was recast from Thomson's tankard. This was a common practice, and an inventory of 26 April 1662 notes that 'Mr. Nickolsons tankard was also at ye same time orderd to be changed into a tunne.'

An inventory of 1718 mentions the tun as being in the Buttery.

Inscription

Waynflete arms ensigned by mitre.

COLL: MAGD. OXON.

Ex dono Samuelis Thomson fil: nat: max:
Gul: Thomson Arm. Londinensi 1657.

The donor's arms with foliated scrolls.

DBR

LITERATURE

E. Jones, *Catalogue of the Plate of Magdalen College*, Oxford, Oxford, 1940.

R. Sheppard, *The Gunstones of St Clement's: The History of a Dynasty of College Servants at Magdalen*, Oxford, 2003, p. 82.

▲ Silver tun
London 1718–19; no maker's mark
original weight marked 11 oz. 11 dwt. 12 gr.
height 9.5 cm

Christ Bearing the Cross attrib.
Juan de Valdés Leal

The art historian T. S. R. Boase (1898–1974), Magdalen's President from 1947 to 1968, recounted the history of this seventeenth-century painting in a Charlton Lecture.

In autumn 1702 James Butler, the Duke of Ormonde, was leading a military force accompanying the English fleet as it returned from an 'ineffective' raid on Cadiz. On 12 October, they overpowered a French convoy at Vigo and captured some Spanish galleons, one of which was carrying the painting. It subsequently came into the possession of William Freeman of Hamels in Hertfordshire, formerly a gentleman commoner of Magdalen, who gave it to the College in 1745. At that time a number of 'painted cloths' were hanging on the lower part of the east wall of the Chapel. These were disposed of in favour of the new altarpiece, which was soon framed by a wainscot and Corinthian columns made of wood. As the stonework now surrounding the painting did not appear until Cottingham's restoration (1829–34), the picture is almost two hundred years older than its Gothicized backdrop.

According to Boase, depictions of a 'calm, lonely' Christ, unaccompanied on the road to Calvary, enjoyed great popularity in the sixteenth and seventeenth centuries. In his lecture he noted similarities between this image of Christ and that used in Seville Holy Week observances, when the statue is 'borne solitary on its great stand'. Over the years, many attributions have been proposed and rejected: to Guido Reni (1575–1642), Lodovico Carracci (1555–1619), Luis de Morales (c. 1520–86), and Francisco Ribalta (1565–1628). Bishop Alexander Forbes of Brechin first connected the painting with the Seville School in 1855, when he reported seeing a copy on a convent wall in Ecija, east of Seville. The compass has recently pointed to Juan de Valdés Leal (1622–90), not only because of the Seville connection but because of what Boase thought was an undeniably 'close kinship' between this painting and a much larger picture of Christ carrying the Cross, then in an American collection, that was signed by Valdés Leal.

The Magdalen painting has been rendered in stained glass for a church at Wanstead in Essex, and often engraved. It has been copied many more times on canvas, making its way to such places as Hereford Cathedral, Findon (Sussex), Bolton Abbey (Yorkshire), Wimborne (Dorset), and Abingdon and Northmoor (Oxfordshire).

MJP

LITERATURE

T. S. R. Boase, *Christ Bearing the Cross, Attributed to Valdés Leal, at Magdalen College, Oxford: A Study in Taste*, Oxford, 1955.

▶ *Christ Bearing the Cross*
attributed to Juan de Valdés Leal
oil on canvas 200 x 159 cm 17th century

Hidden
Magdalen

Joseph Addison by Godfrey Kneller

Joseph Addison (1672–1719), son of the Revd Launcelot Addison (1632–1703), later Dean of Lichfield, came from a line of Anglican clergy. Country-bred, he went to Charterhouse, where Richard Steele (Irish writer and politician, bap. 1672, d. 1729) became a life-long friend. Addison was elected Demy in Magdalen's 'Golden Election' of 1689, after the College had emerged victorious from its struggle with James II (see p. 56): his flowery Latin letter of application for the demyship was printed in 1997 in the Magdalen *Record*. He shared rooms in Cloisters with Henry Sacheverell (p. 58). They strolled in the Water Walks by the river Cherwell, part of which has since become known as Addison's Walk.

While at Magdalen, Addison studied Classics and wrote Latin and English poetry which attracted the attention of John Dryden (1631–1700), the publisher Jacob Tonson (1655/6–1736), and William Congreve (1670–1729), among others. Although Addison was elected Fellow in 1697, it soon became evident that he had no taste for scholarship. He paid early court to such Whig politicians as Lord Somers (1651–1716) and Charles Montagu (1661–1715), later Lord Halifax. A Treasury travel grant allowed him to obtain leave from the College, to remain a layman, and to travel in Europe, especially France and Italy, from 1699 to 1704.

On his return home, Addison established himself as a literary figure in London, where he became a member of the Kit-Cat Club and a frequenter of coffee houses, especially Buttons. He became a principal contributor to the *Spectator* and the *Tatler*, and thus helped set the tone for Augustan England by teaching the eighteenth century 'how it should, and especially how it should not behave'. He had been fortunate in matriculating at Magdalen during its period of Whig favour, when the relations between the political and the literary classes were closer than they had ever been. But as Addison became more staunchly Whig, Magdalen became increasingly Tory, and he eventually resigned his Fellowship in 1711.

Although his time as an MP (1708–19) was undistinguished, his merits as a man of business, literary skill, and patronage enabled him to hold several government appointments, and he ended his life as Secretary of State for the Southern Department (1718–19). Addison bought an estate at Bilton, near Rugby (see p. 188), where he established the gardens and park. He married Lady Warwick (bap. 1680, d. 1731), with whom he had one daughter. He was buried in Westminster Abbey, leaving behind a huge reputation. For a long time his writings were required reading for those wishing 'to attain an English style familiar but not coarse, and elegant but not ostentatious'.

Magdalen has five portraits of Addison. This one, in Hall, signed and dated in 1718 by Godfrey Kneller (1646–1723), was given by Sir Peter Smithers (1915–2006), the author of the authoritative *Life of Joseph Addison*. He read History at Magdalen, gave generously to the College, and helped acquire the gates from Bilton Hall that are now erected in the duckery at the end of Addison's Walk. During the Second World War, Ian Fleming, himself the son of a Magdalen man who was killed in the First World War, recruited Smithers to Naval Intelligence and used him thereafter as the model for James Bond. After the war Smithers became Conservative MP for Winchester (1950–64), and then Secretary-General to the Council of Europe (1964–69). In 1970 he retired to Switzerland to create a famous garden at Vico Morcote on Lake Lugano.

MAJW-B

LITERATURE
P. Smithers, *The Life of Joseph Addison*, 2nd edn, Oxford, 1968.

▶ *Joseph Addison*   Sir Godfrey Kneller, painted 1718
oil on canvas   127 cm x 96.5 cm

145

Hidden
Magdalen

▲ *The Circumcision of Christ*
Cornelis Schut, painted 17th century
oil on panel in an original elaborate gilt frame
84 x 68.5 cm

▶ The 19th-century copy of the Waynflete portrait that had
been painted over Schut's painting

146

The Circumcision of Christ by Cornelis Schut

The painting reproduced on p. 146 is a final oil sketch for a vast picture now in the Ghent City Gallery, and its original purpose was as much political as pious. The principal theme of the composition is blood. The carpenter Joseph, knife in hand, is shown at the moment of performing the circumcision; an angel holds a golden basin in which to catch the drops of blood; in the far right corner the instruments of the Passion are visible; in the bottom left is a lamb about to be slain.

The picture was no doubt intended to flatter the citizens of Catholic Antwerp, where the painter Cornelis Schut (1597–1655) flourished alongside his more famous contemporaries and rivals, Peter Paul Rubens (1577–1640), the two Jan Breughels (1568–1625 and 1601–78), and Antony Van Dyck (1599–1641). One of Antwerp's great churches claimed to possess Christ's foreskin as a relic and Schut's picture was commissioned to proclaim this when the northern Protestant Netherlands were in revolt against their Spanish Habsburg masters, while the southern provinces were determined to demonstrate their loyal Catholic credentials.

Much of Schut's work was ephemeral. He is, for instance, noted for painting the ceremonial arches that were used during city pageants; one such arch was painted to mark the visit of the Habsburg Emperor. Schut's *oeuvre* was mainly commissioned by the Jesuits and his pictures remained in their possession until the order was dissolved in Antwerp in the late eighteenth century. Since then, Schut's pictures have been mainly in storage. His reputation began to rise only in the early twentieth century, when his works started to reappear in sales rooms.

Magdalen has owned this picture since 1936, when a friend of one of the Fellows gave it to the College. But what was actually given, in this same frame, was a portrait of the College's founder, William of Waynflete, a late nineteenth-century diminished copy of the familiar portrait which hangs in the Lodgings (see p 47), the Summer Common Room, New

College, the Provost's Lodgings at Eton, and probably elsewhere. Throughout the 1980s this particular picture lived in a sorry state, leaning against a radiator in the secretary's office in the Lodgings. In 1997 it was sent to Ambrose Scott Moncrieff for cleaning and his X-ray photographs revealed the seventeenth-century underpainting. After several months of meticulous work, Schut's original painting came back into the light of day. We do not know how the picture came to England, who owned it, or who decided to re-use the panel for the Waynflete portrait.

It seems that no other work of Schut exists in Britain, but the National Portrait Gallery possesses two pictures of the second Earl of Arundel which are described as being 'after Cornelis Schut': a notable collection of prints by Schut is held at Princeton.

ADS

147

*Hidden
Magdalen*

San-san-kudo: Prince Chichibu's Sake Frame

San-san-kudo is used during a wedding ceremony conducted according to the Shinto ritual; Shinto is the original Japanese religion and the religion of the imperial family. As a very important part of the ceremony, the bride and groom drink sacred *sake* from these cups and this is called *san-san-kudo*. *San* means three and *kudo* means nine. So *san-san-kudo* refers to

both the bride and groom taking three sips from each of the three cups. The idea of drinking the sacred *sake* from the same cup is symbolic of the union of the two people, and the three cups represent respectively 'heaven' (the smallest), 'earth' (the middle size), and 'human beings' (the largest).

The frame is inscribed in Japanese:

> *Oxford, Magdalen College*
> *In memory of studying at your College*
> **Yasuhito**
> *Year 2586 Kigen calendar*

The Kigen calendar was established in 1872 (Fifth Year of Meiji), with year one being the year when the first Emperor, Jinmu, came to the throne. This calendar is no longer used.

HIH Prince Chichibu (1902–53), also known as Prince Yasuhito, was the younger brother of Emperor Hirohito (1901–89) and matriculated at Magdalen in Michaelmas Term 1926 with the intention of studying History, Politics, and Economics for a year. This was a great coup for President Herbert Warren (1853–1930), worthy of comparison with the matriculation of the Prince of Wales in 1912: indeed, Prince Chichibu was given Prince Edward's former rooms.

Unfortunately, Prince Chichibu had to return to Japan after only a term because of the death of his father. It was later rumoured that the Imperial Palace, anxious about the Prince's exposure to Western values, decided that he should not return to Magdalen. Despite its brevity, the Prince always looked back on his term at Magdalen as one of the happiest periods in his life. Not only did he like his tutor, Stephen 'Luggins' Lee (1889–1962), he also took up rowing and squash and introduced the latter sport to Japan on his return home. He even arranged the furniture of his study in his Tokyo residence and country home along the lines of his study in College.

The Prince was a great anglophile, and the outbreak of the Second World War was a terrible blow to him. In later years Prince Chichibu suffered from

tuberculosis, and died in 1953 aged only 50. His widow, HIH Setsuko, Princess Chichibu, outlived him by four decades, and did much to re-establish Anglo-Japanese relations, not least between the two countries' royal families. The Princess visited Magdalen more than once and remained in close contact with the College until her death in 1995. Magdalen's links with the Japanese imperial family were further strengthened when Prince Chichibu's nephew, HIH Prince Tomohito of Mikasa, was a graduate student here from 1968 to 1970.

DBR/RHD-S

LITERATURE
P. Fullerton, 'Princess Chichibu (1909–1995): An Appreciation', *Magdalen College Record* (1996), pp. 89–96.

◀ Silver *san-san-kudo* cups, the largest inlaid with a gold chrysanthemum and the two smaller ones similarly inlaid; maker: Miyamoto Shoten of Tokyo
largest dish: height 7.6 cm, diameter 22.2 cm

▲ The Japanese inscription on the frame

A Suit of Japanese Armour

The armour was given to Magdalen in *c.* 1937 by Prince Chichibu, who studied here in the 1920s (see p. 148), and it is now on indefinite loan to the Ashmolean Museum. Its form is that of armour from the Muromachi period (1334–1572). But during the long peace of the Edo period (1603–1867) that was established by the Shogun Tokugawa Ieyasu, many suits of armour were made that were copies of older forms. The helmet demonstrably dates from the sixteenth century, but much of this suit may have been made in the Edo period and assembled, with older elements, in more recent years for presentation.

The helmet consists of sixty-two plates riveted together, a style of helmet that was singled out for praise by Shogun Tokugawa Ieyasu in 1585. An inscription inside dates it to the second year of the Eiroku era, which corresponds to 1560, and there is also a maker's inscription which seems to read 'Joshu ju Hiranari saku' (made by Hiranari, resident of Kozuke province). The helmet is crowned with a pair of antler-like *kuwagata* — originally worn to distinguish generals but widely adopted later as a decorative feature by many samurai (mounted warriors). The neckguard is bent upwards at the front to form ear-like projections (*fukiga yeshi*) and a russeted iron mask (*mempō*) covers the face and, no doubt, helped to intimidate the enemy. A pendant throat defence (*yodare kate*) is suspended from the mask.

The body armour is symmetrical (*dō-maru*), with a side opening which allowed the wearer to put it on. It is made up of innumerable lamellae, or small plates of lacquered metal laced together with silk, and these are dyed different colours to form a vivid pattern on assembly. Unlike European armour, which was fastened together with straps and buckles, the elements of Japanese armour were simply tied together. The large shoulder guards (*ō-sode*) are of an earlier type, but these were frequently made for presentation suits of armour. The sleeves (*kote*) have rings of mail and small plates sewn to them as a defence. The skirt, or thigh-defence (*kusazuri*), is also made from lamellae laced together with coloured silk. The legs are protected by heavy shin-guards of plate (*suneate*) that would have been more suitable for a horseman than a foot soldier — but again, these may have been added for presentation.

A plate from the helmet has been examined microscopically and found to be made of low to medium carbon steel. Its hardness on the Vickers Pyramid Hardness scale was 243 kg/mm^{-2}. Modern mild steel is about 120 on the same scale, while the hardened edges of Japanese swords might reach 500–600.

ARW

LITERATURE

H. R. Robinson, *The Manufacture of Armour and Helmets in 16th Century Japan*, London, 1962.

▶ Samurai armour, in the style of the 14th to 16th centuries; suit assembled for presentation

Mount Magdalen

Mount Magdalen rises 4,650 feet on the north-west side of Scoresby Bay at the eastern end of Ellesmere Island in the North-West Territories of Canada. Its official designation is: Lat. 79° 55′ N; Long. 71° 54′ W.

The island was explored (and given its name unofficially) during a survey carried out by an Oxford University Expedition in April–May 1935, of which Edward Shackleton (1911–94; son of the Polar explorer Sir Ernest Shackleton, 1874–1922) was the organiser and surveyor. Edward had been a student at Magdalen from 1931 to 1934 and was made an Honorary Fellow in 1986. He continually pressed the Canadian authorities to allow the name to be made official and was finally rewarded with success after sixty years of effort in April 1994, only months before his death.

In the intervening years Shackleton entered Parliament as a Labour MP, and became a knight and a life peer. He held, among innumerable other offices in industry and politics, those of UK Defence Minister, Lord Privy Seal, Paymaster General, Minister for the Civil Service, and Leader of the Opposition in the House of Lords. During the Second World War he served in Naval and Military Intelligence and in Coastal Command.

The photograph was taken by Steve Williams while engaged in a Royal Navy Reconnaissance Expedition to the Darling Peninsula of Ellesmere Island in July 1983. The earliest recorded climb of Mount Magdalen was carried out by two members of his team on 20 and 21 July 1983.

ADS

LITERATURE

E. Shackleton, *Arctic Journeys*, London, 1937, pp. 210 and 222.

▼ Mount Magdalen, Ellesmere Island, Canada, photographed in 1983 by Steve Williams

Bust of C. S. Lewis by Faith Tolkien

Clive Staples Lewis (1898–1963) was Fellow and Tutor in English at Magdalen from 1925 to 1954 and became an Honorary Fellow after being appointed to the new Cambridge Chair of Mediaeval and Renaissance Literature. He died on 22 November 1963, the day when President Kennedy was assassinated. Walter Hooper (b. 1931), another young American, had first met Lewis in the same year and helped him by acting as his private secretary when Lewis's health was declining and his brother Warren, his usual amanuensis and companion, was absent.

By 1980 Hooper had become literary adviser to the Lewis estate, and privately commissioned this sculpture hoping that it could be placed in the Antechapel as Lewis's principal College memorial. Faith Tolkien (b. 1928), the daughter-in-law of Lewis's friend Professor J. R. R. Tolkien (1892–1973), worked from photographs of Lewis to create the bust, her first commission at a time when she was trying to return to full-time work as a sculptor. Hooper offered the finished bust to Magdalen and the gift was accepted at a College meeting on 3 December 1980, though Hooper was told that the question of its location would require further discussion.

The bust has had a number of homes over the years — the Smoking Room, the Old Practice Room, the Lodgings — but it has not made its way to the Antechapel. Perhaps this can be attributed to fears of theft, or perhaps to a lively mixture of feelings towards Lewis amongst the Fellowship, who may not have been uniformly enthusiastic about his legacy when the matter was considered in 1980. But it is not inconceivable that a gradual shift in attitudes towards the subject, and a secure fixing in the Antechapel, might still lead, eventually, to the realization of the donor's original wish.

MJP

▲ C. S. Lewis sculpted by Faith Tolkien, 1980
bronze   height 35 cm

Chorister Medals

Until the mid-1990s the Head Chorister of Magdalen College Choir wore the Stainer Cross. Sir John Stainer (1840–1901) was Informator (Master of the Choristers) from 1860 to 1872, and the cross was presented to the College in his memory by his family. This splendid piece, in radiant green and white enamel, was stolen from the College in 1999 and, sadly, has still not been recovered. But the President at the time was Anthony Smith, and he, in typical fashion, set about replacing the cross. Soon after its theft, during a visit to the Sultan of Brunei, President Smith was given a large piece of gold from which the magnificent cross was fashioned that is worn by the Head Chorister today. The beautifully conceived design depicts the tree of life, studded with 32 miniature diamonds, and at the tree's base is the College crest.

In May 1996 the College celebrated the eightieth birthday of Bernard Rose (1916–96), Informator from 1958 to 1981. The occasion was marked by a special Choral Evensong that was attended by many former academical clerks (who were in rousing voice). At the beginning of the service, Dr Rose presented the Waynflete Chorister (the deputy head chorister) with a newly fashioned medallion, created specially for the occasion and given to the College by the Rose family. The piece, in silver, was made by Reginald Davies, the High Street jewellers, and is shaped in the form of a Tudor Rose, of the type to be found all over the College. It was named, most appropriately, the Rose Medallion.

This medal was stolen at the same time as the Stainer Cross. Not knowing its provenance, the thief unwittingly tried to sell it to Reginald Davies, who immediately recognized it and sounded the alarm.

When asked about the Stainer Cross, the thief told the police that his accomplice had thrown it into the river. So for all we know, it may yet turn up — on the *Antiques Roadshow* perhaps?

CJGI

▶ The Head Chorister's gold cross and the Waynflete Chorister's silver Rose Medallion

Hidden
Magdalen

The Purchases

Henry Harris as Cardinal Wolsey
by John Greenhill

Henry Harris (1633/4–1704) was an actor and engraver. When, in 1660, Charles II returned to the throne and the London playhouses re-opened following their closure under the Commonwealth, Harris joined the Duke's Company of actors, directed by Sir William Davenant (1606–68). He was first involved in production, but enjoyed immediate success on turning to acting. Pepys (1633–1703) recorded 'the King and everybody else crying him up so high', and his performance as Cardinal Wolsey in Shakespeare's *Henry VIII* was considered outstanding. In 1664, it led to the commissioning of this picture in coloured chalk, almost certainly the oldest extant portrait of a known English actor in costume. Additional copies exist in the Ashmolean Museum and the Garrick Club in London. Another of Harris's noted roles was Ulysses in Dryden's *Troilus and Cressida* (1679), and one of his many accolades was to be awarded the function and the title of Yeoman of the Revels.

Harris also enjoyed considerable professional and financial success in his other profession and became the official engraver of the King's signets, arms, and seals. He gave up the theatre in 1681, and on the accession to the throne of William and Mary in 1689, he became chief engraver at the Mint with special responsibility for making the seals for the American colonies and the English and Irish offices of state.

John Greenhill (1644–76) was a Somerset man who came to London in 1662 aged 20 to join the studio of the painter Sir Peter Lely (1618–80). Most of Greenhill's early work was in crayon and pastel (as here) and depicted contemporary actors in costume. But he was also commissioned to paint the portraits of a number of public figures, including ones of James, Duke of York (1633–1701) — now in the Dulwich Picture Gallery — and the philosopher John Locke (1632–1704) — now in the National Portrait Gallery.

Greenhill's short life came to an abrupt and tragic end when he drowned in a gutter after a bout of heavy drinking.

ADS

PROVENANCE

Probably purchased by the College as a portrait of Wolsey. In the watercolour of President Routh's study painted by George Pyne (1800–84) it can be seen hanging above the door.

▶ The actor Henry Harris in Shakespeare's *Henry VIII*
John Greenhill, 1664
coloured chalk on paper   39.5 x 31.75 cm

158

159

Hidden
Magdalen

Edward Gibbon by Henry Walton

Edward Gibbon (1737–94) was a prodigy who entered Magdalen in 1752 aged fifteen. He was allotted a fine set of three rooms in the New Building (which was then indeed new). He had been sent by an ambitious father who had quarrelled with his own college at Cambridge and who, after a year or more, also quarrelled with Magdalen, blaming it for his son's attraction to Roman Catholicism. He removed Edward from College and sent him to Switzerland, where the phenomenally gifted young man nearly contracted a marriage with the equally endowed Madame de Staël — a union which might have had intellectually stunning consequences. Gibbon dedicated much of his life (1772–88) to his *History of the Decline and Fall of the Roman Empire*, a multi-volume work which has remained the most famous work of history in the English language.

Gibbon resided at Lausanne for much of his life but never forgot his disappointments at Magdalen. In his *Autobiography* he indulged in some famously eloquent attacks on the College, which have coloured most subsequent views of eighteenth-century Oxford. Although he rewrote the autobiography seven or more times and his manuscripts differ substantially, the passages attacking Magdalen pass almost unaltered from version to version:

> The fellows or monks of my time were decent easy men, who supinely enjoyed the gifts of their founder: their days were filled by a series of uniform employments: the chapel and the hall, the coffee-house and the common room, till they retired, weary and well satisfied, to a long slumber. From the toil of reading, or thinking, or writing, they had absolved their conscience; and the first shoots of learning and ingenuity withered on the ground, without yielding any fruits to the owners or the public ... Their conversation stagnated in a round of college business, Tory politics, personal anecdotes, and private scandal: their dull and deep potations excused the intemperance of youth ...

When the College acquired the small portrait that is reproduced here, the Fellows decided that it should hang at precisely that point in the Senior Common Room (see pp. 74–75) from which Gibbon's image would face them for all time when engaged in their 'deep potations'. Alas, in 1992 a casual visitor removed the portrait and took it to Bonhams — where it was unrecognized and sold for £200 as the portrait of 'An Eighteenth Century Gentleman'. But it was then spotted and passed into the antiques trade, rising exponentially in price as it was sold and resold. In 1997 Magdalen's President discovered that a sale had just taken place in Bond Street and unmasked the dealer. Nevertheless, it took two more years before the portrait, thanks to Oxfordshire Constabulary's vigilant art theft unit, was passed back along the train of buyers and sellers and returned to its rightful position — facing the Fellows in the Senior Common Room where they sit, after their academic labours, drinking port during dessert with their guests.

Henry Walton (1746–1813) was a genre painter, a pupil of Johann Zoffany (1733–1810). He was noted mainly for his sentimental painting of a girl plucking a chicken and another with a bowl of cherries. Walton also painted portraits and produced four or five versions of this likeness, which it is interesting to compare with the larger portrait (*c.* 1780) by Sir Joshua Reynolds (1723–92). The Gibbon portraits are the same size and differ only in minor ways; the identity and provenance of this particular portrait was proved beyond doubt because of a tiny patch of light that falls on a single button. Shortly before the theft a Fellow had photographed the picture to serve as the frontispiece of a new edition of the *Autobiography* — happily removing any doubt as to which of Walton's portraits belonged to Magdalen.

ADS

PROVENANCE
Purchased from Mrs A. M. Onslow in 1937.

▶ Portrait of Edward Gibbon
by Henry Walton
oil on panel   20 x 17 cm

Hidden
Magdalen

Travelling on the Liverpool and Manchester Railway

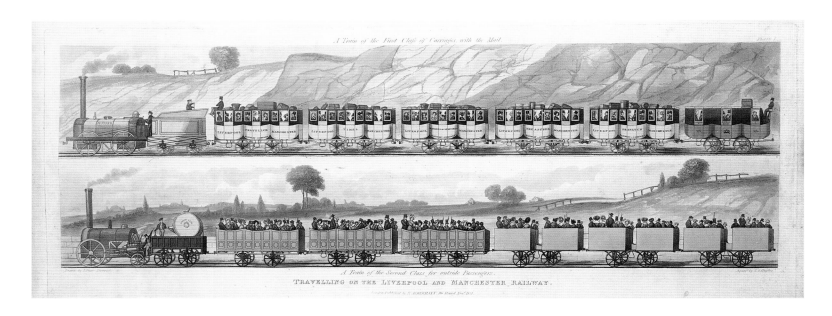

The Liverpool–Manchester railway was proposed in 1824 and opened in 1830. Magdalen's two prints, from the first (Ackermann) edition of November 1831, were found recently, rolled up in a decorated cardboard tube at the back of a cupboard in a desk in the Old Library. In his book on early railway prints Rees describes them as 'Perhaps the most famous of all railway prints'. A slightly altered version appeared in 1833: the passenger train has one less first-class carriage; a flat-bed truck behind the mail coach carries a horse-drawn coach with passengers but no horses; and the three box-like second-class carriages are replaced by two more comfortable-looking carriages and all have canopies. An 'imitation of the original' (Rees) was published by Raphael Tuck and Sons in 1894.

The engine pulling the first-class carriages is clearly marked 'Jupiter', though Rees notes that it was incorrectly drawn with equal-sized wheels. The second-class carriages are drawn by 'North Star', an improved version of 'Rocket'. The engine pulling the goods carriages is called 'Liverpool', while the train with livestock is drawn by 'Fury'. The line was a great success, with trains achieving speeds of up to 30 mph on its 31-mile track, and it stimulated the introduction

of railways throughout the country, despite the accidental death of the Liverpool MP, William Huskisson (1770–1830), who fell into the path of the 'North Star' at the opening.

These hand-coloured aquatints are on cloth-backed paper and the colours are remarkably vivid, almost certainly because they have been protected from daylight for a very long time. The drawings are by Isaac Shaw (*fl.* 1830–50) and the engraver was S. G. Hughes (*fl.* 1830s). Shaw produced a series of uncoloured lithographs of mansions in Lancashire about 1845.

There is no record of these prints in Magdalen's archives. But Burgon recounts that the aged President Routh (see p. 60) was told that a gentleman commoner had arrived early one term. Whereupon Routh commented that the roads were bad at that time of year. On being told that it was now possible to come to Oxford by railway, Routh allegedly refused to believe what he was hearing — 'I don't know anything about *that!*' This suggests a possible explanation for Magdalen having these prints: they could have been presented to President Routh some time after 1844 (when the Great Western Railway opened the station in Oxford), to demonstrate the

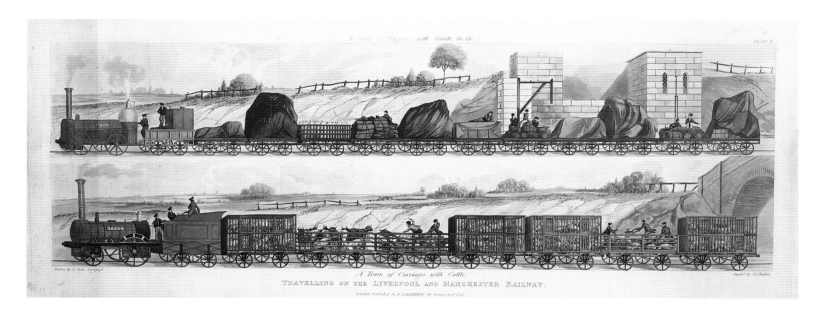

A Train of Waggons with Goods &c &c.

PLATE II

A Train of Carriages with Cattle.

TRAVELLING ON THE LIVERPOOL AND MANCHESTER RAILWAY.

existence and nature of railways. Certainly, by 1847, Magdalen's Butler was travelling by train to London to buy provender for dessert after Gaudies.

DBR

LITERATURE

J. W. Burgon, *Lives of Twelve Good Men*, 2 vols, London, 1888, vol. 1, p. 7.

G. Rees, *Early Railway Prints: A Social History of the Railways from 1825 to 1850*, Oxford, 1980.

R. Sheppard, *The Gunstones of St Clement's: The History of a Dynasty of College Servants at Magdalen*, Oxford, 2003, p. 29.

◀▲ Two early prints from 1831, the year after the Liverpool–Manchester railway opened, drawn by Isaac Shaw; engraved by S. G. Hughes
aquatint   25 x 66 cm

Mary Magdalene Washing Christ's Feet
by Edward Burne-Jones

Edward Burne-Jones (1833–98) once famously argued that art should ignore the real world in favour of the possible worlds of the imagination: 'I mean by a picture a beautiful romantic dream, of something that never can, never will be . . . in a land no one can define, or remember, only desire.' If this accounts for the somewhat other-worldly appearance of human figures in his pictures, it might also help to explain the sense of loss and yearning that hovers around his religious subjects. Like many of his Victorian contemporaries, Burne-Jones spent his adult life struggling with religious doubts. He came up to Exeter College in 1853 and quickly abandoned his teenage intention of entering the Church. But he never entirely lost his Christian convictions, and a struggle between the two sides of a personality described by one friend as 'half monk, half Puck' can be traced throughout his later career as a painter and designer of stained glass.

Burne-Jones's first artistic allegiance was to the Pre-Raphaelite Brotherhood. He became the pupil of D. G. Rossetti (1828–82) in the late 1850s, before going into business in 1861 with his Exeter contemporary William Morris (1834–96) as one of the founding members of Morris & Co. Like Morris, Burne-Jones was obsessed by Arthurian legends, confessing a year before his death that the Holy Grail legend was 'ever in my mind and thoughts'. This chalk drawing brings together his religious and literary interests, for although the subject is taken from the Bible (Mary Magdalene is traditionally associated with the female sinner in Luke 7:36 who weeps over and anoints Christ's feet), the posture also owes something to another fallen woman, Guinevere, whom Tennyson's *Idylls of the King* describes grovelling at Arthur's feet.

The hard outlines of the bodies indicate that this drawing was originally undertaken as a preliminary design for a stained-glass window, and this is confirmed by a note on the back which states that it was a Morris & Co. commission for St Michael's Church in Torquay and 'fixed in the year 1878'. The church was demolished in the 1960s, but similar versions of the same scene survive as windows in the church of St Ladoca in Ladock (1863) and St Chad's Church in Rochdale (1872/3). Like these other examples, Magdalen's drawing shows Burne-Jones's movement towards an increasingly monumental style: a form of medievalism that had been filtered through his knowledgeable love of the Italian Renaissance and Greek sculpture. Given how much Burne-Jones wanted to squeeze into each design, it is not surprising that the figures of Christ and his disciples seem to be straining against their frame. One might even wonder how far Burne-Jones intended the kneeling woman to be drawn in a style that was more modern and Aesthetic than the angular figures above her. To eyes grown used to Rossetti's languishing maidens, it looks oddly like a Pre-Raphaelite figure paying homage to the past.

RJD–F

PROVENANCE
Bought by the College in Burford in 1946.

▶ Design for a stained-glass window by Sir Edward Burne-Jones, 1878
black chalk on two sheets of paper   81 x 71 cm

165

The Lowther Sideboard

It is not known how Magdalen acquired this fine oak sideboard (or buffet), but it has stood for many years in the ante-room to the New Room, where it is used for serving drinks on occasions such as Degree Days and Schools dinners. It bears the date 1608, but there are strong reasons for believing that it is in fact an example of nineteenth-century antiquarianism. In 1608 the three-shelved open 'court cupboard' was evolving into the 'livery cupboard' that had an enclosed storage compartment in the top section. In Cotgrave's *Dictionarie of the French and English Tongues* (1611), the French word *buffet* is defined as 'a court cupboord or high standing cupboord', and *dressoir* as 'a cupboord; a court-cupboord (without box or drawer) onely to set plate on'. As our sideboard differs from these historical models, the piece is probably of a later date.

The sideboard displays prominent inscriptions and is finely decorated in the manner of later press cupboards. '1608' is carved on the two pendants and repeated in the middle of the lower shelf. The upper shelf bears the words 'SIR IOHN LOWTHER KNIGHT AND DAME ELEANOR', while the frieze along the top proclaims 'I AND MY HOVSE WILL SERV THE LORD' (Joshua 24:15). The picture on the door of the small central cupboard represents a crowned king and queen with fleurs-de-lis and bears the legend 'KYNGE EDWARD Y^E 1ST AND ELEANOR Y^S QVENE'. The central panel of the upper section portrays a queen or princess kneeling before a king, whose plumed helm sits on a bed beside him while three attendants bear drinks and a towel.

Sir John Lowther was born *c.* 1582 into one of England's oldest armigerous families, from Lowther, near Penrith in Westmorland. He was the second son, but became the heir when his elder brother died. Sir Hugh de Lowther, Attorney-General to Edward I, was the first of the family to be knighted, which may explain his family's devotion to that king. Sir John's wife, Eleanor Fleming of Rydal, near Grasmere, whom he married in 1602, also had the same first name as Edward I's queen, Eleanor of Castile.

Cartouches on the sideboard's front pillars bear the arms and crest of Lowther on the left and those of Fleming on the right. Other notable features are the carved figures framing the panels in the upper section (imploring or praying female figures on the outside, male Stuart worthies on the inside), the stylized flower and strapwork patterns elsewhere, the gadrooned fronts to the shelves, and the ornate pillars with sunflowers at their base and bulbous 'melons' between the cartouches.

Sir John, who was at the Inner Temple from 1600 to 1617, was MP for Westmorland in four parliaments (1623–30), and two of his sons became baronets. He is not known to have had any connection with Magdalen and the significance of 1608 is also unknown. But his grandfather Richard (with whom his father Christopher had been at enmity) died in January 1607/8, and although his father was still alive, aged 50, John may have inherited a major share of the family's estates at that time. On the other hand the date may simply be a mistake.

The sideboard may have been created as part of the furnishings for the new Lowther Castle, which was built in the Gothic style by the second Earl of Lonsdale in the early nineteenth century.

JSTG

LITERATURE

V. Chinnery, *Oak Furniture: The British Tradition*, Woodbridge, 1979.

C. B. Phillips, 'Lowther, Sir John', *ODNB*.

▶ Oak sideboard, dated 1608 but probably 19th century

Hidden
Magdalen

168

*Hidden
Magdalen*

The Gargoyles by Gerald Wilde

Gerald Wilde (1905–86) was a remarkable man and an outstanding exponent of expressionist painting, though his later work gradually became more abstract. He was highly esteemed by contemporaries such as Graham Sutherland (who was one of his principal teachers) and Henry Moore, by successors such as Lucian Freud and Frank Auerbach, and by critics such as Kenneth Clark and David Sylvester. The Labour peer and art connoiseur Lord Strabolgi claimed that 'his genius burns with the brightness of acetylene'.

It was once thought that Gerald was a son of Oscar Wilde, but even if he were not, he was a *protégé* of Wilde's nemesis Lord Alfred Douglas (see pp. 22–23), who paid for Gerald's education at the Chelsea College of Art. He may not even have been the model for Gulley Jimson in *The Horse's Mouth* by Joyce Cary (1888–1957) — though many believed he was — since the novel was published in 1944, five years before Wilde first met Cary in Oxford. Wilde's appearance, one-eyed and pallid, and his lifestyle, drunken and chaotic, certainly fitted that of the archetypical bohemian painter.

Wilde was commissioned to provide the front cover of the catalogue for the Arts Council's exhibition that formed part of the Festival of Britain (1951), and most of his best, less abstract work was done in the first decade after the Second World War. He painted *The Gargoyles* in 1950, and Magdalen acquired it through the short-lived SCR art fund, perhaps through the influence of the historian A. J. P. Taylor (1906–90), who was then a powerful figure in College and a friend of Wilde.

The Gargoyles is a typically robust and dense oil on canvas, and the paint has been applied so thickly that the surface is raised into strong relief. Like much of Wilde's best early work, the composition, especially its figures, has a very dark outline and background, reminiscent in some ways of the work of Georges Rouault (1871–1958). The subject is loosely based upon the gargoyles in Cloisters, and it has also been remarked that it might equally well have been based on those sitting at High Table. But unlike the former, the shapes in the painting are coloured green and red, with the occasional orange eye-socket, and unlike their models those shapes are intertwined, with a restless, writhing energy.

CFHT

PROVENANCE
SCR art fund (probably).

LITERATURE
C. Hawes, ed., *Gerald Wilde*, London, 1988.

◀ *The Gargoyles*   Gerald Wilde, painted 1950
oil on canvas   100 x 75 cm

The Library

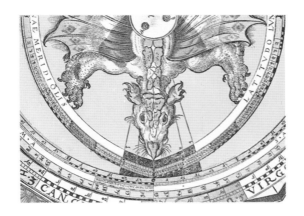

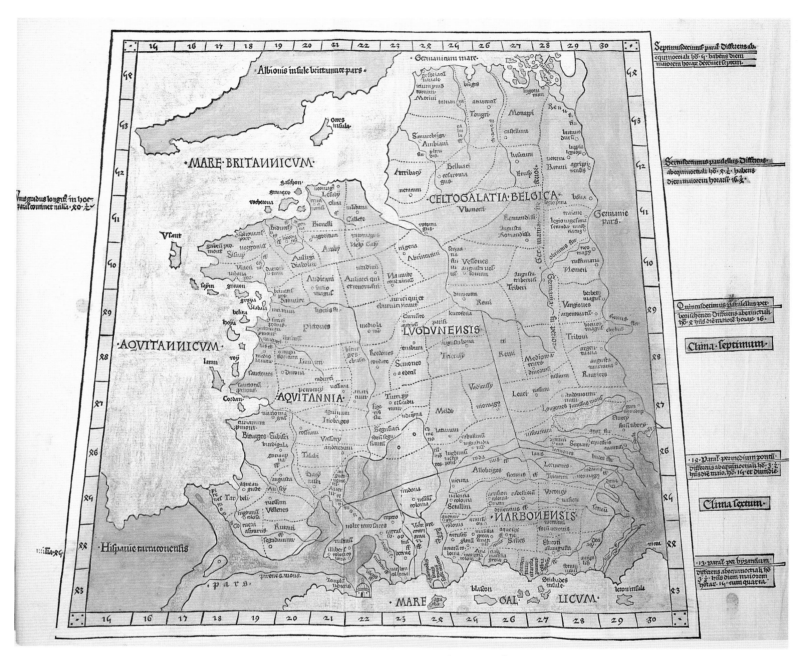

▲ Map of western Europe from the 1482 edition of the
Geographia

Hidden
Magdalen

Ptolemy's *Geographia*

Ptolemy (*c.* 90–*c.* 168), the mathematician, astronomer, and geographer, worked hard to establish a scientific basis for the study of Geography. *Geographike Hyphegesis*, or *Geographia* as it is commonly known, is a treatise on map-drawing as well as an atlas, and represents all that was known of world geography in the second century. Ptolemy's work was lost after the fall of the Roman Empire and rediscovered in the West only in the fifteenth century. The *Geographia* was translated into Latin in *c.* 1405 and circulated in handwritten form until 1477, when the first printed edition was published in Bologna. Magdalen's copy is the very rare first German edition of 1482, edited by Nicholaus Germanus and printed in Ulm by Lienhart Hol. The earlier Italian editions had copperplate engraved maps, whilst this volume has woodcut maps by Johannes Schnitzer ('John the Wood-Carver') of Armsheim. As he usually cut his capital letter Ns the wrong way round, they appear in reverse when printed and make his work fairly easy to identify.

The hand-coloured map illustrated here shows western Europe, including the Roman provinces of Narbonensis (taking its name from the Roman colony Narbo, now Narbonne) and Aquitania, as well as the territory of the continental Celts, Celtogalatia-Belgica. There should be thirty-one other maps here, but unfortunately nine — including a stunning map of the world signed by the Wood-Carver — are missing, and probably have been for centuries. This loss is partly compensated for by the fact that the Oxford humanist John Claymond (1467/8–1536), was clearly one of the first owners of this copy: he records that it cost him 20s. 4d. (the equivalent of over £420 today).

This is just the sort of book that would have attracted Claymond, whose greatest work was a deeply learned but unpublished commentary on Pliny's *Natural History* (*c.* 77), part of which was based on manuscripts that were once in Magdalen's library. Claymond was a serious book-owner. He added numerous notes to the *Geographia*, as well as seventeen pages of indexes to the maps — ending each with 'the end' and his signature. Claymond was President of Magdalen from 1507 to 1517, but then his friend Richard Fox (1447/8–1528), the Bishop of Winchester, persuaded him to become head of his new Oxford foundation, Corpus Christi College, and it was to this college library that Claymond left most of his books. Fortunately, this volume ended up decades later with John Budden (1566–1620), Praelector in Natural Philosophy and Waynflete's first biographer, who presented it to Magdalen's library.

CYF

Eboracensis

Verum tamen ut ad recensitionem epor̄ quos p̄ dictam digressionem i callem reḡdiar̄
expulso patruis ut dictum e Wilfrido q̄ totius nordanimbrorū regionis erat eps̄ duo
p eo constituti sunt. In eboraco bosa in haugustald eata defuncto q̄ eata iohes ordinat̄
eps̄. Ipso ū alfridi regis redditu in episcopatū totū Wilfridus v annis expulsis iohe
de haugustaldo 7 bosa de eboraco. Post v annos Wilfrido r̄tiab alfrido expulso
illis sedibus suis restituti sunt. Defuncto ū alfrido. Wilfridus in creiculā recepit sedem ap̄
haugustaldū habuit. iohe in eboracū migrante q̄ iā bosa defunctus erat. Iohes ur̄
exumiarū virtutū notissimū predicatore habet. bedā in gestis anglorū. S; nec in trinos
est laudibus suis. n̄ adhuc defunctus miraculis. Celebrimū illud habet. q̄d habitato
res beuerleicū p̄ spectaculo solebant exhibere. Tauri ferocissimi q̄ nodosissimis vinculis
astricti magno virorū fortiū sudore adducunt. statū ut curriculū ingressi fuerint ita ō
feritate soporita conquescunt. ut oves simplicitate putes. Laxatis q̄ nodis dimittuntur
patrū pludere. q̄ an̄ q̄d obstabat solebant cornibus 7 pedibus impetere. Ei successit in
eboraco Wilfridus prior suus. q̄ transcend c̄pora bede. Nā et illo anno q̄ obiit fu
it ille in eboraco epm̄ asseilat. Hoc defuncto. eminuit in pontificale speculū egbertus
frater egberti eiusd̄ puincie regis. Is 7 sua prudentia 7 germani potentia sedem sua
illam in genuinū statū reformauit. Nāq̄ q̄d cui ū gesta legenti anglorū in ppl̄
est passim ap̄ Rofecestrū. insigne pallii moriens reliq̄. Ceci p̄ eū urbis psules n̄
dui simplici epi vocabulo alti de lelariant. Ac ille egbertus metropizat cogitans
animosioris ingenii homo. q̄d sit superbū si appetat indebita ita ignauiū si negli
gas debita. pallii appellatione apostolica reparauit. Hic omnium libaliū artiū ar
mariū ita dicā fuit. 7 nobilissimā bibliothecā eboraci constituit. Cui rei teste
idoneū adduco. Alcuinū. q̄ dixit in epla ad karolū augustū. Date in eo quo situ
res eruditionis scolasticę libellos. quales in patria habui p̄ bona 7 deuotissi
mā magistri mei archiepi industriā. vel si placet excellentie uestre. remittā
aliquos epueris nostris. q̄ excipiant in eis q̄ necessaria. 7 reuehant in flandria flo
res britannie. Sepultus e cū fr̄e suo in una porticu ap̄ eboracū p̄ xxxiiii annos
epatibus successor conge. substituto est eanbaldus. prefati Albini discipuli industri.
Unde in epla ad eund̄ dixit. Laus 7 gloria deo. q̄ dies meos in prosperitate bona seruta
uit. ut in exaltatione filii mei karissimi gauderem. q̄ laboraret uice mea in eccla
ubi ego nutritus 7 eruditus fueram. pesse thesauros sapientie in quibus me magi
ster meus dilectus archieps̄ egbert̄ heredem reliquit. Ipse e eanbald̄ q̄ cū echelardo ar
chiepo cantuariensi mutuis pb̄rans officiis. inuasionem q̄ offa rex mertior super
cantuariense ecclam fecerat. ad nichilū redeg. Q̄d albini epla significare ui
detur in epla ad eund̄ adelardū ita dicens. Audiens salutem 7 prosperitate uestra
7 conuentū cū eboracensi archiepo filio meo eanbaldo. satis n̄ placuit. propter tanta
sopite colloquio sanitatis. unitate sc̄e ecclę recoisiginari. q̄ partim discussa ut ratio
nabili consideratione s; q̄dā potestatis cupiditate. Post eū hi fuer archiepi
Wlfsius. Wimundus. Wlfere. echelbald. Rodewald. Wlstan. Hic eadm̄ regis
ed̄uuerd̄ fri echelstani priuatoribus studiis irae emeruit. q̄d danis cū eum
rebellantibus fauet. ita quietū 7 benignū exillarū animū uter eum in uincla coniecer.
S; in multos p̄ actus penitudine. 7 respectu clericalis reuerentie. indempne abire
permisit. quis ille data si fuerit ut animi indignatio. iuxta uestigio exienti. Post eū oslu
vel q̄dū accipiens honoris. floruit q̄rtū oswdc̄i 7 emii 7 edgari regū. habuit q̄
successores oswaldu 7 aldulsum. Wlstanū. q̄ omnes epi 7 wigornenses fuere. hac
de causa. Oswaldus n̄ epali p̄genie oriundus. utpote odonis archiepi nepos. apud

[marginal note, right side:] Ecclesia igitur recoisiuit metropolitaniam cantuariensis 7 eboracensis usuale q̄ dicunt. c. se. q̄ servare habet. et e concordant hunc unionem ab archiepo odone cantuar̄ e lata.

William of Malmesbury's
Gesta pontificum anglorum

The *Gesta pontificum anglorum* (*History of the English Bishops*) chronicles English ecclesiastical history from *c.* 600 to William of Malmesbury's time and includes a history of William's own Benedictine monastery. William (*c.* 1090–*c.* 1142) was an immensely erudite and prolific historian. His major works include his *Gesta regum anglorum* (*History of the English Kings*, a secular companion piece to the *Gesta pontificum*), a history of the antiquities of Glastonbury Abbey, and lives of saints. These well-researched accounts helped to establish William as the foremost historian of the time and the most important English historian since Bede. Indeed, the *Gesta pontificum* still remains a primary source for modern scholars of early English ecclesiastical history.

This particular copy (MS 172) was written *c.* 1125 and is one of the most important manuscripts in Magdalen's collection. Both the text and the many authorial amendments are by William himself, which suggests that this manuscript was his working copy of the first version of the *Gesta pontificum*. Many of William's corrections were incorporated into a second version of the book (*c.* 1140). The manuscript is not only one of the earliest in the hand of an English author, it is also the earliest closely datable book in William of Malmesbury's hand.

Some other marks in the book were made by the historian John Bale (1495–1563) and his close friend and collaborator John Foxe (1516/17–1587; see pp. 52–54). This is not surprising, for the *Gesta pontificum* was one of Foxe's main sources for his *Actes and Monuments* — notes in his distinctive, spiky handwriting appear on almost every page of the *Gesta*, here listing in the margin the names of bishops mentioned in the text. The volume formed part of Foxe's library and was given to the College, along with thirteen other manuscript books, by his eldest son Samuel (1560–1630) in 1614 soon after his own son Thomas (1592–1662) had become a Fellow of Magdalen. Most of the volumes from the Foxe gift are still in the College library, along with presentation copies of the first two editions of Foxe's *Actes and Monuments* (p. 54).

CYF

LITERATURE

R. M. Thomson, *William of Malmesbury*, rev. edn, Woodbridge, 2003.

William of Malmesbury, *Gesta pontificum anglorum*, ed. M. Winterbottom and R. M. Thomson, 2 vols, Oxford, 2007.

The *Gesta pontificum anglorum* written in Malmesbury's own hand (*c.* 1125) and annotated by Foxe (magnified)

A Cypriot 'Model Book'

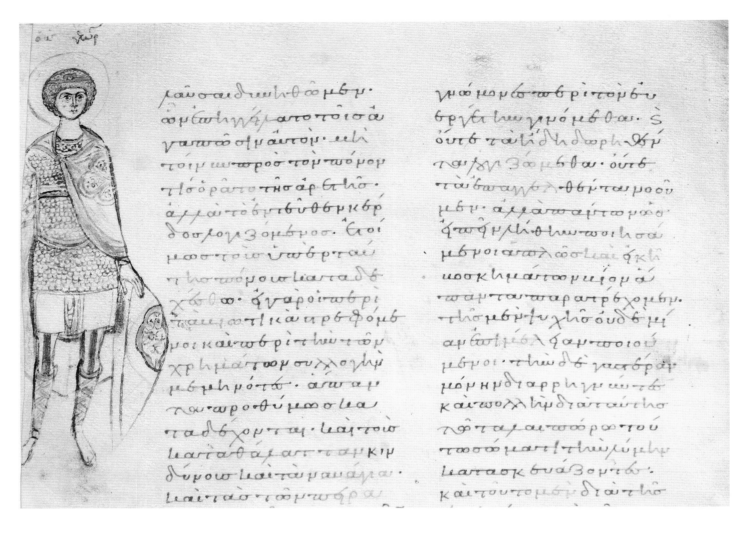

At first glance, Magdalen Greek Manuscript 3 does not seem a particularly notable book. It is the second volume of the commentary on Genesis by St John Chrysostom (c. 347–c. 407), copied some time in the first half of the eleventh century, and its present binding is a fairly ordinary sixteenth-century one, probably made about the time when Magdalen acquired the book. The large number of wax stains suggests that the book was regularly used.

But the book's original generous margins inspired its transformation into an artists' model book. It initially contained about 145 drawings, but some have been cut out, leaving 112, and many of those have suffered further damage under the binder's guillotine. There

are two published theories about the artists and their book — the more plausible and recent of which is that of Irmgard Hutter, who has become convinced that Magdalen's manuscript had been

> adapted to serve as a model book and was actually used as such; that three painters [whom she calls A, B and C] were involved in its production, two working simultaneously and a third slightly later; and that the artists copied both wall paintings and icons, in part with the intermediary of tracings or cartoons.

The marginal drawings cover the whole range of Byzantine saints, including apostles, patriarchs, women, bishops, martyrs, and monks. Military saints, such as St George (who is illustrated above), are particularly numerous. The other drawing depicts Sarah, Rachel, Rebecca, and Aseneth, women of the Old Testament, with their heads framed by roundels. The drawings were produced on Cyprus or Cyprus-Sinai in the late twelfth or early thirteenth centuries, and were probably copied from a programme of existing icons.

A fifteenth-century pen trial in the book mentions a Michael Frangopoulos, but that is too common a name to identify a possible owner more precisely. The volume was certainly at Magdalen by 1598, when Thomas James (1572/3–1629), Bodley's first Librarian, recorded it. It is also known that Sir Henry Savile (1549–1622) used Magdalen's manuscript for his edition of Chrysostom's *Homilies* (1612). Otherwise nothing is known about how this volume came to be in Magdalen's library.

CYF

LITERATURE

I. Hutter, 'The Magdalen College "Musterbuch"', in N. P. Sevenko and C. Moss, eds, *Medieval Cyprus*, Princeton, 1999, pp. 117–48.

◄ Manuscript page with a model drawing of St George for artists to copy, from the 12th or 13th century (detail)

▶ Page of models of Old Testament women (detail)

Law Teaching in Medieval England

One of the most marked features of the intellectual renaissance of the twelfth century was the revival of the study of Roman law. It began in northern Italy around 1100, with its most notable centre in Bologna, and spread to England within a few decades. Modern scholarship has questioned the story that one Master Vacarius (1120–c. 1200) was lecturing on the subject in Oxford about 1150, but it is virtually certain that Roman law was being studied and taught at a number of centres — including Oxford — well before 1200. Dating probably from the early years of the thirteenth century, Magdalen MS 258 is a product of this teaching. The manuscript is English and could have originated in Oxford. But since we know that law was also being studied in Northampton and Lincoln at this time, it is as well not to be dogmatic.

The usual, though not the only, way of analysing the Roman legal texts was through glossing. The text being studied here, the *Institutes of the Emperor Justinian* (c. 482–565), occupied the main body of the page, with comments being added either between the lines or, more commonly, in the margins. Both types are visible here. These glosses took different forms: grammatical explanations, definitions of legal terms, cross-references to other texts, short summaries forming bridges between consecutive passages, standardized explanations of legal doctrine, example cases, marginal notes signalling passages worthy of particular attention, the drawing of distinctions between superficially similar legal ideas, questions and queries, and indications of points on which legal scholars had taken different views. All of these are exemplified in MS 258.

The glosses here are largely derived from the north Italian scholars of the mid-twelfth century, reflecting both the orthodox analysis associated with the school of Bulgarus (before 1100–c. 1167) and also the more exuberant heterodoxy of Martinus Gosia (d. 1167). If the author of the glosses was himself an Italian who had come to England, the most plausible candidate would be Johannes Bassianus of Cremona (*fl.* 1190).

He may have been in England in the 1190s: several of his writings survive primarily in English manuscripts and some of the glosses here come directly from his works. But it is more likely that the glosses were written by a native English lawyer who had studied under Bassianus at Bologna, perhaps Simon of Sywell, who is known to have been teaching canon law in Oxford in about 1200. The manuscript has been thoroughly analysed by Pierre Legendre in the *Tijdschrift voor Rechtsgeschiedenis*.

DJI

LITERATURE

P. Legendre, in *Tijdschrift voor Rechtsgeschiedenis*, 33 (1965), pp. 353–429.
P. Stein, *The Teaching of Roman Law in England around 1200*, London, 1990.

▶ Manuscript of the *Institutes of the Emperor Justinian*, glossed for teaching purposes; probably from the early 13th century

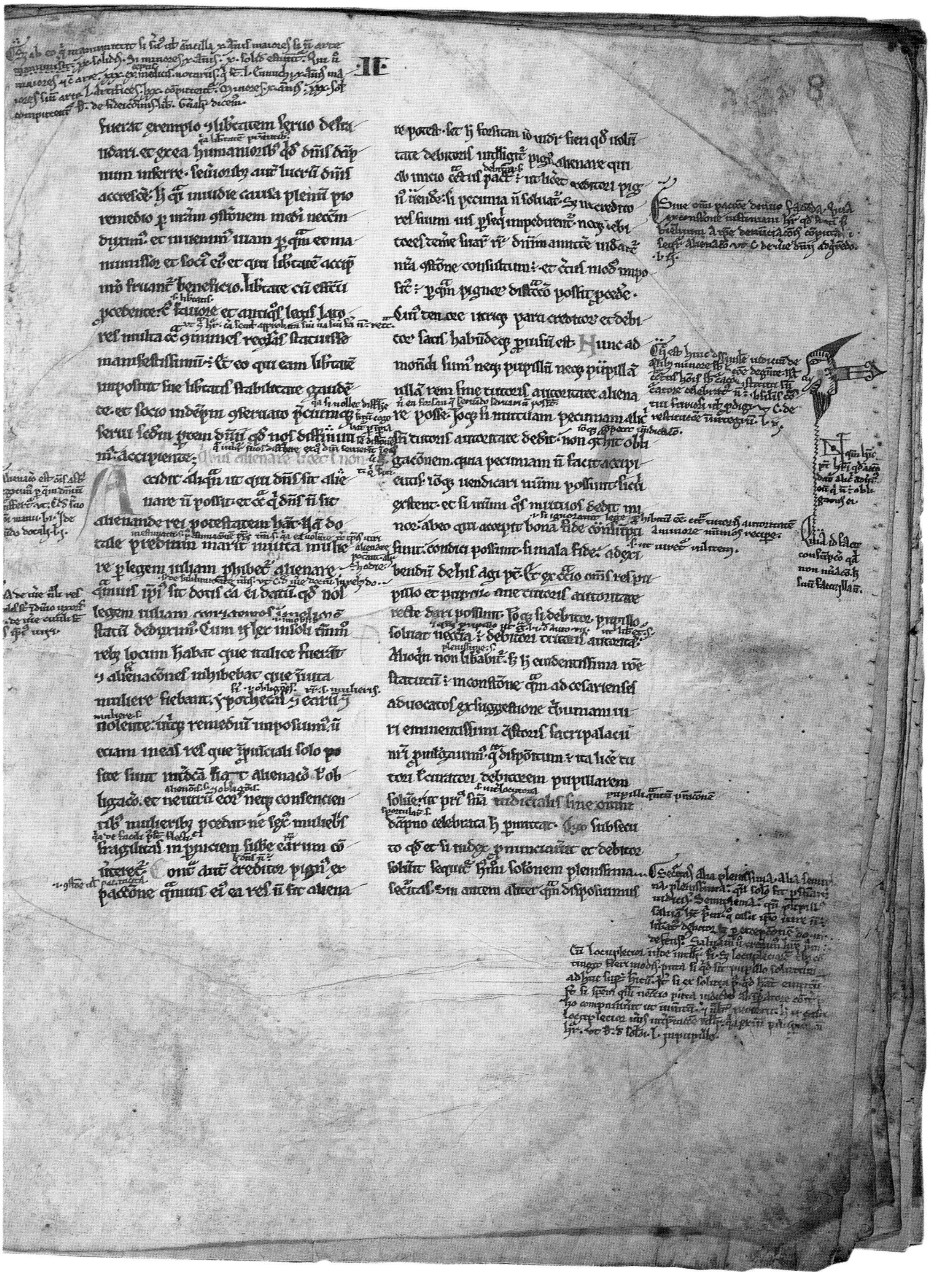

omniũ populorum. Lumen ad re
uel.itionem gentium: et gloriam
plebis tue israel.

In . . . . scē Frediswide.

Scd̄ . . . . Matth. xxv.

IN illo tempore.
Dixit I E S V S
discipulis suis pa
rabolam hanc. Si
mile est regnum ce
lorum decem vir
ginibus: que accipientes lampa
des suas: exierunt obuiam spon
so et sponse. Quinꝗ autem ex
eis erant fatue: et quinꝗ prudē
tes. Sed quinꝗ fatue acceptis
lampadibus: non sumpserunt
oleum secum. Prudentes vero

Hidden
Magdalen

Cardinal Wolsey's Lectionary

Many regard Cardinal Wolsey's gospel-lectionary as Magdalen's most beautiful manuscript book. Along with its counterpart, an epistle-lectionary now in the Christ Church collection, it was commissioned by Wolsey in the late 1520s. The two books contain gospel and epistle readings for high feast days and specific saints' days that were associated with Wolsey's chief offices and foundations. For example, St Frideswide, the patron saint of Oxford, is shown here with the city of Oxford in the background.

Wolsey spared no expense on these books. The scribe was one of the best, the well-connected Pieter Meghen (1466–1540), whose other patrons included Henry VIII. He had lost one eye — Erasmus called him Cyclops — but was still able to write in this beautiful, spacious hand. Although Meghen is known to have worked with illuminators such as Hans Holbein the younger (c. 1497–1543) and the Horenbout family, the identity of the Magdalen illuminator(s) remains elusive and he, she, or they are currently known as 'the Master of Cardinal Wolsey'. The illuminator, who had stylistic associations with the Low Countries, was also of the highest calibre and the velvety-smooth surface of the vellum matches the quality of the artists. One of Henry VIII's inventories suggests that the two volumes may originally have been bound in a treasure binding of gold, silver, and possibly jewels, but this cannot be proved.

When Wolsey died in 1530, Henry VIII confiscated his property, and when the lectionaries became Henry's property they were bound in the leather binding that still encases Magdalen's volume. After Henry's death in 1547 the gospel-lectionary was removed to Winchester, since the text of an oath made in 1556 by Thomas White, who was standing in for his brother-in-law John White (1509/10–1560), the new Bishop of Winchester, is written on its first pastedown (the blank leaf of paper pasted to the upper board of the binding). Such a proxy oath suggests that by the mid-sixteenth century the lectionary may well

◀ Page from Wolsey's gospel-lectionary, with an illustration of St Frideswide with Oxford in the background

▲ Detail

have found a temporary home in the Bishop of Winchester's library.

John White, the last Roman Catholic Bishop of Winchester, was deprived of his bishopric in 1559 and died the following year. This may have been when Samuel Chappington, whose signature is on the first flyleaf, acquired the lectionary. Little is known about him, except that he came from a Devon family of organ-makers that had associations with Winchester. It was also probably one of Samuel's relations who built the organ for Magdalen's Chapel in 1597, since the College's account books for that year record that John Chappington (c. 1540–1606) was paid £33 13s. 8d. for constructing that instrument. Consequently it seems likely that Magdalen acquired the lectionary through John's family in the early seventeenth century.

C Y F

John Stanbridge's *Long Parvula*

Magdalen's account books record that in 1502 the College spent 46s. 6d. at the local St Frideswide's Fair on a seven-volume set of Hugo of Vienna's biblical commentary. It had been printed between 1498 and 1502 by Johann Amerbach (1441?–1513) in Basel for Anton Koberger (c. 1440–1513) in Nuremberg. That purchase in itself says something about how seriously the College regarded its academic responsibilities, for most Oxford colleges did not buy many books and encouraged donations instead: Magdalen did both.

The volumes were bound at about the same time, almost certainly by an Oxford binder, and some of the materials used add to the interest of these volumes. Binders commonly used 'waste' paper to make pastedowns and endpapers, and this could come from dismembered manuscript books or comprise unwanted sheets from printed books. In this case, our binder used sheets from a little grammar book printed by Richard Pynson (c. 1449–1529/30). They, and the copy presented to the British Library, are now the only evidence for the existence of this grammar.

The *Long Parvula*, as this particular textbook was called, was part of the curriculum followed in late medieval grammar schools, including Magdalen College School. Students were first instructed in the basics of parsing and sentence construction in English, before they were allowed to apply those principles to Latin. This little textbook, written in English with Latin examples, covered the simple rules of construction. Its method is set out in its first paragraph (right-hand page illustrated):

What shalt thou do whanne thou hast an englisshe to make in laten? I shal reherce myn englissh ones twies or thries and loke oute my prinicipal verbe & aske this question who or what and that worde that answereth to the question shalbe the nominatyve case to the verbe. ... as in thys exaumple. The mayster techeth scolers.

The English example at the top of the opposite page — 'I am wery of my life' — suggests the rigorous life of the fifteenth-century schoolboy.

The *Parvula* is part of a series of grammar books attributed to John Stanbridge (1463–1510), who became Usher of Magdalen College School in 1486, and Master after the death of John Anwykyll in 1487. Stanbridge's contribution was based on the work of earlier grammarians, particularly that of John Leylond (d. 1428), which he rewrote and updated to modern humanistic standards.

Textbooks, like most other books of the time, were usually purchased in sheets. These were then folded and sewn but probably not protected by anything more than a paper cover. As they would have had little defence against schoolboys' vigorous reading, few have survived. The unsewn sheets of this one did so only by sheer good luck, saved by the binder.

CYF

LITERATURE

N. Orme, *Education in Early Tudor England: Magdalen College Oxford and its School*, Oxford, 1998.

in the stedde of an accusatif case. as I am wery of
my life. Tedet me vite mee. Unde versus.

Penitet et tedet miseret pudet et piget ista
Accusatiuos poscunt/simul et genitiuos.

Natura primum sed transitione secundum.
These verbes impsonals in theses ꝑses folowing
Will haue an accusatif case in the sted of a noiatyse
case/as I must go to the mayster. Oportet me ire
ad ꝑceptore. Goode scolers haue a plesure to lerne
Bones scolares iuuat discere. nat wytstandynge
somtyme they be verbes psonals ꝫ haue nompna
tyf case before theym. Exemplum. Hic cibus dele
ctat me. hec res latet me. Versus.

Quarto iunge iuuat decet ac delectat oportet
Et latet illorum numero vult associati
These iii. ꝗbes impsonals Refert. Interest/et Est
set for ꝑtinet wil be ꝯstrued with a genitif case of
nownes/and an ablatyf case of v. pronownes, as
mea/tua/sua/nostra/and vestra/as in this ensau
ple. It is for my ꝑfite. Mea interest. It is for thy
profite. Tua interest It is for his profite Sua in
terest. Also this verbe interest after preciane is con
strued with an ablatyue case of the femynyne gen
der of this nowne possessyue. Cuius cuia cuium.
Unde versus.

Refert intet et est genitum pro pertinet adde.

Et sextum proprie donat pronomina quinꝗ

Nanꝗ refert nostra me/tu/su/cu/ quoꝗ vestra
The verbes impsonal in theise verses folowynge
Wil be ꝯstrued wyth a datif case. Exeꝑlu we may

Hat shalt thou do whanne thou
hast an englisshe to make in laten
I shal reherce myn englissh ones
twies or thries and loke oute my
principal verbe ꝫ aske this questi
on who or what/and that worde that answereth
to the question shalbe the nominatyue case to the
verbe. except it be a verbe impersonall. as in thys
exaumple. The mayster techeth scolers. techethe is
the verbe. who techeth. the mayster techeth. thys
worde mayster answerethe to the questyon here/ꝫ
therfore it shalbe the nominatyf case and the wor
de that cometh after the verbe shalbe the accusatyf
case comonly. as magyster docet me And whanne
I haue an adiectif nowne/ pronowne or a particy
ple adiectyue/or relatyfe I shal aske this questyon
who or what/and that worde that answereth to
the questyon shalbe substantyfe to the adiectif and
the anticedent to the relatyfe.

Han two substantyues come togeder lon
gynge bothe to one thynge they shalle be
put both in one case. as my fader a man lo
ueth me a childe. Pater meus vir diligit me pue
tu. ⸿ Howe shalt thou knowe the principal verbe
in a reson if thou haue in it more verbes than one.
Euermore my first verbe shalbe my principal ꝗbe
except he come nye a relatyf or a coiunctyo or be ly
ke the infynitif mode. wherby knowest thou wha
he cometh nye a relatif. Euermore wha he cometh
ny any of these englissh wordes that whom or the

ꝫ

▲ Surviving pages from an early 16th-century school
textbook

F III

184

Peter Apian's *Astronomicon Caesareum*

Like Ptolemy (*c.* 90–*c.* 168), whose *Geographia* features elsewhere in this volume (pp. 172–73), Peter Apian (1495–1552) studied Mathematics, Astronomy, and Cosmography and produced important works on those subjects. Indeed, Apian based much of his first major book, *Cosmographia* (1524), a practical introduction to *inter alia* Astronomy, Geography, and mathematical instruments, on Ptolemy's findings. It came with three ingenious paper volvelles — movable circles — that allowed readers to construct their own paper scientific instruments. When the famous instrument-maker Gemma Frisius (1508–55) published a very popular revised and enlarged edition of *Cosmographia* in 1533, he added a fourth volvelle.

Apian's second major work, *Astronomicon Caesareum*, appeared in 1540. This was a more elaborate book than the *Cosmographia*, both in content and physical form. Among his innovative scientific ideas, Apian suggested here that solar eclipses might help to determine longitude. He also described five comets, including Halley's, and was the first to observe that the tail of a comet always points away from the sun. The *Astronomicon* also contained far more movable parts than the earlier books.

The new owner or his bookbinder needed ingenuity and some dexterity to assemble this volume, since numerous volvelles had to be cut out, coloured, assembled and sewn together, sometimes six deep, before the book would work properly. But once constructed, the paper scientific instruments could be used for calculating tides, the position of the planets, etc. The volvelle of the dragon shown here is for calculating the points where the moon crosses the path of the sun (the ecliptic), for the years between 7000 BC and AD 7000. These intersections (the lunar nodes) form the head and tail of the dragon at diametrically opposed positions on the ecliptic. By combining these positions with the moon's motion, the volvelle can be used to predict the times and nature of lunar and solar eclipses. Worked examples are given on the page opposite it (not shown) for the birth dates of the two Caesars, or German Emperors, whom Apian addresses in his *Astronomicum Caesareum*: Charles V and Ferdinand I.

The book's binding is of richly blind-tooled leather over oak board, and was possibly made by Dominick Pinart (d. 1619) in the second half of the sixteenth century. The volume formed part of a gift of books and money given to Magdalen's library by the Revd Dr John Fitzwilliam (Servitor 1652 and Fellow 1661; d. 1699). Fitzwilliam was a staunch non-juror who left the College in 1666 to become Chaplain to James, Duke of York. Although his refusal to take the oaths to William and Mary later forced him to retire from public life, his loyalty to his old college remained undiminished to the end of his life.

CYF

◀ A page from the *Astronomicon Caesareum*, showing a paper construction that could predict solar and lunar eclipses

Nachrichten für die Truppe

> 2.5.45.
>
> Magdalen College,
> Oxford.
>
> This is the complete run of a "subversive" and unofficial Newspaper dropped over Germany 1944/5 by the 8th U.S. Air Force, and compiled by a mixed Anglo-American and German refugee team (The run is actually complete, as of copies passed for printing. Numbers missing were either suppressed in the proof stage or never were issued. Three pre-publication trial copies are also included). A considerable part was played in its production by C E Stevens, Fellow of the College. As my knowledge of this Publication and its dissemination is governed by the provisions of the Official Secrets Act, it should not be made available for study until this is specifically allowed by Act of Parliament or Official Decree.
>
> C E Stevens

During the Second World War a 'Black Propaganda Unit' was set up, with C. E. Stevens (1905–76), commonly known as 'Tom Brown', as a member. He had been a Fellow and Tutor in Ancient History at Magdalen since 1933, and during the Second World War he was involved in the *Soldatensender*, which broadcasted news and propaganda in German. Stevens published the name of a Swedish export company which bought ball bearings in Sweden and exported them to Germany, thus undoing the effect of Allied bombing. He announced the names and honours for U-boat men before they were announced in Germany, having worked this out from the number of tons a ship had to sink before the crew received the appropriate decorations. At a meeting of the V Committee whose task was to plan the 'V for Victory' campaign of the BBC European Service, he proposed that the BBC should transmit the opening bars of Beethoven's Fifth Symphony on the grounds that this was the Morse Code for V and, for Germans, represented the sound of 'fate knocking at the door'.

Stevens later became involved in the publication of *Nachrichten für die Truppe*. This newspaper did not claim to be issued by the Allied Command or published by dissident Germans, but was dropped 'as an offering of the sublime objective truth' (Sefton Delmer). Up to a million copies were dropped daily on or behind the German lines from 25 April 1944 until the war's end. But an analysis published in the *American Sociological Review* in 1949 claimed that the credibility of BBC broadcasts actually declined because of *Nachrichten für die Truppe*.

Stevens returned to Magdalen after the war and deposited a complete set of *Nachrichten für die Truppe* in the College library, with the stipulation that it was to remain secret until an act of Parliament or a decree said otherwise. The entire run was published by Kraus Reprint and Periodicals in 1973.

This issue is of 7 June 1944, the day after D-Day, and bears the headline 'Reinforcements stream through the breach in the Atlantic Wall', while another item states that no more tungsten will be coming from Portugal.

DBR

LITERATURE
S. Delmer, *An Autobiography*, 2 vols, London, 1961–62, vol. 2.

◀ C. E. Stevens's letter dated 2 May 1945

▶ A copy of *Nachrichten für die Truppe* no. 52 (7 June 1944), stamped 'This document is graded confidential'

Nr. 52, Mittwoch 7. Juni 1944 — **NACHRICHTEN** *FÜR DIE TRUPPE*

Verstärkungen strömen durch die Breschen im Atlantikwall

Invasionstruppen vereinigen sich hinter den Befestigungen; Besatzungen abgeschnitten

Durch die Breschen im Atlantikwall zwischen Cherbourg und Le Havre stossen starke anglo-amerikanische Verbände in den heutigen Morgenstunden weiter landeinwärts vor.

Die Alliierten führen Verstärkungen heran, die sie trotz des hohen Seegangs im Kanal während der Nacht landen konnten.

Sturmgeschütze und mittelschwere Artillerie eröffneten mit dem Morgengrauen ein verstärktes Feuer auf die deutschen Kampfstellungen, das von den 35½ und 20 cm- Geschützen der alliierten Schlachtschiffe und Kreuzer unterstützt wird. Ein starkes Schlachtgeschwader kreuzt vor Cherbourg.

Gleichzeitig mit dem Artillerie-Bombardement stossen Hunderte von Jägern und Bombern im Tiefangriff auf die deutschen Truppen nieder.

An der Landefront vom Norden der normannischen Halbinsel bis Trouville müssen sich die deutschen Truppen an vielen Stellen vor der anglo-amerikanischen Übermacht zurückziehen.

Zwei Landungsgruppen der Anglo-Amerikaner die gestern nordwestlich und nordöstlich von Bayeux den Atlantikwall durchstossen und sich hinter den Befestigungen vereinigt hätten, drängen die 716. Infanterie-Division weiter zurück, die gestern den ganzen Tag in verlustreichen Kämpfen versucht hatte, diese Vereinigung zu verhindern.

In Caen toben noch Strassenkämpfe zwischen Einheiten der 21. Panzerdivision und anglo-amerikanischen Truppen.

Deutsche Ortung war lahmgelegt

Auf der normannischen Halbinsel stehen die deutschen Truppen an der Strasse Valogne-Carenton in schweren Kämpfen mit alliierten Truppen, die im Laufe der Nacht Panzerverstärkungen erhielten.

Von Westen, wo die ersten Landungen erfolgt waren, bis dicht an die Befestigungen an der Ostküste, ist die normannische Halbinsel zum grössten Teil von den Anglo-Amerikanern überrannt. Einige deutsche Verbände sind isoliert.

Deutsche Truppenbewegungen hinter dem Atlantikwall wurden während der Nacht durch schwere Bombenangriffe gegen Eisenbahn- und Strassenverbindungen gestört.

Deutsche Pioniere konnten während der Nacht wieder einige Behelfsbrücken über die Seine schlagen, nachdem die alliierten Luftangriffe sämtliche Strassen und Eisenbahnbrücken über die Seine zwischen Paris und der Flussmündung zerstört hatten.

Diese Behelfsbrücken sind jetzt nördlich Paris die einzige Verbindung zwischen Frankreich ostwärts der Seine und Frankreich westwärts der Seine.

Die Hauptgründe für den unerwarteten Landungserfolg der Alliierten trotz aller Abwehrvorbereitungen sind : 1. Vollständige Beherrschung der Meere und der Luft. 2. Das Versagen der Unterwasser-Hindernisse. 3. Die unerwartete Durchschlagskraft der neuen Bomben der Anglo-Amerikaner.

Durch ihre Luftüberlegenheit konnten die Angreifer vor Beginn der Landungsoperationen die deutschen Ortungsstationen in Trümmer legen, so dass die Landungsflotten nicht rechtzeitig erfasst wurden.

Bombenteppiche erledigten in kurzer Zeit die Unterwasserhindernisse. Das darauffolgende Bombardement der schweren Schiffsartillerie, unterstützt durch Tausende von Bombern, übertraf alles, was deutsche Soldaten an irgend einem Kriegsschauplatz bisher erlebt haben.

Die ungeheure Explosivgewalt schlug Breschen in die Betonbefestigungen, durch die die Panzer dann nach dem Inneren vorstiessen.

Sie kommen angefahren

Fliegeraufnahme einer der anglo-amerikanischen Invasionsflotten kurz vor der gestrigen Landung in der Normandie.

Reserven werden im Osten eingesetzt

Alle verfügbaren Kräfte werden jetzt vom OKH in die Schlacht von Jassy geworfen, um zu versuchen, mit einer deutschen Offensive die Sommer-Gross-Offensive der Sowjets im Keime zu ersticken.

Seit Wochen haben die Sowjets starke Angriffsverbände, Artillerie und Panzerkräfte im Raum von Jassy, sowie am unteren Dnjestr zusammengezogen.

Im OKH wird angenommen, dass die Sowjets beabsichtigen, die deutsch-rumänische Front zu durchbrechen, sobald die Anglo-Amerikaner ihre Landungsoffensive im Westen entfaltet haben.

Unter den Truppen, die in der Schlacht von Jassy eingesetzt sind, befinden sich die 349. Infanterie-Division, sowie die SS-Panzer-Divisionen „Hohenstaufen" und „Frundsberg", die erst kürzlich aus dem Westen nach dem Vorfeld des Karpathenwalls gebracht wurden.

Immer neue Reserven werden herangezogen, um den Karpathenwall zu verteidigen.

Kein Wolfram mehr aus Portugal

Die portugiesische Regierung gab heute früh bekannt, dass sie mit sofortiger Wirkung die gesamten Wolframlieferungen an das Reich einstellt.

Die Einstellung der Lieferungen des lebenswichtigen Härtungsmetalls Wolfram erfolgt vier Wochen, nachdem die spanische Regierung ihre Wolframlieferungen an das Reich unter dem Wirtschaftsdruck der Anglo-Amerikaner um 90 Prozent gekürzt hat.

Nach dem Verlust der Mangangruben von Nikopol und der Einstellung der türkischen Chromlieferungen war portugiesisches Wolfram das letzte unentbehrliche Härtungsmetall, das die deutsche Rüstungsindustrie aus dem Ausland beziehen konnte, um die schweren Materialverluste der Wehrmacht im Osten, Süden und jetzt auch im Westen wieder wett zu machen.

De Gaulle in London

Aus Lissabon wird gemeldet dass General De Gaulle in England eingetroffen ist.

Petain in Vichy

Der französische Staatschef Marschall Petain ist gestern Nachmittag von St. Etienne nach Vichy zurückgekehrt und hat den französischen Ministerpräsidenten Laval empfangen.

Neue Kämpfe an der Balkanfront

In schwere Kämpfe mit den Partisanenverbänden Titos sind Truppen des Heeres und der Waffen-SS in Kroatien verwickelt.

Den Truppen, die unter dem Oberbefehl von Generaloberst Rendulic stehen, sind Kampf- und Schlachtfliegerverbände beigegeben worden, die den deutschen Truppen in Italien und Frankreich fehlen.

Besonders blutige Verluste erlitten, wie aus dem OKW-Bericht hervorgeht, die Truppen der 7. SS-Gebirgsdivision „Prinz Eugen", unter Führung von SS-Oberführer Kumm, und die Truppen des SS-Fallschirmjägerbataillons 500, unter Führung von Hauptsturmführer Rybka.

OBERST BECK TOT

Aus Bukarest wird gemeldet, dass der ehemalige polnische Aussenminister, Oberst Beck, gestern in einem Dorf bei Bukarest nach langer Krankheit gestorben ist.

HOLLÄNDISCHE LANDWACHT VERSAGT

Nur 15 Prozent der Mannschaften der Landwacht in den Niederlanden trat gestern bei der Invasions-Alarmierung an.

Selbst die Offiziere in zahlreichen Standorten, darunter Tilburg, Arnhem und Kindhoven, sind unter allen möglichen Entschuldigungen weggeblieben.

Die wenigen Angehörigen der niederländischen Landwacht, die der Einberufung gefolgt waren, wurden wieder nach Hause geschickt.

Paris gebombt

Das Gebiet von Paris wurde heute früh von starken Bomberverbänden angegriffen.

Library Furniture

Joseph Addison (1672–1719; see pp. 144–45), the founder of English journalism through the creation of *The Spectator* (1711), matriculated as a Demy at Magdalen (1689) and subsequently became a Fellow (1697). The plaque on Magdalen's 'Addison's chair' tells us that it had once belonged to this publicist, poet, and statesman and was acquired by him, together with other furniture from Bilton Hall — the thousand-acre estate just outside Rugby which Addison acquired from William Boughton for £8,000 in about 1711. The Bilton estate remained in Addison's family until the death of his only child

(1797), and apart from the pictures the contents were auctioned off two years later. The Hall was remodelled in the second half of the nineteenth century and its gates, probably removed in the process, were discovered in a junkyard in the 1950s and presented to Magdalen by a group of old members (see p. 144). Adorned with Addison's initials, these now lead into the water meadow just opposite the duckery that is situated at the north-east corner of Addison's Walk.

The chair was presented to Magdalen in 1888 by the lawyer Reginald Bird MA (1832–91), Demy (1849–63), *quondam* member of the Australian mounted police (*c.* 1859), member of the Middle Temple (1862), and non-resident Fellow of Magdalen (1862–91). It would originally have been part of a set of furniture, and although it derives stylistically from the late seventeenth century, it was probably made between 1710 and 1720, possibly even for Addison when he purchased Bilton Hall. As its back is rather low for that period, it may have been cut down in the second half of the century in an attempt to update it. We know nothing of the chair's history between 1799 and 1888, but its Morocco leather is not original and probably dates from the late nineteenth century. When its seat was restuffed in the early 1990s, as much extant material as possible was left in place.

Magdalen's medieval library was Gothicized in the mid-1820s to form what is now the College's Old Library. The set of sixteen library stools may have been made as part of this process, since one stool belongs against each of the Old Library's sixteen stacks. Although the stools may have been loosely modelled on the famous set that Chippendale made for Christ Church's library in 1764, their design is far simpler and less elegant, leading some experts to suggest that they may even have been made in the last third of the nineteenth century.

What is now Magdalen's New Library was built in 1849–51 to house Magdalen College School according to the designs of John Chessell Buckler (1793–1894). It became the College's main library in the early 1930s when the school was moved across the High Street and Longwall Quad was opened. In the early 1990s, two scroll-back Windsor chairs stamped with the name of S. Hazell were found in the New Library's basement. They were covered with layers of paint and had to be restored.

Stephen Hazell (1819–90) was born in Summertown. He was probably trained by William E. Wardell (1801–73), Oxford's first maker of Windsor chairs, and he became one of Oxford's most significant nineteenth-century chair-makers. He first advertised in 1846, when he was 27 and working from South Parade, Summertown. He subsequently moved to workshops at 18 Friar Street, 36 Speedwell Street, and 10 Albert Street. He ceased work in 1875 and was succeeded in the trade by his son, Stephen Charles Hazell (c. 1846–98). Hazell senior's most impressive chairs are still used in the Reading Room of the Bodleian Library, and when evaluating his more vernacular work Bernard Cotton wrote: 'Nowhere was [the Windsor chair] made with greater finesse … than in the City of Oxford.'

Magdalen's two Hazell chairs are rather battered by now. Made of beech and elm, they have seats with mitred back corners and a scored line around their fronts and sides; they also have concave turned legs with a single ring, plus a lower ring and straight front feet — a design that Hazell almost certainly took over from Wardell. Such features date the chairs to c. 1850, and this suggests that they were part of the furniture that was commissioned for Magdalen's new school building. If this is so, then they are the only such pieces of furniture to have survived.

R W S

LITERATURE

B. Cotton, *The English Regional Chair*, 3rd edn, Woodbridge, 2000, pp. 91–94.

P. Macquoid and H. Edwards, *Dictionary of English Furniture*, rev. edn, 3 vols, London, 1954), vol. 2, pp. 255–59.

◀ Addison's chair

▲ One of the sixteen steam-moulded library stools

▶ One of the two scroll-back Windsor chairs

Three Modern Carvings in the Old Library

▲ Mike Strutt

▲ Alan Mount

In 1992, to mark the end of the renovation of the Old Library, it was decided to replace three of the many missing carvings on the neo-Gothic stacks with three likenesses of long-standing members of Magdalen's support staff: Mike Strutt (holding two keys); Alan Mount (holding mason's tools); and Jasper Scovil (holding two books). Mike (1932–2000) began his working life as Magdalen's Lodge Boy (1946–50). After national service in the RAF he joined the Thames Valley Police, rose to the rank of sergeant, and played a major part in 'Operation Julie', a large anti-drugs operation in the 1970s. He then spent 21 years as Magdalen's Head Porter (1976–97). Alan (1929–2006) grew up in Herne Bay, trained as a stonemason, and became master stonemason at St Paul's Cathedral (1973–78). He was appointed Magdalen's Clerk of Works (1978–94) and oversaw the repairs and refurbishment of nearly all of Magdalen's major buildings — including the Old

Library. He was awarded the MBE for services to conservation (1996). His ashes are buried under an inscribed stone in Magdalen's Antechapel. Jasper (b. 1932) read History at Merton (1951–54). After national service in RAF Intelligence, he worked for the British Council Books Department in London, Libya, and Tunis. He became Deputy Librarian in Oxford's History Faculty (1964–70) and Magdalen's Deputy Librarian (1971–93).

The carvings were executed by an Oxford carver, John Bye (b. 1932), who has done other work for the College. John was apprenticed as a church carver with A. R. Mowbray (1949–54) and spent his final year learning figure carving with Jethro Harris, a local sculptor. During his national service with the Royal Engineers John carved regimental badges for visiting officers: this work now exists in such far-flung places as Australia, Canada, and Nepal. After Mowbray's workshops had closed (c. 1954), John worked with

▲ Jasper Scovil

Harris and his partner for seventeen years. He set up
on his own in 1973, since when he has produced a
great variety of work: organ cases for organ builders in
Scotland, Denmark, and the USA; and carvings for
many churches, most Oxford colleges, and St George's
Hall at Windsor Castle after the great fire (1997). At
the time of writing John is working on two four-foot
figures of St Peter and St Paul for the Oxford church
where he and his late wife worshipped for nearly fifty
years.

RWS

LITERATURE

R. Sheppard, 'Alan Mount M.B.E. (1929–2006)' (obituary),
Magdalen Record (2007), pp. 283–89.

The Science Memorabilia

The Magdalen Mammoth Tusk

As one walks through Magdalen it is slightly unsettling to remember that woolly mammoths, bears, and lions roamed there long before humans. In 1922 the discovery of the site of a natural spring in the north-west corner of the Grove yielded Magdalen's oldest treasure, the tusk of an adult mammoth, *Mammuthus primigenius*.

Workmen creating a drinking place for the deer discovered a bed of river-gravel and were ordered to extract and spread it on College paths. A labourer noticed ivory mixed with the gravel and thereafter his colleagues tested each fragment with a pickaxe. But this first tusk was lost. In February 1922, Robert Gunther (1869–1940; Fellow and Tutor in Natural Science 1896–1921) was alerted to the uncovering of the tip of what proved to be another tusk. The original might have been two metres long, but a large, gently curved piece 114 cm long and 17 cm in diameter was carefully recovered. Beside many skull fragments too poor to preserve, three fine teeth of a younger mammoth were also retrieved (for a photograph, see Gunther, 1925). The lower jaw of a brown bear was also found, the first in Oxfordshire: an impressive cast of it is displayed in the Oxford University Museum of Natural History.

The Magdalen Grove gravel is part of the complex sequence of deposits of silty sands and gravels comprising the Summertown–Radley Formation. Excavations in the Grove in 1984 revealed an upper layer of flood-plain silt that abounded in fossil bivalves and molluscs and contained the humerus of a lion. This upper layer of silty gravel correlates with the Stanton Harcourt Channel deposits. But these are considered to be the earlier of the two strata within the Formation and date to around 200,000 years ago. At Magdalen the deposit fills a channel cut by the proto-Cherwell, a relatively large and vigorous river, into the lower, much older, cold-climate gravel that contained the mammoth remains. Sandford described the tusk deposit as a 'charnel-house of elephant remains' including several molars, several milk teeth, and the lower jaw of a very young mammoth (p. 142).

The Oxford palaeontologist Tom Kemp says: 'Magdalen is very fortunate to possess such a splendid specimen found in her own grounds, which were once like Siberian tundra. Mammoth remains are not common, and most tusks found are shattered fragments' (personal communication). In 2007 the tusk was cleaned and conserved by Mr Philip Powell, who kindly advised on this note.

RH

LITERATURE

R. T. Gunther, *The Daubeny Laboratory Register 1849–1923*, Oxford, 1925.

K. S. Sandford, 'The river-gravels of the Oxford district', *Quarterly Journal of the Geological Society* 53 (1924), pp. 113–79.

▲ Mammoth tusk discovered in the Grove in 1922

John Goodyer

John Goodyer (*c.* 1592–1664) has been described as 'a forgotten Botanist of the Seventeenth Century', and Magdalen's early custodianship of his books and manuscripts may have significantly contributed to this neglect. Goodyer could read and write both Latin and Greek, suggesting that he may have attended grammar school in Alton, Hampshire, where he was born, but nothing is known of his education. Although he travelled frequently to London and Oxford and occasionally further afield, he spent most of his life in and around Petersfield, Hampshire, as steward and land agent to Sir Thomas Bilson, the lord of the manor of Mapledurham in the parish of Buriton.

Robert Gunther, Magdalen's Fellow Librarian from 1920 to 1923 and himself a biologist (see p. 194), described Goodyer's approach to botany thus: 'though mindful of the medicinal and economic value of plants, [he] clearly saw that the science of botany could not be advanced without detailed morphological descriptions from living plants'. So Goodyer's extensive notes are an important contribution to our knowledge of early English gardening and botany. He not only described plants as he saw them, with occasional notes on their habitats, he also frequently named them, many years before the standardization of botanical names in the eighteenth century.

Thus Goodyer writes of his discovery of the woolly thistle (now known as *Cirsium eriophorum*) on 29 June 1621: 'I found this wild in Hampshire in greate plentie by Haliborne in a feild called Marborne, nere a bridge called Habridge, beinge the land of Wm. Balden, & also in the next feild to it.' On 13 August he described the plant at length: 'ech leafe havinge as it were fower rowes of small leaves betwene which groweth uppe a stalk 3 or 4 foot high somewhat woollie'. On the 'vertues' of the recently introduced Jerusalem artichoke Goodyer wrote: 'where this plant groweth naturallie I knowe not ... but in my iudgement, which way soever they be drest and eaten they stirre and cause a filthie loathsome stinking winde within the bodie'. Goodyer contributed to Thomas Johnson's

revised edition of Gerard's *Herbal* (1633), and translated Theophrastus' *Enquiry into Plants* from the Latin (1623) and Dioscorides' *Herbal* from the Greek (1653–55).

Goodyer had no surviving children and left all his 'books *de plantis* ... to Magdalen College Oxon to be kept entirely in the library of the said College for the use of the said College'. He made this bequest probably because his father had been a tenant of the College. Moreover, his favourite nephew, Edmund Yalden (d. 1682), was a Fellow of the College from 1633 to 1642 before becoming Rector of Compton, Surrey. Goodyer's collection of botanical works from the fifteenth to the mid-seventeenth century is one of the most significant in Britain. According to Gunther, the collection consisted of '239 separate printed treatises bound into 134 volumes' and Goodyer recorded the cost and date of purchase of just over a quarter of these on the first flyleaf.

His first recorded purchase, on 31 January 1615 for 20s., was '*Opera quae extant omnia*, ed. Caspar Bauhino. fol. Basil 1598' by Petrus Andreas Matthiolus (1501–77). Goodyer also owned two copies of Matthiolus's *Commentaries on the Materia Medica of Dioscorides*, one in the original Latin, the other a French translation. One of his last recorded purchases (21 March 1660) was *A compleat history of animals and minerals*, octavo, Oxford, 1661 by Robert Lovell (1630?–1690). Goodyer's first edition of John Gerard's (1545–1612) *The Herball, or, Generall Historie of Plants Gathered by John Gerarde of London* (1597) is missing, but the enlarged and amended edition by Thomas Johnson (1595/1600–1644), which includes Goodyer's own contributions, still forms part of the collection. The edition of Theophrastus' (*c.* 300 BC) *De historia plantarum* and *De causis plantarum* that Goodyer used for his translation had been published by Aldus in Venice (1497), and Goodyer also bought a copy of Dioscorides' works (first century AD), published by the same press, for 8s. 6d. on 15 June 1654. There is not the space here to show the significance of this

3 Marcij. 1653
Exam. 4 ffeb. 1655
2071

1. Πεδαχις Διοσκοριδα Αναζαρβεως

Of Pedacius Dioscorides ye Anazarbean

2. περι ιατρικης ὑλης τεταρτον

of medicinall matter, ye 4th

3. βιβλιος

booke

4. Εν τοις τρισι βιβλιοις προ τουτο φιλτατε Αρειε

In the three bookes before this most louing Arius

5. παραδοντες περι αρωματων, και ελαιων,

hauing spoken of Aromaticall matters, and oyles,

6. ἠ μύρων, ἠ δενδρων, ἠ ζωων, και σιτηρων,

and oyntments, & trees, & liuing creatures, and Corne,

7. ἠ λαχανων, ἠ ριζων, ἠ χυλισματων, ἠ βοτανων,

& pot herbs, & rootes, & iuices, and herbes,

8. ἠ σπερματων. εν τουτω οντι τεταρτω

& of seeds. In this being the fourth

9. διαλεξομεθα περι των βοτανων, και ριζων.

wee will discourse of ye herbes, and rootes

10. λειπομενων

left vnspoke of

remarkable collection, but a full catalogue appeared in Gunther's book, cited below.

For nearly 250 years Magdalen's record as custodian of the collection was poor. Gunther notes: 'at first the books were more or less kept together, but the changing needs and views of successive generations led to their being scattered throughout the library, some being removed to a distant room in the Founder's Tower'. Gunther also records that in *c.* 1745

Magdalen's Librarian sold off a copy of Matthiolus' *Compendium de plantis omnibus*, but that in the 1920s its then owner, Mr Gilbert R. Redgrave, noticed the Magdalen bookplate and generously returned the book 'after an absence of a century and three quarters'.

During his time as Fellow Librarian, Gunther reassembled the Goodyer collection — not an easy task as the transcript of the list of the books had disappeared and he had to use an old list from the

Book of Benefactors. But he brought together and catalogued all the surviving books that could be identified, thus at last fulfilling Goodyer's bequest.

DBR

FURTHER READING

R. T. Gunther, *Early British Botanists and their Gardens Based on Unpublished Writings of Goodyer, Tradescant and Others*, Oxford, 1922.

◀ The first page of Goodyer's translation of Dioscorides, with both the Greek and English in his own hand. (He started by copying the Greek on to paper, leaving space between the lines for his translation.)

▲ A hand-coloured thistle from one of the books in Goodyer's collection: Fuchs Leonhart's *Historia stirpium* of 1542

Fritillaria meleagris: The Snake's-Head Fritillary

Why should the fritillary, recently voted the county flower of Oxfordshire and found in abundance in the Meadow, be considered 'hidden'? While it is locally abundant, the disappearance of damp, grassy meadows — its favoured habitat — has made it a national rarity. As it flowers in the Easter vacation, many of our undergraduates never see it in full bloom. Its very origins are also a mystery and for centuries botanists have debated whether the species is native to Britain or merely a garden escape. Although we know that the plant had been introduced from France into England by the late sixteenth century, its first accepted record in the wild dates from 1736, in a Middlesex

meadow. Locals maintained, however, that it had been established there for about forty years.

The plant's origins in the College grounds are also uncertain. The first printed record occurs in *Flora Oxoniensis* (1794) by John Sibthorp (1758–96), the third Sherardian Professor of Botany (1784–96). The botanist and clergyman John Lightfoot (1735–88) had also seen the plant in the Meadow some years previously, for he noted this occurrence in a marginal (but undated) entry in a copy of the third edition of John Ray's *Synopsis methodica Stirpium Britannicarum* (1724). Yet when George Claridge Druce (1850–1932) summarized these records in the first edition of his

Flora of Oxfordshire (1886), he observed: 'It is not a little singular that the Fritillary, so conspicuous a plant of the Oxford meadows, should have for so long remained unnoticed by the various botanists who had resided in or visited Oxfordshire.'

In *Flora Britannica* (1996), Richard Mabey devotes one of the longest entries to the fritillary. Following Druce, he notes that the mid-eighteenth century was one of the less active periods in the College's intellectual history and remarks that the 'men of books and laboratories' were not always the best at fieldwork. But could the annual display really have been missed by the botanists of the time, given that the purple sheen over the Meadow is visible from within many College rooms?

Although Magdalen may have 'slept' scientifically during part of the eighteenth century — or at least taken a rather extended nap — the same cannot be said of the seventeenth century, described by Carl Linnaeus (1707–78) as the golden age of botany in England. The botanists Walter Stonehouse the Divine (1597–1655), William Hooper (1622–95), and William Browne (*c.* 1629–78) were all Fellows of the College. John Goodyer (1592–1664), the great botanist of Petersfield (pp. 195–97), was a regular visitor, and his nephew, Edmund Yalden, was a Demy and later Fellow of Magdalen (see p. 195). The Botanic Garden, then known as the Physic Garden, the earliest still-surviving garden of its kind, was founded on Magdalen land in 1621. Robert Morison (1620–83) became Oxford's first Professor of Botany in 1669. During this time the first comprehensive accounts of the country's native flora were being produced, relying heavily on the field observations of these and other eminent botanical pioneers. So as the garden historian Geoffrey Grigson wrote in 1955, it 'seems not only singular, but impossible' to believe that the fritillary could have been overlooked by all these scientists.

So how did the fritillary come to Magdalen? Perhaps we are looking at the problem the wrong way round. What if they were so familiar in the Meadow by the seventeenth century that they were not thought worthy of note? When compiling their accounts of the native flora, these early botanists sought to exclude species that were known to be introductions or garden escapes. Grigson recommends the scrutiny of wild fritillary sites for evidence of nearby gardens at some time in the past, and the archaeologist and historian John Steane has shown that planted gardens were well established to the north-west of where the New Building now stands. Moreover, by the early seventeenth century the fritillary was well-known in knot gardens and parterres and prized for its exotic flowers, which Gerard (1597) described as 'surpassing ... the curiest painting that Art can set down'.

Another famous botanist possibly joins up the strands of this story. John Tradescant the elder (d. 1638), the country's most famous gardener, had an

◀ ▶   Reddish-purple and white fritillaries in the Meadow

Hidden
Magdalen

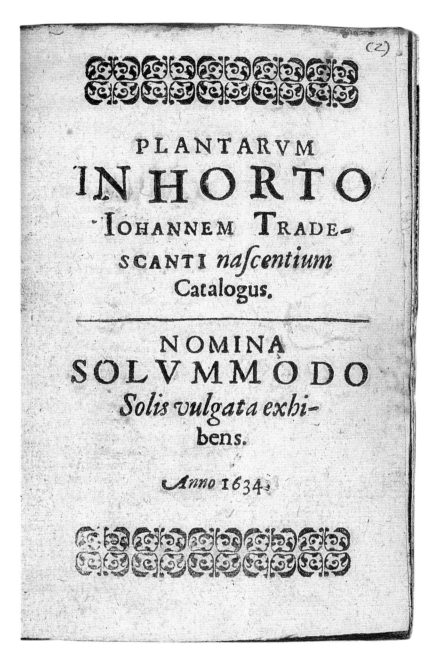

PLANTARVM
IN HORTO
·IOHANNEM TRADE-
SCANTI *naſcentium*
Catalogus.

NOMINA
SOLVMMODO
Solis vulgata exhi-
bens.

Anno 1634.

Oxford connection. He helped provide the new Physic Garden with plants, and in 1636 the Earl of Danby (Henry Danvers, 1573–1644) asked him to become its first Superintendent. In November, Tradescant delivered a letter from Danby to President Frewen to negotiate a stipend: it explained that 'Mr John Tredeskine is willinge to persever in his worke with some assurance of Estate'. He was appointed, only to die in April 1638.

Hard evidence links Tradescant to the fritillary. He had purchased forty in Haarlem in 1611 and the species then appeared in his complete plant list of 1634, *Plantarum in Horto Iohannem* [sic] *Tradescanti nascentium Catalogus*, the only surviving copy of which is in the Goodyer Library. Furthermore, the Bobart herbarium of 1648, the Physic Garden's first catalogue, contains a page of magnificent fritillary plants, including the white variant characteristic of the Meadow. The fritillary was evidently well established in the Physic Garden by the mid-seventeenth century, and Tradescant may well have introduced it there himself.

So could there be a connection between the fritillaries in the Garden and the Meadow? Both sites

▶ Fritillary entries
  from Tradescant's
  plant list

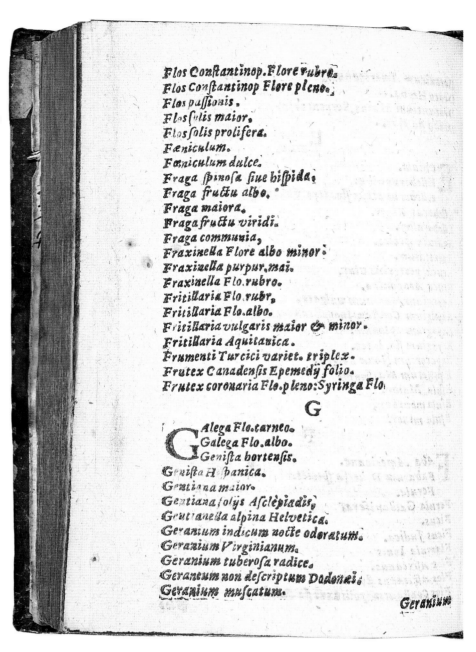

Flos Constantinop. Flore rubro.
Flos Constantinop Flore pleno.
Flos passionis.
Flos solis maior.
Flos solis prolifera.
Fœniculum.
Fœniculum dulce.
Fraga spinosa siue hispida.
Fraga fructu albo.
Fraga maiora.
Fraga fructu viridi.
Fraga communia.
Fraxinella Flore albo minor.
Fraxinella purpur. mai.
Fraxinella Flo. rubro.
Fritillaria Flo. rubr.
Fritillaria Flo. albo.
Fritillaria vulgaris maior & minor.
Fritillaria Aquitanica.
Frumenti Turcici variet. triplex.
Frutex Canadensis Epemedÿ folio.
Frutex coronaria Flo. pleno: Syringa Flo.

G

Galega Flo. carneo.
Galega Flo. albo.
Genista hortensis.
Genista Hispanica.
Gentiana maior.
Gentiana folÿs Asclepiadis.
Gentianella alpina Helvetica.
Geranium indicum nocte odoratum.
Geranium Virginianum.
Geranium tuberosa radice.
Geraneum non descriptum Dodonæi.
Geranium muscatum.

Geranium

regularly flooded and cultivation in the Garden could not begin in earnest until 1633, when the soil level had been raised by 'four thousand loads of mucke and dunge' and the wall completed. But even then the Garden still flooded, and in spring 1663, for example, a 'prodigious flood', extending almost at street level right across to Christ Church meadow, inundated the Meadow. The Water Walks around the Meadow would not be improved for some decades. Under these conditions, flood waters could easily have transported fritillary seeds from the Garden across the short distance to the Meadow, where a more extensive, low-lying, and equally wet site was well suited to their further propagation.

If, perhaps, the fritillary was well established in the Meadow in the seventeenth century, but was recognized as an introduction, botanists would not have thought it worthy of note in the first serious floras of the time. Although the true origins of this extraordinary plant will remain hidden from us for a while longer, the above story does at least provide a plausible solution to the riddles surrounding its origins in Magdalen.

JACS

The Daubeny Lecture Room and Laboratory

Charles G. B. Daubeny FRS (1795–1867) ranks among Magdalen's finest by virtue of being a polymath, a liberal educationalist, and a leader of the nineteenth-century scientific renaissance in Oxford. He was elected Fellow in 1815 and became the Aldrichian Professor of Chemistry from 1822 to 1854, the Sherardian Professor of Botany in 1834, and the Sibthorpian Professor of Rural Economy in 1840. A Fellow of Magdalen for fifty-two years, he served as the College's Bursar and Vice-President. He also corresponded with such significant scientists of his day as Charles Darwin (1809–82) and Michael Faraday (1791–1867).

Daubeny's chemical research paralleled that of Justus von Liebig (1803–73) into the function of plant and nitrogen cycles. He helped revolutionize agricultural practice by the use of mineral fertilisers and his book on volcanoes (1826) accompanied Darwin on the *Beagle* (1831–36). After 1834 Daubeny extended and rearranged Oxford's Physic Garden to become the Botanic Garden.

In 1847, as one of his many attempts to establish practical science teaching in the University, Daubeny initiated the first (unsuccessful) campaign to establish a University Museum that would house the six professors of Natural Science and their collections. He also initiated the petition of 1849 for an Honours School of Natural Sciences. When this was granted in 1850 — the reformers' first victory — the building of a museum became inevitable.

Meanwhile, in 1848, he had built the Daubeny Lecture Room and Laboratory opposite Magdalen, where he gave practical demonstrations to students from any college. From this advanced base he and his successor Edward Chapman (1839–1906) led Oxford's scientific revolution. Twelve subjects, four new to the University, were taught in the Laboratory during seventy-nine years of vigorous scientific activity. Daubeny was genial, diplomatic, always late to Chapel, and famed for his demonstration experiments going wrong!

Daubeny's was the first purpose-built college laboratory in Oxford, and in Tony Simcock's expert opinion it

> stands at the very beginning of the important laboratory-building phase in the history of universities. It also benefits from being a discrete building of architectural elegance with a high degree of internal and external preservation. It has great significance architecturally, and due to its special role in the history of science, in Oxford and generally. The large amount and variety of interesting scientific work done there as documented in R. T. Gunther's *Daubeny Laboratory Register* (1924 edition) lends it unique significance, for we know more about what went on there than in any other comparable laboratory anywhere.

Daubeny also gave Magdalen his Professor's House, a fine telescope, and an endowed science scholarship. He then left his valuable science library and collections of apparatus and specimens to the College, together with money to maintain them. His library of books, extended by his successors, has been catalogued and conserved, and his Lecture Room, which is unique in remaining intact except for its movables, has been restored by bequests from modern benefactors.

RH

LITERATURE

A. V. Simcock, *The Ashmolean Museum and Oxford Science 1683–1983*, Oxford, 1984.

◀ The Daubeny Laboratory

◀ Charles Daubeny by an unknown artist
oil on canvas 48 x 38 cm

◀ The signatures of Charles Darwin and Michael Faraday on correspondence with Charles Daubeny

The Cary Globes

◄   The terrestrial globe, made in 1822 or later

The earliest extant celestial globes are metal Islamic globes from the eleventh century, although it is thought that classical Greek astronomers had used similar globes much earlier. The earliest surviving terrestrial globe was made in Nuremberg in 1492 by Martin Behaim (1459–1507) and the constellations of the southern hemisphere first appeared on a celestial globe in 1601.

The two globes depicted here are a terrestrial globe and a celestial globe and were made by the firm of J. & W. Cary who, together with William Bardin (1740–1803) and John Newton (1759–1844), were the main globe-makers in early nineteenth-century England. John Cary (1755–1835) was a cartographer and his brother William (1759–1825) a maker of scientific instruments. Their globe-making business started in 1791, when they advertised 3.5, 9, 12, and 21-inch terrestrial and celestial globes 'from entire new Plates'. From the inscription, the terrestrial globe was made after 1822 while the celestial globe may be earlier, even though they were presumably bought as a pair. At about this time the Carys marketed two types of celestial globes—one, as here, with cartoons of the constellations, and the other with the boundaries of

Inscription on the celestial globe

CARY'S
New and Improved
CELESTIAL GLOBE,
ON WHICH
Is carefully laid down the whole of the
STARS AND NEBULÆ,
Contained in the ASTRONOMICAL CATALOGUE, *of the*
Revd Mr WOLLASTON, F.R.S.
Compiled from the Authorities of
FLAMSTEED, DE LA CAILLE, HEVELIUS, MAYER
BRADLEY, HERSCHELL, MASKELYNE &c
With an extensive number from the Works of Miss Herschel
The whole adapted to the Year 1800, and the
Limits of each Constellation determined
by a Boundary line

LONDON:
Made and sold by J & W Cary, N° 181 Strand Mar. 1, 1799:

▶ The celestial globe, showing the constellations as cartoon
drawings

the constellations indicated by a simple line. The latter
was considered more scientific. We do not know how
Magdalen acquired these globes. The College had
possessed globes in an earlier period as there is a
record of a table being made for globes in 1549, and
the *Libri computi*, the College's annual accounts for
domestic expenditure from *c.* 1480–*c.* 1880, record that
the College's globes were repaired by Christopher
Wade in 1568 for 2*s*. 6*d*. So the Cary globes may have
been given to or bought by the College to replace the
earlier ones.

Magdalen's globes are mounted on mahogany stands
with three reeded legs and a central compass. The
spheres are 21 inches in diameter and coated with
plaster, to which the printed paper maps have been
affixed. Information on each globe is contained within
a printed cartouche. They were conserved by Sylvia
Sumira in 2003.

DBR

LITERATURE
E. Dekker and P. van der Krogt, *Globes from the Western World*,
London, 1993.

Hidden
Magdalen

The James Short Reflecting Telescope

Perhaps William of Waynflete's introduction of Natural Philosophy into Oxford's curriculum explains why Magdalen was the only Oxford college to have an astronomical observatory in the eighteenth and nineteenth centuries. Certainly, the surviving instruments are interesting.

Richard Persehouse of Reynolds Hall, Walsall, Staffordshire, matriculated at Magdalen in 1751 as a gentleman commoner and presented the College with this state-of-the-art telescope in about 1763.

James Short (1710–68) of Edinburgh began to make Gregorian-type telescopes in 1732. Light from the celestial or terrestrial object under observation falls upon a concave polished mirror at the base of the tube. It is then reflected up to a small, secondary concave mirror, and back through a hole in the centre of the first mirror to the eyepiece, which can be focused.

The telescope is made of brass and stands on a 40 cm pillar and tripod with cabriole feet. The tube is 617 mm long; the objective mirror is 97 mm in diameter and mounted on three springs in a slightly larger cell. The altazimuth mount can be finely adjusted in the vertical and horizontal planes by turning square ivory handles. A square silver plate bears the College and the Persehouse coats of arms together with the donor's Latin inscription, which includes the date of his graduation ('A. M. A. D. 1755'). One of James Short's price lists includes instruments of this size at 20 guineas.

Short moved from Edinburgh to London in 1736 and was elected a Fellow of the Royal Society in 1737. The Magdalen telescope dates to 1762 or 1763 and bears the serial 216/1237–18. This means that it is his 216th of that size, the 1,237th he made, and of 18 inches focal length.

Short's genius was to master the techniques for producing superb paraboloid mirrors in a wide range of sizes. He refined his own formula to cast non-tarnishing alloy; devised an accurate moulding process; perfected his grinding and polishing methods; and then exercised unusual dexterity and patience. His telescopes were the finest in Europe because they could gather more light and magnify better than refracting telescopes. Short's brighter, more distinct images allowed him to charge double his rivals' prices. At his London workshop (established in 1740) he made telescopes ranging from 28 mm hand-held, to 45.8 cm aperture of 386 cm focal length. About 10 per cent of his total production of 1,380 telescopes survives.

Persehouse's gift is the first known Magdalen telescope. He may have been moved to make this gift by attending the Physics and Astronomy lectures that were given in Oxford by the Astronomer Royal, James Bradley (1692–1762), or he may have been enthused by the vogue for astronomical observations among gentlemen and academic scientists.

RH

◀ Magdalen's first telescope, the state-of-the art reflecting telescope of 1762/3

▲ The donor's inscription with the College's and his coats of arms

Hidden
Magdalen

Hidden
Magdalen

The George Dollond Altazimuth Refractor

Magdalen's first known telescope is discussed on p. 206; Magdalen's second telescope is the magnificent brass altazimuth refractor by George Dollond of London. The achromatic object glass has an aperture of 7 cm and is set in a tube that is 140 cm long. This pivots vertically upon a trunnion in a brass yoke mount (77.5 cm tall), which rotates on an adjustable base that is supported by a folding mahogany tripod. Beside a set of eyepieces of different magnifying powers, there is also an eyepiece micrometer, a masterpiece of Dollond's art. A tiny oil lantern attached to the mount admits just enough light to illuminate cross-hairs in the eyepiece which then allow the positions of celestial objects to be measured. Although of modest aperture, such a high-quality instrument sufficed for amateur research and was especially suitable for practical instruction in position measurement for time-keeping or navigation.

According to Robert Gunther (see p. 194), who apparently had sight of original documentation, the telescope was purchased in 1836 for £78 15s. by the Revd Dr Joseph Cox, a Demy who had benefited from a rapid career change. He was elected Fellow on 25 July 1824 but married five days later and so had to resign his Fellowship. He had, however, provided for this eventuality by being elected Master of Queen Mary College, Guernsey, in February 1824. Such a handsome gift twelve years after leaving Magdalen suggests his affection for the College.

In 1857 the College built a telescope room observatory beside the Daubeny Laboratory (see pp. 202–03). The former supported Magdalen's third telescope, a 14 cm Cooke refractor of 1855 that was given to the College by Professor Charles Daubeny (see p. 203). The Short and Dollond telescopes were also kept in the observatory until 1902 and then in the Laboratory until about 1927. In the late 1940s David Kendall (1918–2007; Fellow and Tutor in Mathematics 1946–62) used the Dollond in Longwall Quad to show his friends the rings of Saturn. In the early 1950s his undergraduates Robert Exell (Exhibitioner 1954–61) and Gordon Cave (Demy 1954–57) found its optical quality so good that they could discern the tiny discs of Uranus and Neptune.

RH

◀ Magdalen's second telescope, the refracting telescope of 1836

The Sporting Memorabilia

The Magdalen Cricket Ground

The view in the picture is from Cowley Marsh towards the city: Magdalen's Great Tower is visible on the right and the Radcliffe Camera and the spire of St Mary's are easily recognizable. The land was part of Cowley Common and Bullingdon Green in an area of East Oxford that is now bordered by Magdalen Road and has been completely developed (with a pub called 'The Magdalen' on the junction with Iffley Road). A cricket match is in progress, presumably between Magdalen Cricket Club and that of another college. The date is unknown but probably pre-1840s (when the land was enclosed).

In Magdalen Cricket Club's early days, cricket was a school activity that had started somewhere between 1800 and 1805, and the Club was in fact the forerunner of the University Cricket Club. During the Revd Henry Jenkins's time as Master (1810–28), the Club grew in popularity with the choristers and the growing number of non-chorister boys. Jenkins later gave the University the common land that he had annexed.

Under the Enclosures Act of the 1840s, Cowley parish began to part with its common — where many colleges played cricket. The Magdalen ground was put up for auction and bought by the University for £2,000. An agreement was then signed by the Vice-Chancellor and the Steward of the University Cricket Club, by which Magdalen became the permanent lessee of the now enclosed ground. After mentioning the price, the Act of Convocation goes on to confirm that the land is preserved for the playing of cricket by students. Other college grounds soon did

likewise and became enclosed on the common. Cowley parish encouraged this development as it provided employment for local men and boys — not just in the care and preparation of the grounds but also through the catering and ancillary needs of the players. In the mid-nineteenth century, John Pimm, the landlord of the Coach and Horses in St Clement's, catered for the College ground: in 1860 lunch cost 3s. 6d. and dinner 1s. per head.

Until 1862 the affairs of Magdalen Cricket Club were managed in a somewhat haphazard manner. No captain was ever elected but there were three treasurers (or stewards) of equal authority, no one of whom had specific responsibility for anything. This caused problems, and an entry in the Magdalen Score Book of 30 May 1828 records that they were each fined ten shillings for not turning up to a match.

In the mid-1860s suggestions were starting to circulate that Cowley Marsh should be given up — principally because it was so often flooded — and that cricket pitches should move to the Parks. This did not happen for fear that pavilions would proliferate there, and on the whole colleges made their own arrangements on their own lands. Had it happened at that time it is likely that the boundary of the Parks would have been extended to include land even as far away as the present Magdalen ground.

MRB-B

LITERATURE

R. S. Stanier, *Magdalen School*, Oxford, 1958.
G. Bolton, *History of the O.U.C.C.*, Oxford, 1962.

▲ View of the Magdalen cricket ground on Cowley Marsh
in the early 19th century, engraved by L. V. Richardson
collotype (a technique for large-volume printing before
offset lithography) engraving 48 x 71cm

213

Bow	C. R. Cudmore.	11.	10.
2	J. A. Gillan.	12.	9.
3	D. Mackinnon.	12.	12.
Str	J. R. Somers-Smith. (Steerer).	10.	10.

▲ The diploma awarded for Magdalen's win in the four-oared rowing event of the 1908 Olympics

The 1908 Olympic Games Diploma

The modern Olympic Games were twelve years old when London hosted the fourth Olympiad in 1908. As the structure of the event was still being shaped, each sport tried to adapt to the facilities available rather than build anew. For rowing, it was therefore natural to use the Royal Regatta course and facilities at Henley, and the regatta stewards agreed to a request from the Amateur Rowing Association to retain the infrastructure from the annual event in early July for use at the Olympic Regatta at the end of that month. The course was also lengthened by 330 yards to give a total distance of a mile and a half.

Although only seven nations entered crews for the 1908 games, they represented a large section of the world rowing community of the day. As in other sports, it was then possible for there to be more than one entry per nation per event. The United Kingdom (not Great Britain as today) entered two crews for the four-oared race: Magdalen College, Oxford, and Leander Club. Magdalen were coached by Guy Nickalls (Magdalen 1887–90; see p. 216) and the crew consisted of:

Bow: C. R. Cudmore (11 st. 10 lb)
   2: J. A. Gillan (12 st. 8 lb)
   3: D. Mackinnon (12 st. 12 lb)
Stroke: J. R. Somers-Smith (10 st. 10 lb) – steersman

In their first heat Magdalen raced the Canadians and won by two-and-a-quarter lengths in 8 minutes, 34 seconds. The second heat, between Leander Club and the Dutch, was won by the local crew in 9 minutes, 4 seconds. The final was therefore a host-nation contest. The race reporter records that 'Magdalen steered better than their rivals, and led by their forward canvas at the top of the Island.' But when they led by about a length at the halfway mark,

Leander came out into the mid-stream. A good race continued, but despite a strong spurt by the stroke of the Leander crew, Magdalen won by a length and a half in 8 minutes, 34 seconds.

Champions at the 1908 games were presented with gold medals (solid gold, not gilt as now) about the size of the modern two-pence piece, in the form of a coin (but without the later eyelet and ribbon). They also received a model silver oar and a diploma. The commemoration medal was given to all participants, including medal winners. The 1908 medal ceremony was accompanied by the drums and bugles of the Irish Guards, and the medals were presented by Lady Desborough, the wife of the Chairman of the Organizing Committee.

The diploma pictured here, drawn by Bernard Partridge (1861–1945), hangs in the room of the Captain of Boats. Such diplomas were presented to each gold medal winner, plus one for their club. This one is an example of the latter: above the names of the crew and the title of the event they won is a scene of Greek gods and goddesses at the Temple of Hera, Olympia, the site of the ancient games.

At the banquet which concluded the games, the Reverend Robert de Courcy-Laffan, an International Olympic Committee member, said: 'I must warn those who organise future Olympiads that they must be prepared for times of trial.' *Plus ça change, plus c'est la même chose.*

MRB-B

LITERATURE

T. Cook, *Henley Races 1903–1914*, London, 1919.

D. Miller, *Athens to Athens: The Official History of the Olympic Games and IOC*, Edinburgh, 2003.

J. Swaddling, *The Ancient Olympic Games*, London, 1980.

The Henley Blade

▲ The pencil blade used by Guy Nickalls in the 1922
Henley Royal Regatta

The Henley Blade is a memento from a particularly successful period of College rowing history. To commemorate the success of his sons, Guy (Commoner 1886–91) and Vivian (Commoner 1890–93), at Henley Royal Regatta, Tom Nickalls added the Nickalls' Cup to the Silver Goblets for the pair-oared competition in 1895. Guy Nickalls's son (also Guy, or Gully; Commoner 1920–23) together with R. S. C. Lucas (Commoner 1914 and 1919–21) competed for this cup, representing either Magdalen or Leander Club, on five occasions, and won the event in 1920 and 1922. This pencil blade was used by Guy in the 1922 regatta and it now hangs in the room of the Captain of Boats.

In the final round of the 1922 Regatta, Nickalls and Lucas beat H. E. West and K. Vernon of Thames Rowing Club to win the Silver Goblets. Nickalls and Lucas each won six medals during this period, having also been in winning College and Leander Club crews in the Grand Challenge Cup. But perhaps their most entertaining Henley story concerns their first race in the Goblets of 1924, when they rowed for Leander against their Magdalen contemporaries G. K. Hampshire (Exhibitioner 1920–23) and W. Phillips (Commoner 1920–22), who rowed in College colours. Their story is told in the race report:

> The result of this race was entirely unexpected for Nickalls and Lucas were considered the probable winners of the Goblets. It was not generally known, however, that as well as being famous oarsmen they were no mean amateur carpenters and always carried a set of tools. Whilst waiting at the Start, Stroke, thinking that the boat was unnecessarily heavy, cut away some of the bigger timbers and on the first stroke of the race Bow pushed his stretcher through the skin and she started to leak.
>
> However, they soon took the lead and before going far, Hampshire and Phillips hit the booms and Nickalls and Lucas waited for them.
>
> On re-starting, Nickalls and Lucas again took the lead and were a long way ahead at Fawley, reached in 5.30. Here it became obvious that something was wrong for the boat was floating lower and lower in the water. In spite of the handicap they kept well ahead and it became more of a race against the leak than against their opponents. At the Mile Post it was clear that the leak was gaining on them fast and at the bottom of the Enclosure the cut-water disappeared and then the boat sank amidst execrations that were visible but inaudible at the Winning Post.
>
> All the time Hampshire and Phillips were entirely unconscious of what had happened to their opponents whom they had not seen since about half way up the Island. When they came up with them they were not a little surprised to find them swimming and so stopped rowing. Ultimately they paddled in to complete the Course in 12.0 and immediately offered to row the race again. The Committee, however, could not allow this, pointing out that as they had passed the Winning Post the race was over and that a boat must abide by its accidents.

MRB–B

LITERATURE

C. T. Steward, *Henley Records 1919–1938*, London, 1939.

The Deed of Foundation

To all and each of the Sons of Holy Mother Church to whom and to whose attention these present letters may come, and whom the matters written below concern or may in future concern, William Waynflete by divine permission Bishop of Winchester, eternal salvation in the Lord. Since our most Christian and illustrious Prince and Lord, Lord Henry, presently King of England and France and Lord of Ireland, sixth [of that name] since the conquest, to the praise, glory and honour of almighty God, Father, Son and Holy Spirit and of the chaste Blessed Virgin Mary Mother of Christ, together with Blessed Mary Magdalen, Saint John the Baptist and the Apostles Peter and Paul and other patron saints of the diocese of Winchester, for the rooting out of heresies and errors, the increase of clergy, and ornament of Holy Mother Church, whose ministries should be entrusted to suitable persons, who like stars may cast light over their watch and enlighten the people equally by teaching and example, of his special grace and of his own accord and sure knowledge, recently by his letters patent, for himself and his heirs insofar as in his power, granted and gave us licence, to the praise, glory and honour of God and of the said Blessed Virgin Mary, Mother of Christ and of the aforesaid Blessed Mary Magdalen, Saint John the Baptist, the Apostles Peter and Paul and other patron saints of the diocese of Winchester, to set up, found, create and establish in the University of Oxford, to last for all future time, a certain perpetual College of learning in the sciences of sacred theology and philosophy, consisting of a President and a number of graduate scholars engaged in studying those same sciences, according to ordinances and statutes to be composed, set forth, constituted and established thereafter by us in this matter, on a certain piece of land outside the east gate of the town of Oxford, abutting on the east the stream called Cherwell, on the south the highway leading from the said gate to the bridge called Eastbridge, on the west the highway leading from the said gate to the place called Canditch, and on the north certain lands called Halywell, and that we should have the right to appoint, create and choose a suitable person in holy orders as President and in the office of President of that same College as well as other persons willingly associating with him as Scholars of the same College, to be elected and added according to ordinances and statutes to be made thereafter by us concerning [their] rule, correction, deprivation and removal. The aforesaid King willed also and granted by the said letters patent that once set up, founded, created and established the aforesaid College should be known in perpetuity as the College of Blessed Mary Magdalen, in common speech Maudeleyne College, in the University of Oxford; and that the aforesaid President and Scholars and their successors should likewise be known in perpetuity as President and Scholars of the College of Blessed Mary Magdalen in the University of Oxford; and that the same President and Scholars and their successors under the title President and Scholars of the College of Blessed Mary Magdalen in the University of Oxford should be persons fit, capable and permanent at law in the seeking and receiving of lands, holdings, rents and possessions of all kinds, to be held by them and their successors in perpetuity notwithstanding the statute preventing the placing of lands and holdings in mortmain: and that the same President and Scholars by and under the same title should be able to plead and be impleaded in any court and tribunal of the aforesaid King, his heirs and successors, as also in the courts and tribunals of whatsoever other persons within his Kingdom of England according to the laws and customs of that Kingdom; and that in order to do and receive all other things, they should plead and be impleaded, do and be able to do, in the aforesaid courts and tribunals according to the aforesaid laws and customs, to the extent and in the same manner as other liege persons of the said King are fit and capable; as also that the aforesaid President and Scholars and their successors should have a common seal to be used in perpetuity in carrying out their transactions. And since our beloved in Christ John Horley, President of the Hall of Blessed Mary Magdalen in the aforesaid University of Oxford, and the Scholars of that Hall have by certain letters patent given, granted, and confirmed to us by those letters the aforesaid piece of land, namely the site or piece of land outside the east gate of the town of Oxford, lying between the stream called Cherwell on the east, and the highway leading from the said gate to the place called Canditch on the west, and between the highway leading from the said gate as far as the bridge called Eastbridge on the south and certain lands called Halywell on the north, to have and to hold, to us our heirs and assigns in perpetuity, to the intention and effect that we should set up and found on the aforesaid site or piece of land a College of the kind specified above, as is fully evident to us:

LET IT BE KNOWN TO YOU ALL that we, after very deep and profound thought, deeming these proposals to be pious and worthy, and desiring to carry them out and put them into full effect, having first been accorded the authority and licence of the holy Apostolic See in this matter, proceeding in the name of the undivided Trinity, Father, Son and Holy Spirit towards the setting up, foundation and establishment of a College of this kind, to the praise, glory and honour of almighty God and of the blessed Virgin Mary, Mother of Christ and of the aforesaid Saint Mary Magdalen as of Saint John the Baptist, the Apostles Peter and Paul and the other patron Saints of the Diocese of Winchester, and to the fulfilment of certain good works, we do set up, found, create and establish to last for all future time a certain perpetual College of learning in the sciences of sacred theology and philosophy according to the tenor of these present [letters] consisting of, and to the number of, one President and a number of graduate scholars studying the same sciences according to statutes and ordinances to be composed, instituted, made and established hereafter in this matter, in the aforesaid University, that is to say on the site and piece of land specified

and delineated above, and we appoint, create and ordain Master William Tybard Bachelor of Sacred Theology as President and in the office of President of the same College, and Master Robert Calthorp, Master William Laughton, [and] Master Henry Fisher Masters of Arts, [and] Simon Godmanston, Richard Bernes and Robert Rous. Bachelors of Arts, as graduate Scholars of the same College, in willing association with the aforesaid President, they being chosen and appointed by us according to ordinances and statutes to be set out by us hereafter concerning [their] rule, correction, deprivation and removal. We also will, establish, grant and ordain by these present [letters] that the same President and Scholars and their successors, Presidents and Scholars of the same College according to the ordinances and statutes to be composed and made known by us as proposed, shall have power to elect, associate and admit further Scholars according to those ordinances and statutes for [their] rule, correction, deprivation and removal; moreover we, by these present [letters] will, grant, establish and ordain, for ourselves and our successors in perpetuity, that the Scholars and their successors thus elected, associated and admitted according to such statutes and ordinances of this kind for rule, correction, deprivation and removal, shall be Scholars of the College and be taken, held and in all matters considered as Scholars and Members of the same College. Furthermore, we will, grant, establish and ordain that when the aforesaid President retires or departs or is removed or deprived for any other reason, the Scholars of the same College for the time being according to the form and effect of the statutes and ordinances to be made as aforesaid, shall be able to elect another suitable man as President of that College without seeking or waiting for a licence from us or our successors: and by the tenor of these present [letters], for ourselves and our successors for the time being bishops of Winchester, we have caused the person thus elected to be admitted and confirmed as President and in the office of President of the same College, and thus we will, grant, establish and ordain by these present [letters] that it should be done according to the aforesaid ordinances and statutes proposed for the making of a free election from time to time of a new President of the College, that he be admitted and confirmed as President of that College in the aforesaid manner, and being admitted and confirmed according to the ordinances and statutes aforesaid for rule, correction, deprivation and removal, that he and no other be permanent President; nor should it be in any other manner. We also will, grant, establish and ordain that when in the future Fellows of the aforesaid College retire or depart or are deprived or removed, the aforesaid President and Scholars and their aforesaid successors shall have in perpetuity according to the ordinances and statutes, free election and confirmation of new Scholars in their place without in the future seeking or waiting for licence in the matter from us or our successors; and we will, grant, establish and ordain, for ourselves and our successors in perpetuity, that persons thus elected, confirmed and admitted, and no others, shall be Scholars of the aforesaid College and be held, taken and considered Scholars and Members of the same College according to the ordinances and statutes for rule, correction, deprivation and removal. Moreover we, by virtue and authority of the aforesaid licence of our Lord King obtained in the proposed matter, give,

grant and confirm to the aforesaid President and Scholars of the College by these present [letters], the aforesaid site or piece of land with its appurtenances, lying within the aforesaid limits and boundaries, to have and to hold for themselves and their successors both in respect of the houses and buildings and the dwellings and other necessary outbuildings to be built and erected on and upon that site or piece of land, and in respect of the increase of livelihood of the President and Scholars and their successors in perpetuity. However, each and all the other ordinances and statutes specified above, which are necessary and opportune for the above matters but which are treated summarily in these present letters, we defer to others to be composed, ordained and established by us. In pledge and testimony of each and all the above proposals we have caused our Seal to be affixed to these present [letters]. Given at our Manor of Southwark in our diocese of Winchester on the twelfth day of June 1458, in the thirty-sixth regnal year of the aforesaid Lord King Henry, the sixth since the Conquest and the eleventh year of our Consecration.

TRANSLATED FROM THE LATIN BY GLH

Index

A Turn or Two I'll Walk to Still my Beating Mind (by Richard Brocklebank) 92

Ackermann, Rudolph (publisher) 162

Actes and Monuments (by John Foxe) 52, 53, 54, 175

Adams, Arthur White (Fellow of Magdalen and Dean of Divinity) 74

Addison, Joseph (Fellow of Magdalen) 38, 58, 130, 144, 188

Addison, Revd Launcelot (father of Joseph and Dean of Lichfield) 144

Addison's Walk and water-meadow 38, 144

Adorno, Theodor Ludwig Wiesengrund (philosopher and musicologist) 89

Agas, Ralph (cartographer) 26

Alexander, George (theatre producer) 67

Alexander I (Tsar) 84, 85

Alkaloids 70

Amerbach, Johannes (printer) 182

American War of Independence 63

Anatolia (Turkey) 118

Anne (Queen) 58

Anwykyll, John (Master of Magdalen College School) 182

Apian, Peter (cosmographer) 185

Apollonius of Rhodes (Greek poet) 20

Arthur, Prince (son of Henry VII) 132, 133

Arundel, Thomas Howard (2nd Earl of Arundel and Surrey) 147

Aseneth (Old Testament figure) 177

Ashmolean Museum (Oxford) 150, 158, 203

Ashurnasirpal II (King of Assyria) 129

Astronomical observatory (Oxford) 209

Astronomicon Caesareum (by Peter Apian) 185

Auerbach, Frank Helmut (painter) 169

Bale, John (historian) 175

Barbieri, Giovanni Francesco (Il Guercino) (painter) 106, 107

Bardin, William (globe-maker) 204

Barlow, Thomas Oldham (engraver) 63

Bassianus, Johannes (lawyer) 178

Bathsheba (Old Testament figure) 133

BBC European Service 186

Bede, the Venerable (historian) 175

Beethoven's Fifth Symphony 186

Behaim, Martin (cartographer) 204

Bellhouse, Francis Hewitt (engineer) 86

Bennett, Jack Arthur Walter (Fellow of Magdalen) 74

Bereblock, John (artist) 26

Berenson, Bernard (art historian) 94, 95, 96, 98

Betjeman, Sir John (Magdalen undergraduate and poet) 22, 23

Bicester (Oxfordshire) 124

Bilson, Sir Thomas (Lord of the Manor of Mapledurham, Hampshire) 195

Bilton Hall near Rugby (Warwickshire) 144, 188

Bird, Reginald (Fellow of Magdalen) 188

Blauet, Dionisia (donor) 10

Bloxam, John Rouse (Fellow of Magdalen) xi, 20, 30, 31, 35, 40, 49, 56, 57, 58, 60, 61, 64, 65, 81

Blue Mosque (Istanbul) 118

Blunderbuss 82

Boase, T[homas] S[herrer] R[oss] (President of Magdalen) 74, 107, 124, 125, 142

Bodleian Library (Oxford) 26, 189

Bodley Head (publishers) 69

Boer War 92

Bol, Hans (painter) 104

Bologna (Italy) 106, 107, 173, 178

Bonhams (London auction house) 160

Books of Names (*Libri nominum*) 16

Boskovits, Miklós (art historian) 94, 95, 96, 98, 99

Botanic Garden (Oxford) 40, 199, 200

Bouncer, Little Mr *see* Ward, William

Boydell, John (publisher) 108, 110, 114

Brackley (Northamptonshire) 10, 12

Bradley, James (Astronomer Royal) 205, 206

Bradley, Revd Edward ('Cuthbert Bede', author and clergyman) 68

Bramley, Harry Ramsden (Fellow of Magdalen and Dean of Divinity) 9

Brazil 112

Breughel, Jan, the elder (painter) 147

British Museum (London) 110, 118

Brocket Hall (Hertfordshire) 122
'portraits' of Elizabeth I 122

Brocklebank, John Ralph Auckland (Magdalen undergraduate and son of Richard) 92

Brocklebank, Richard Hugh Royds (Magdalen undergraduate, father of John, and donor) 92, 95, 96, 98, 104, 108, 112, 120

Brocklebank Bequest 92, 95, 96, 98, 100, 102, 104, 108, 110, 112, 114, 116, 118, 120

Brocklebank Collection (Magdalen) 2, 92, 120

Brown, Lancelot ('Capability') (landscape gardener) 38

Browne, John (father of William) 135

Browne, William (Fellow of Magdalen, College Manciple, and son of John) 135, 199

Buckler, John (architect, father of John Chessell Buckler) 26, 40

Buckler, John Chessell (architect, son of John Buckler) 188

Budden, John (William of Waynflete's biographer) 173

Bulganin, Nikolai Alexandrovitch (Prime Minister of the Soviet Union) 76

Bulley, Frederick (President of Magdalen) 56

Bulley Jr, Frederic (Magdalen undergraduate) 89

Burne-Jones, Sir Edward Coley (painter) ix, 164

Burton, James (Fellow of Magdalen) 20, 21

Butler, James (2nd Duke of Ormonde) 142

Bye, John (wood-carver) 190

Calixtus III (Pope) 7

Canterbury, Archbishop of 9, 50, 81

Captain of Boats (Magdalen) 215, 216

Carracci, Lodovico (painter) 142

Carter, Joseph (bell-founder) 36

Cartulary of the Hospital of St John (Oxford) 10

Cartwright, John (brother of Edmund and political activist) 63

Cartwright, Revd Edmund (Fellow of Magdalen, inventor and brother of John) 20, 63

Cary, [Arthur] Joyce [Lunel] (novelist) 169

Cary, John (cartographer and brother of William) 204, 205

Cary, William (instrument maker and brother of John) 204, 205

Catherine of Aragon (wife of Prince Arthur and King Henry VIII) 132, 133

Hidden Magdalen

Cave, Gordon Russsell (Magdalen Demy) 209

Cecily, Duchess of York 14, 15

Chalgrove Field (Oxfordshire) 55

Chamberlain, Henry (diplomat and father of Henry) 112

Chamberlain, Henry (soldier and painter and son of Henry) 112

Chapel, Magdalen College:
misericords 35
ornamental carvings 35
plate 135
stained glass, medieval 30
stalls 35
vestibule 30
West Window 30

Chapman, Edward (Fellow of Magdalen) 203

Chappington, John (organ-builder) 181

Chappington, Samuel 181

Charles I (King) 1, 26, 32, 33, 55, 136, 138

Charles II (King) 138, 158

Charles V (Holy Roman Emperor) 100, 185

Charles IX (King of France) 100

Chasteilain, George (book-binder) 10

Chichibu [also known as Prince Yasuhito] (Magdalen undergraduate and Crown Prince of Japan) 148, 149, 150

Chippendale, Thomas (cabinet maker) 188

Choir and choristers ix, xi, 16, 20, 49, 64, 89, 154, 212

Chorister medals 154–55

Christ Church (Oxford) 50, 116, 181, 201

Christmas carols 9

Chyles, Nathaniel (Fellow of Magdalen) 138

Cilgerran Castle (Pembrokeshire) 108, 109

Cirsium eriophorum see Woolly thistle

Civil War (English) 46, 55, 135, 136, 138, 140

Clark, Kenneth Mackenzie [Baron Clark] (Fellow of Magdalen and art critic) 169

Claymond, John (President of Magdalen) 173

Clouet, François (painter and son of Jean) 100

Clouet, Jean (painter and father of François) 100

Coach and Horses public house, St Clement's (Oxford) 212

Cole, Walter (donor) 10

Collins, Thomas (Master of Magdalen College School) 58

Congreve, William (playwright) 144

Constable, John (painter) 108

Cooke, Colin Arthur (Fellow of Magdalen and Senior Bursar) 74

Copley Fielding, Anthony Vandyke 116

Corpus Christi College (Oxford) 173

Cosmographia (by Peter Apian) 185

Cottingham, Lewis Nockalls (architect) 35, 142

Courtauld Institute (London) 106, 107

Cowley Marsh (Oxford) 212

Cox, George Valentine (memoirist) 20

Cox, Joseph (Fellow of Magdalen) 209

Cox, William (Fellow of Magdalen) 138

Crawford, Gerald Norman Cullen (Fellow of Magdalen) 74

Crick, Francis Harry Compton (molecular biologist and Nobel Laureate) 73

Cromwell, Elizabeth (mother of John Hampden) 55

Cromwell, Oliver (Lord Protector) 30, 33

Cudmore, Sir Collier Robert (Magdalen undergraduate) 215

Cup of the Restored Fellows (Magdalen) ix, 138

Cupid Restraining the Enraged Mars (painting by Il Guercino) 106

Cuthbert Bede see Bradley, Revd Edward

d'Halluin, Antoine (Grand Louvetier de France and father of Jeanne) 100

d'Halluin, Jeanne (French aristocrat and daughter of Antoine) ix, 100, 102

da Modena, Barnaba (painter) 96

Dale, John (Fellow of Magdalen) 135

Dalton, Richard (art dealer) 107

Danvers, Henry (1st [and only] Earl of Danby) 200

Darnley portrait 122

Darwin, Charles Robert (naturalist) 203

Daubeny, Charles Giles Brindle (Fellow of Magdalen) ix, 61, 202, 203, 209

Davenant, Sir William (theatre manager) 158

David (King, Old Testament) 133

Davies, Reginald (jeweller) 154

Dawe, William (bell-founder) 36

de Camvill, Hugh (benefactor) 12

de Joyeuse, Anne (first husband of Margaret of Lorraine) 102

de Lorraine, Louise (Queen and sister of Margaret) 102

de Lorraine, Nicolas (Duc de Mercoeur, Comte de Bar, and father of Margaret) 102

de Luxembourg, François (Duc de Piney and second husband of Margaret) 102

de Medici, Catherine (Queen) 100

de Morales, Luis (painter) 142

de Moryn, Christian (organist and husband of Catharina van Hemessen) 102

de Staël, Anne Louise Germaine (author) 160

de Valera, Éamon (Prime Minister of the Republic of Ireland) 73

de Vries, Adriaen (sculptor) 104

Dead Sea Scrolls 130

Delmer, [Denis] Sefton (author) 186

Demy (pl. Demies) xi, 9, 15, 20, 23, 58, 60, 63, 64, 130, 138, 144, 199, 209

Devonshire, Duke of 110

di Baldese, Ambrogio (painter) 98

di Bartolo, Taddeo see Taddeo di Bartolo

di Cione, Jacopo (painter) 98

di Nardo, Mariotto (painter) 98

di Puccio, Piero (painter) 96

Diggle, Edmund (Fellow of Magdalen) 138

Dioscorides Pedanius (physician and botanist) 195, 196, 197

Dirac, Paul Adrien Maurice (theoretical physicist and Nobel Laureate) 73

Dollond, George (instrument maker) 209

Dom João (King of Portugal and Emperor of Brazil) 112

Dom Pedro (Emperor of Brazil) 112

Douglas, Lord Alfred [Bruce] (Magdalen undergraduate and poet) x, 22, 23, 68, 130, 169

Driver, Sir Godfrey Rolles (Fellow of Magdalen) 74

Druce, George Claridge (botanist) 198, 199

Dryden, John (poet) 144

Duccio (di Buoninsegna) (painter) 94

Dulwich Picture Gallery (South London) 158

Earlom, Richard (printmaker) 110, 114

Easling, J[ames?] C[row?] (engraver) 114

Eccles, Sir John Carew (Honorary Fellow of Magdalen and Nobel Laureate) 89

Edward I (King) 166

Edward IV (King) x, 15

Edward, Prince of Wales (Magdalen undergraduate, later King Edward VIII) x, 22, 23, 42, 148

Edwards, Peter (artist) 73

Eginton, Francis (decorative artist) 30, 31

Eleanor (Queen and wife of Edward I) 166

Elizabeth I (Queen) ix, 52, 100, 122, 135,

Elizabeth of York (Queen) 15

Ellesmere Island (Qikiqtaaluk Region of the Canadian territory of Nunavut) 152
Royal Navy expedition to 152

Elliot, William (engraver) 108

Eppewelle or Epwell, Richard (scribe) 10

Erasmus of Rotterdam (humanist) 181

Eton College (Berkshire) 7, 89

Exell, Robert Harold Buchanan (Magdalen exhibitioner) 209

Exeter College (Oxford) 164

Expulsion [extrusion] of the Magdalen Fellows ix, 56, 57

Faraday, Michael (chemist) 202, 203

Fawkes, Guy (terrorist) 1, 58

Ferdinand I (Holy Roman Emperor) 185

Ferdinand II (King of Aragon; together with Isabella, the Catholic Monarchs) 132

First World War 23, 42, 43, 92, 144

Fitzwilliam, John (Fellow of Magdalen and non-juror) 185

Fleming, Eleanor (wife of Sir John Lowther) 166

Fleming, Ian [Lancaster] (author) 144

Fletcher, Charles Robert Leslie (Fellow of Magdalen) 55

Flora Britannica (by Richard Mabey) 199

Flora of Oxfordshire (by George Claridge Druce) 199

Flora Oxoniensis (by John Sibthorp) 198

Florence (Italy) 94, 95, 98, 107

Florey, Howard Walter [Baron Florey] (Honorary Fellow of Magdalen and Nobel Laureate) 89

Forbes, Alexander Penrose (Bishop of Brechin) 142

Forman, Abraham (Fellow of Magdalen) 138

Founder of Magdalen see Waynflete, William of

Fox, Richard (Bishop of Winchester) 173

Foxe, John (Fellow of Magdalen, martyrologist, and father of Samuel) 52, 53, 54, 175

Foxe, Samuel (son of John) 52

Foxe, Thomas (Fellow of Magdalen and son of Samuel) 53

François I (King of France) 100

François II (King of France) 100

Frangopoulos, Michael (one-time owner of the Cypriot 'Model Book') 177

Fraser, Antonia [Margaret] (author) 133

Frederick William III (King of Prussia) 84

Freeman, William (gentleman commoner of Magdalen and donor) 142

Freemasonry 68

Freud, Lucian Michael (painter) 169

Frewen, Accepted (President of Magdalen) ix, 32, 40, 47, 136, 200

Fritillary, Snake's-Head (Fritillaria meleagris) 198–201

Fulton, Robert (painter and inventor) 63

Gainsborough, Earls of 107

Gardner, Percy (archaeologist) 92

Gellée, Claude (painter) see Lorrain[e], Claude

Gemma Frisius (instrument-maker) 185

Gennari brothers (nephews of Il Guercino) 107

Geographia (by Ptolemy) ix, 172, 173, 185

George III (King) 20, 107

George V (King) 22, 23

Gerard, [John] (herbalist) 195, 199

Gerard's Herbal 195

Gesta pontificum anglorum (by William of Malmesbury) 195 175

Gesta regum anglorum (by William of Malmesbury) 175

Ghent (Belgium) 147

Gibbon, Edward (Magdalen undergraduate and historian) 160, 161

Gibson, Thomas (artist) 58

Gillan, Sir James Angus (Magdalen undergraduate) 215

Gilpin, William (clergyman and writer on art) ix, 124, 125

Giotto [di Bondone] (painter) 94

Globe, celestial ix, 204, 205

Globe, terrestrial ix, 204, 205

Glyndwr, Owain (freedom fighter) 108

Godington (Godendun) (Oxfordshire) 12

Golden Election of 1689 58, 144

Goodyer, John (botanist) 195–97, 199

Gordon, George Stuart (President of Magdalen) 53, 73

Gosia, Martinus (lawyer) 178

Grayson, Cecil (Professorial Fellow of Magdalen) 74

Greenbury, Richard (painter) 30, 32, 33, 47

Greenhill, John (painter) 158

Gregg, John Francis (Fellow of Magdalen) 86

Griffiths, James Howard Eagle (President of Magdalen) 74

Grigson, Geoffrey Edward Harvey (writer) 199

Guercino, Il (painter) see Barbieri, Giovanni Francesco

Guinevere (Queen) 164

Gundelach, Matthäus (painter) 104

Gunther, Robert William Theodore (Fellow of Magdalen) 194, 195–97, 203, 209

Halifax, Lord (Foreign Secretary) 73

Hampden, John (Magdalen undergraduate, MP and son of William) 55

Hampden, William (father of John) 55

Hampshire, G[eorge] K[enneth] (Magdalen exhibitioner) 216

Hardie, Colin Graham (Fellow of Magdalen) 74

Harding, John (President of Magdalen) 55

Harris, Henry (actor and engraver) 158

Harris, Jethro (sculptor) 190, 191

Hayter, Sir William Goodenough (diplomat) 76

Hayward, John (historian of silver) 135

Hazell, Stephen (Oxford chair-maker and father of Stephen Charles) 189

Hazell, Stephen Charles (Oxford chair-maker and son of Stephen) 189

Heaney, Seamus [Justin] (Honorary Fellow of Magdalen, poet and Nobel Laureate) 73

Hedging and Ditching (by J. M. W. Turner) 114, 115

Heisenberg, Werner Karl (physicist and Nobel Laureate) 73

Henley Royal Regatta x, xi, 215, 216

Henry III (King) 10

Henry VI (King) 7

Henry VII (King) 15, 132

Henry VIII (King) 16, 181

Hertford College (Oxford) 10

Hiranari (Japanese armourer) 150

Hirohito (Japanese Emperor) ix, 148

History of the Decline and Fall of the Roman Empire (by Edward Gibbon) 160

Hitler, Adolf 73

Hoefnagel, Joris (painter) 104

Hoffman, Hans (painter) 104

Hol, Lienhart (printer) 173

Holbein, Hans, the younger (painter) 181

Homilies (by St John Chrysostom) 177

Hooper, Walter (donor and C. S. Lewis scholar) xi, 153

Hooper, William (Fellow of Magdalen) 199

Horenbout family (miniaturists and painters) 181

Hospital of St James and St John (Brackley, Northamptonshire) 12

Hospital of St John the Baptist (Oxford) 7, 10, 36

Hospital of St Stephen and St Thomas (Romney, Kent) 19

Hough, John (President of Magdalen) 56

Hughes, S[amuel?] G[eorge?] (engraver) 162, 163

Huleatt, Revd Charles (Magdalen undergraduate, donor, and papyrologist) 130

Hunt, Arthur Suridge (Magdalen Demy and papyrologist) 130

Huskisson, William (MP) 162

Hutter, Irmgard (art historian) 177

Idylls of the King (by Alfred, Lord Tennyson) 164

Isabella I (Queen of Castille; together with Ferdinand, the Catholic Monarchs) 132

Istanbul (Turkey) 118, 120

Iznik (Turkey) ix, 92, 118, 120

James, Duke of York *see* James II

James, Thomas (Bodley's librarian) 177

James I (King) 26, 32

James II (King) 56, 144, 158, 185

Japanese armour xi, 150

Jenkins, Henry (Master of Magdalen College School) 212

Jenkins, Roy Harris [Baron Jenkins of Hillhead] (Chancellor of Oxford University and politician) 83

Jennings, Alexander (Fellow of Magdalen) 138

Jimson, Gulley (character in *The Horse's Mouth* by Joyce Cary) 169

Jinmu (Japanese Emperor) 148

Johannes Schnitzer of Armsheim (wood-carver) 173

John, Augustus [Edwin] (painter) ix, 92

John, Jeffrey Phillip Hywel (Fellow of Magdalen and Dean of Divinity) 9

Johnson, P[atrick] (Fellow of Magdalen) 74

Johnson, Thomas (herbalist) 195

Joseph (husband of Mary, mother of Jesus) 147

Kemp, Tom (palaeontologist) 194

Kendall, David George (Fellow of Magdalen) 209

Kennedy, John F[itzgerald] (President of the United States of America) 153

Kent, William (landscape gardener) 38

Khrushchev, Nikita Sergeyevich (Chairman of the Council of Ministers, Soviet Union and father of Sergei) 76

Khrushchev, Sergei (son of Nikita) 76

King Henry VIII (by William Shakespeare) 158

Kneller, Sir Godfrey (painter) 58, 144

Knight, Ellis (bell-founder) 36

Koberger, Anton (publisher) 182

Kozuke Province (Japan) 150

Kütahya (Turkey) 118

Lady Warwick [Charlotte Myddleton] (wife of Joseph Addison) 144

Lady Windermere's Fan (by Oscar Wilde) 68, 69

Lang, Cosmo Gordon (Fellow of Magdalen and Dean of Divinity) 9, 81

Langton, George (Fellow of Magdalen) 138

Langton, William (President of Magdalen) 19, 55

Lawrence, Thomas Edward (Fellow of Magdalen) 89

Layard, Austen Henry (archaeologist) 129

Le Brocquy, Melanie (sculptor) 67

Leal, Juan de Valdés *see* Valdés Leal, Juan de

Leander Club 215, 216

Lee, Stephen ['Luggins'] (Fellow of Magdalen) 148

Lely, Sir Peter (painter) 158

Lever, Stuart Mordecai (Magdalen undergraduate and donor) 30

Lewis, C[live] S[taples] (Fellow of Magdalen, theologian, and poet) 23, 74, 153

Leylond, John (grammarian) 182

Leyser, Karl Joseph (Fellow of Magdalen) 76

Liber studiorum (*Book of Studies*) (by J. M. W. Turner) 110, 114

Liber veritatis (*Book of Truth*) (by Claude Lorrain[e]) 110, 114

Libri computi (*Books of Accounts*) 205

Libri nominum see Books of Names

Liddell, Henry George (Dean of Christ Church [Oxford]) 116

Lightfoot, John (botanist) 198

Lindemann, Frederick Alexander [1st Viscount Cherwell] (physicist and scientific adviser to Winston Churchill) 73

Linnaeus, Carl (botanist) 199

Lloyd, Brian Beynon (Fellow of Magdalen) 74

Locke, John (philosopher) 158

Loggan, David (artist and engraver) 40, 42

Long Parvula (by John Stanbridge) 182

Lorenzetti, Ambrogio (painter and brother of Pietro) frontispiece, 94, 95, 96

Lorenzetti, Pietro (painter and brother of Ambrogio) 94, 95

Lorrain[e], Claude, [Gellée, Claude] (painter) 108, 110, 114

Lorraine, Margaret of (courtier) ix, 102

Lovell, Robert (botanist) 195

Lowther, Christopher (father of Sir John) 166

Lowther, Richard (grandfather of Sir John) 166

Lowther, Sir Hugh de (Attorney-General) 166

Lowther, Sir John (MP and son of Christopher) 166

Lucas, Richard Cockle (sculptor) 49

Lucas, Richard Saville Clement (Magdalen undergraduate) 216

Luxor (Egypt) 130

Mabey, R[ichard] (naturalist) 199

Mackenzie, W[illiam] J[ames] M[iller] (Fellow of Magdalen) 73

Mackinnon, D[uncan] (Magdalen undergraduate) 215

McMillan, Minnie (donor and wife of John Richards) 30

Macray, W[illiam] D[unn] (Fellow of Magdalen) xi, 12, 30, 31, 129, 133

Magdalen College, Oxford:
  Antechapel 30, 32, 35, 49, 58, 153, 190
  archives 10, 12, 15, 20, 26, 28, 29, 55
  attendance register ix, 16
  bells ix, 36
  Boxe 136
  Bridge 27
  Buttery Book 56
  bylaws 80
  chests 29
  Cloisters 2, 31, 38, 40, 42, 50, 65, 144
  College School 16, 50, 54, 58, 182, 188, 212
  College School, Master of 50, 58, 74, 182
  crest 82, 154
  Cricket Club 212
  dessert ix, 74, 86, 89, 160, 163
  foundation of 6, 7, 218–20
  Founder's Cup ix, 135, 136, 140
  Founder's Tower 40, 196
  gargoyles 169
  Gothicization of 38, 40, 65, 142, 188
  Great Tower 2, 10, 16, 36, 40, 50, 212
  Grove 40, 194
  High Table ix, 169
  kitchens 10, 27, 68
  library 61, 64, 162, 171, 173, 175, 177, 185, 186, 188–91, 195–97
  Longwall Quad 189, 209
  matriculation x, 2, 22, 23, 148
  Muniment Room ix, 3, 12, 28, 29
  New Building 2, 40, 65, 83, 160

New Library 188
New Room 166
Oak 83
Old Library 61, 162, 188, 190, 191
Old Practice Room 153
open-air pulpit ix, 9, 81
Oscar Wilde Room 68
Port Railway ix, 74, 86, 87
President's Lodgings 26, 33, 50, 73, 133, 140
Professor's House 203
Pulpit Cloth ix, 81
St John's Quadrangle 9, 42, 83
St Swithun's Quadrangle 40, 76
SCR scales and weights book 73, 89
seal 7, 80
Senior Common Room 2, 74, 86, 160
silver 135, 136, 138, 140, 141, 148, 154
Smoking Room 89
statutes 7, 8, 9, 15, 28, 52, 56, 218–20
Summer Common Room ix, 74, 147
Tapestries 132, 133
the Hall 56, 74, 86
War Memorial xi, 42, 43
water meadow and walks 2, 38, 83, 144, 188, 198–201
Magdalen Hall (Oxford) 7, 10, 55
Mammoth (*Mammuthus primigenius*) 194
Manchester Victoria University 70
Margaret of Lorraine *see* Lorraine, Margaret of
Mars as a Warrior (painting by Il Guercino) 106
Martini, Simone (painter) 94, 96
Mary I (Queen) 26, 50
Mary II (Queen) 158, 185
Mary Rose (16th-century warship) 135
Master Vacarius (lecturer in law) 178
Matthiolus, Petrus Andreas (botanist) 195, 196
Maudeleyn Hall (Oxford) *see* Magdalen Hall
May Morning in Oxford 64
Mayew or Mayhew, Richard (President of Magdalen) 132, 133
Meghen, Pieter (scribe) 181
Merton College (Oxford) 190
Mesopotamia 129
Mews, Peter (Bishop of Winchester) 56
Michelangelo (painter and sculptor) 30
Monaco, Lorenzo (painter) 98
Moncrieff, Ambrose Scott (picture restorer) 147
Montagu, Charles [Earl of Halifax] (Whig politician) 144
Moore, Henry Spencer (painter and sculptor) 169
Moring, T[homas] (engraver) 80

Morison, Robert (botanist) 199
Morris, William (designer and visionary socialist) 164
Mosul (Iraq) 129
Mount, Alan Frederick (Magdalen's clerk of works) 190
Mount Magdalen (Canada) 152
Muniments 7, 28, 29
Muromachi period 150
Musée du Louvre (Paris) 106, 120
Musée National du Château et des Trianons (Versailles) 102

Nachrichten für die Truppe 186, 187
Napoleon I (Emperor of France) 84
National Gallery (London) 110
National Portrait Gallery (London) 33, 52, 122, 158
Neighboure, George (Magdalen's surveyor) 19
New College (Oxford) 33, 36, 76, 86
New, Edmund (draughtsman) 42
Newman, John Henry (cardinal) 64, 65
Newton, J[ohn] (globe-maker) 204
Nicholaus Germanus (editor) 173
Nickalls, Guy (Magdalen undergraduate and brother of Vivian) 215, 216
Nickalls, Guy ['Gully'] Oliver (Magdalen undergraduate and son of Guy) 216
Nickalls, Tom (father of Guy and Vivian) 216
Nickalls, Vivian (Magdalen undergraduate and brother of Guy) 216
Nimrud (modern-day Kalhu, Iraq) ix, 129
Nineveh (Iraq) 129
Nobel Prize ix, 3, 70, 73
Noble, Sir John (donor) 140
North-West Territories (Canada) 152

Olympic Games
    diploma x, 215
    gold medal 215
Orsanmichele, the church of (Florence) 98
Oxford, Mayor of 27
Oxfordshire Constabulary 160

Padua (Italy) 96
Palazzo Publico (Siena) 95
Papyrus ix, 3, 130, 131
Parr, Samuel (schoolmaster) 84
Partridge, Sir John Bernard (cartoonist) 215
Pater, Walter Horatio (author) 68

Patten, Christopher Francis [Baron Patten of Barnes] (Chancellor of Oxford University and politician) 83
Penegoes (Montgomeryshire) 108
Pepys, Samuel (diarist) 158
Perkin, William Henry (Professor of Chemistry) 70
Persehouse, Richard (gentleman commoner of Magdalen) 206
Petersfield (Hampshire) 195, 199
Phillips, Wogan (Magdalen undergraduate) 216
Pimm, John (publican) 212
Pinart, Dominick (bookbinder) 185
Piret, Revd Michael John (Fellow of Magdalen and Dean of Divinity) vii, 9
Planck, Max Karl Ernest Ludwig (physicist and Nobel Laureate) 73
Plantarum in Horto Iohannem Tradescanti nascentium Catalogus (by John Tradescant) 200
Pliny the Elder (historian) 173
Poole, Reginald Lane [Mrs Rachel Emily] (art historian) xi, 33, 47, 55
Porsuk river (Turkey) 118
Pottery, Turkish ix, 92, 118
Poussin, Nicolas (painter) 108, 110
Prague (Czech Republic) 104
Pre-Raphaelite Brotherhood (painters) 164
Prince of Peace (poem by Edmund Cartwright) 63
Prince Regent (later King George IV) 84
Princeton University (New Jersey) 147, 177
Prout, Samuel (painter) 116
Ptolemy (geographer) ix, 173
Pugin, Augustus Welby Northmore (architect and interior designer) 40, 41, 49, 64, 65
Puritanism at Magdalen 32, 47, 55
Pynson, Richard (printer) 182

Quantum theory 73
Queen's College (Oxford) 52, 60

Rachel (Old Testament figure) 177
Railways ix, 3, 74, 86, 162, 163
Raitt, Alan William (Fellow of Magdalen) 74
Raphael Tuck & Sons (publishers) 162
Rassam, Clive (Magdalen undergraduate, great-grandson of Hormuzd) xi
Rassam, Hormuzd (donor and archaeologist) 129

Rawlins, Thomas (friend and contemporary of Richard Rawlinson) 26

Rawlinson, Richard (antiquarian) 26

Ray, John (naturalist) 198

Rebecca (Old Testament figure) 177

Red Book 38

Redgrave, Gilbert (donor) 196

Reformation 47, 140

Regner the Painter 12

Reliquiae Sacrae (by President Routh) 84

Reni, Guido (painter) 142

Repton, Humphry (landscape gardener and father of John) 38

Repton, John Adey (landscape gardener and son of Humphry) 38

Restoration of King Charles II 33, 135, 138

Restoration of the Magdalen Fellows 56, 138

Reynolds, Sir Joshua (painter and President of the Royal Academy) 160

Rhodian Pottery 118

Ribalta, Francisco (painter) 142

Ribbentrop, [Ulrich Friedrich Wilhelm] Joachim von (wine salesman, later Nazi Foreign Minister and war criminal) 73

Ricci, Marco (painter) 108

Richard III (King) [Richard, Duke of York] x, 15

Richards, John ['Jack'] Hall (Waynflete Fellow, donor and husband of Minnie McMillan) 30

Rijksmuseum (Amsterdam) 104, 120

Rio de Janeiro (Brazil) 112

Robert Taylor and Sons (Oxford) (bell-founders) 36

Robertit, Florimond [Baron d'Alluye] (Secretary of State) 100

Roberts, Colin Henderson (papyrologist) 130

Robinson, Sir Robert (Professorial Fellow of Magdalen and Nobel Laureate) 3, 70

Robinson, William (father of Robert) 70

Rogers, Edward (Fellow of Magdalen) 138

Roman Catholicism 47, 64, 160

Roman law 178

Romney (Kent) 19

Rose, Bernard William George (organist, *informator choristarum*, and Fellow of Magdalen) 154

Rose Medallion *see* Chorister medals

Rossetti, Dante Gabriel (painter) 164

Rothenstein, Sir William (painter) 74

Rouault, Georges Henri (painter) 169

Routh, Eliza Agnes Blagrave (wife of President Routh) 129

Routh, Martin Joseph (President of Magdalen), x, 2, 38, 40, 60, 61, 63, 84, 129, 158, 162

Roxelana, Hürrem (wife of Süleyman the Magnificent) 118

Royal Academy of Arts (London) 108

Rubens, Sir Peter Paul (painter) 147

Rudhall, Abel (bell-founder) 36

Rudhall, Abraham (bell-founder) 36

Rudolf II (Holy Roman Emperor) 104

Rundell, Philip (silversmith) 84

Ruskin, John (critic and artist) ix, 114, 116

Rüstem Pasha (Grand Vizier) 118

Ryle, Gilbert (Professorial Fellow of Magdalen) 74

Sacheverell, Henry (Fellow of Magdalen) 58, 144

St Cecilia 95

St Frideswide 181

St Frideswide's Fair 182

St George 176

St Germans, Edward Granville Eliot (3rd Earl of St Germans) 55

St Giles 98

St John, Oliver (counsel) 55

St John Chrysostom 177

St John the Baptist 7, 10

St John the Baptist's Day 81, 83

St John's College (Oxford) 27

St John's Day 83

St John's Day sermon (Magdalen) 9, 81

St Mark's Day 81

St Mary Magdalene 7, 10, 80, 136

St Matthew's Gospel ix, 130

St Paul's Cathedral (London) 58, 133, 190

St Romuald 98

St Ursula 96, 110

St Valerian 95

Sake Frame 148

San-San-Kudo (Japanese ceremony) 148

Santa Maria della Scala (Siena) 94

Santa Maria Maggiore (Florence) 98

Sarah (Old Testament figure) 177

Savery, Hans (nephew of Roelandt) 104

Savery, Jacob (brother of Roelandt) 104

Savery, Roelandt (painter) ix, 104

Savile, Sir Henry (classical scholar) 177

Schools Dinners 166

Schrödinger, Erwin Rudolf Josef Alexander (Fellow of Magdalen and Nobel Laureate) ix, 73, 89

Schut, Cornelis (painter) 147

Scott, Sir Walter (writer) 63

Scovil, Jasper (Magdalen's deputy librarian) 190

Second World War 42, 92, 144, 148, 152, 169, 186

Selim I (Sultan) 118

Setsuko, Princess Chichibu (wife of Crown Prince Chichibu of Japan) 148

Seville (Spain) 142

Sex hormones 70

Shackleton, Edward Arthur Alexander [Baron Shackleton] (Magdalen undergraduate, explorer, MP and son of Sir Ernest) 152

Shackleton, Sir Ernest Henry (father of Edward) 152

Shakespeare, William (playwright) 122, 158

Shaw, Isaac (painter) 162

Shaw, John (Fellow of Magdalen) 20, 21

Shelley, Edward (office clerk) 69

Shinto (a religion of Japan) 148

Short, James (instrument maker) xi, 206, 209

Shuttleworth, Philip Nicholas (Warden of New College, Oxford) 86

Sibthorp, John (Sherardian Professor of Botany) 198, 203

Siena (Italy) 94, 96

Simon of Sywell (teacher of canon law) 178

Sinclair, Hugh Macdonald (Fellow of Magdalen) 74

Skelton, Joseph (engraver) 26, 27

Smith, Anthony David (President of Magdalen) vii, 141, 154

Smithers, Sir Peter Henry Berry Otway (Magdalen undergraduate and donor) 144

Snargate (Kent) 19

Somers, John [Baron Somers] (Whig politician) 144

Somers-Smith, John Robert (Magdalen undergraduate) 215

Sorrell, Alan Ernest (painter) 74

Spectator 144, 188

Spithead Sketchbook (by J. M. W. Turner) 114

Spranger, Bartholomeus (painter) 104

Stainer, Sir John (organist, *informator choristarum*, and Honorary Fellow of Magdalen) 9, 89, 154

Stainer Cross *see* Chorister medals

Stalin, Josef 76

Stanbridge, John (Master of Magdalen College School and grammarian) 182

Stanier, Robert Spenser (Master of Magdalen College School) 74, 212

Steane John (archaeologist) 29, 199

Steele, Sir Richard (writer and politician) 144

Stephyns, William (supplicant) 15

Stevens, Courtenay Edward ['Tom Brown'] (Fellow of Magdalen) 76, 186

Steward of Hall 16

Stonehouse, Walter (Fellow of Magdalen) 199

Stradling, Edward (Magdalen undergraduate) 140

Strong, Sampson (painter) 47, 50

Strong, Sir Roy Colin (art historian) 122

Strutt, Michael ['Mike'] (Magdalen's head porter) 190

Süleyman the Magnificent (Sultan of Turkey) 118, 120

Sultan of Brunei 154

Sutherland, Graham Vivian (painter) 169

Sylvester, David Bernard (art critic) 169

Synopsis methodica Stirpium Britannicarum (by John Ray) 198

Taddeo di Bartolo (painter) 96

Tate Collection (London) 108

Tatler 144

Tayler, John (Fellow of Magdalen) 138

Taylor, A[lan] J[ohn] P[ercivale] (historian and Fellow of Magdalen) 169

Tennyson, Alfred, Lord (poet) 164

Theophrastus (peripatetic philosopher and botanist) 195

Thiede, Carsten Pieter (papyrologist) 130

Thomson, Samuel (Magdalen undergraduate) 140

Tokugawa Ieyasu (Shogun) 150

Tolkien, Faith (sculptor) 153

Tolkien, J[ohn] R[onald] R[euel] (philologist and writer, father-in-law of Faith) 153

Tomohito of Mikasa (Magdalen graduate student and Japanese prince) 149

Tonneau, Joseph (painter) 56

Tonson, Jacob (publisher) 144

Touchet, Marie (mistress of Charles IX) 100

Tradescant, John, the elder (gardener and collector) 197, 199, 200

Tradescant, John, the younger (gardener and collector) 1

Tuckwell, William (memoirist) 20

Turner, J[oseph] M[allord] W[illiam] (painter) ix, 108, 110, 114, 116

Tybard, William (President of Magdalen) 7, 219

University Museum 194, 203

University Parks 212

University Sermon ix, 9, 81, 83

Valdés Leal, Juan de (painter) 142

van Hemessen, Catharina (painter and daughter of Jan) 102

van Hemessen, Jan Sanders (painter and father of Catharina) 102

van Vianen, Paulus (silversmith) 104

Vasari, Giorgio (painter and biographer) 96

Viana, Paulo Fernando (engineer and architect) 112

Visitor of Magdalen (see also Winchester, Bishop of) 20, 46

von Liebig, Justus (chemist) 203

von Ribbentrop see Ribbentrop

Wadham College (Oxford) 108

Wainflete (birthplace of William of Wayneflete) 80

Walker, James (firearms dealer) 82

Walton, Henry (painter) 160

Ward, Miles (executed felon) 140

Ward, William ('Little Mr Bouncer', Magdalen undergraduate) 2, 67, 68

Wardell, William E. (chair-maker) 189

Warren, Sir [Thomas] Herbert (President of Magdalen) 42, 133, 148

Wayneflete, William of (Founder of Magdalen College) ix, 7, 12, 15, 19, 28, 30, 40, 46, 47, 49, 80, 83, 136, 147, 173, 218–20

Wayneflete Professor of Chemistry 70, 203

Web or Webb, William (cartographer) 19

Wells Cathedral (Somerset) 135

West, Benjamin (artist and President of the Royal Academy) 63

What is Life? (book by Erwin Schrödinger) 73

White, John (Bishop of Winchester) 181

White, Sir Thomas of South Warnborough (Hampshire) 181

Wilde, Gerald (painter) 169

Wilde, Oscar [Fingal O'Flahertie Wills] (Magdalen undergraduate and writer) ix, 2, 67–69, 130, 169

Wilkinson, John (Principal of Magdalen Hall) 55

William III (King) 158, 185

William of Malmesbury 175

Williams, Steve, RN 152

Wilson, John (father of Richard and clergyman) 108

Wilson, Richard (painter and son of John) ix, 108

Winchester, Bishop of (see also Visitor of Magdalen) 7, 20, 46

Winchester College (Hampshire) 7, 47, 49

Windsor chairs 189

Witt, Sir Robert (art collector) 107

Witt Collection, Courtauld Galleries (London) 107

Wolsey or Wulsy, Thomas (Fellow of Magdalen and cardinal) ix, 16, 50, 53, 158, 181
  gospel-lectionary commissioned by ix, 3, 181

Wood, Antony (antiquary) 30

Woolly thistle (Cirsium eriophorum) 195

Worcester College (Oxford) 64

Yalden, Edmund (Fellow of Magdalen) 195, 199

Yeates, Alfred (architect) 42

Yerbury, Henry (Fellow of Magdalen) 135, 138

Zoffany, Johann (painter) 108, 160